T0330164

Restoring Demand in the World Economy

Restoring Demand in the World Economy

Trade, Finance and Technology

Edited by

Joseph Halevi

University Pierre-Mendès France and Stendhal, Grenoble, France and University of Sydney, Australia

Jean-Marc Fontaine

University of Paris, Sorbonne and the Sorbonne Institute of Development Studies (IEDES), France

Edward Elgar
Cheltenham, UK • Northampton, MA, USA

Published by
Edward Elgar Publishing Limited
Glensanda House
Montpellier Parade
Cheltenham
Glos GL50 1UA
UK

Edward Elgar Publishing, Inc.
6 Market Street
Northampton
Massachusetts 01060
USA

A catalogue record for this book
is available from the British Library

Library of Congress Cataloguing in Publication Data
Restoring demand in the world economy: trade, finance, and technology
/edited by Joseph Halevi, Jean-Marc Fontaine.
  A collection of 13 essays by international authors.
  1. Consumption (Economics) 2. Demand (Economic theory) 3. Supply
and demand. 4. Economic history—1945– 5. Economic policy.
I. Halevi, Joseph. II. Fontaine, Jean-Marc, 1942–
HC79.C6R47   1998
339.4'7—dc21   97-50057
                                                                          CIP

ISBN 1 85898 458 0

Printed and bound in Great Britain by
Biddles Ltd, Guildford and King's Lynn

Contents

Tables

Contributors

Yilmaz Akyüz, United Nations Conference on Trade and Development, Geneva

Wladimir Andreff, University Paris 1 Panthéon Sorbonne, director of the ROSES (Reforming and Opening post-Socialist Economic Systems), CNRS

Amit Bhaduri, Centre for Economic Studies and Planning, Jawaharlal Nehru University, New Delhi 110067

Victoria Chick, University College, London

Renato Di Ruzza, Université de Aix en Provence

Louis Haddad, University of Sydney

Joseph Halevi, Centre d'Etudes sur la Pensée Economique, Université Pierre Mendès-France et Université Stendhal, Grenoble; University of Sydney

Jan A. Kregel, University of Bologna, Italy

Peter Kriesler, University of New South Wales, Sydney

Jacques Mazier, Université de Paris 13

El Mouhoub Mouhoud, Université d'Evry and Commissariat Général au Plan, Paris

Alain Parguez, Université Franche Comté and University of Ottawa

Prabhat Patnaik, Centre for Economic Studies and Planning, Jawaharlal Nehru University, New Delhi 110067

Sunanda Sen, Centre for Economic Studies and Planning, Jawaharlal Nehru University, New Delhi 110067

Acknowledgements

We thank the organizations and the people which made possible the articulation of the ideas contained in this volume in a Conference held at the Maison des Sciences de l'Homme in Paris at the end of September 1994, where the first draft of the bulk of the essays published in this volume was presented. The official financial sponsors of the Conference 'Rehabilitation of Demand' were: The University of Sorbonne Paris 1 and its centre for development studies (IEDES), the Department of Economics of the University of Sydney and the School of Oriental and African Studies of the University of London (SOAS). We gratefully acknowledge also the contributions of the British Council in Paris, of the Franco-Indian cooperation programme and of the Universities of Sydney and of New South Wales for providing travel grants. Professors Georges Haddad, president of the University of Sorbonne, Jean Racine, of the Maison des Sciences de l'Homme (Paris), Laurence Harris, head of the economics department at SOAS, Warren Hogan, then head of the economics department of the University of Sydney, and Jean Masini of the IEDES, are to be thanked for giving crucial institutional backing to the project. Technical support from the staff of the Department of Economics of the University of Sydney – Ms Valerie Jones, Mr Jack Towe and Mr Phong Le – and of the sister Department at the Université Pierre Mendès France in Grenoble – Mlle Christine Capoccioni – was absolutely essential for the successful completion of the volume. Finally, as some of the essays were originally in French, we note that Chapters 3, 9 and 11, were translated into English by Joseph Halevi, while Chapter 12 was translated by Jean-Marc Fontaine.

Introduction

The concept of effective demand acts as the central category informing and guiding the themes discussed in each of the four parts of the book. Part I presents three overall perspectives as to the role of effective demand in a global context, Part II discusses some instances of world economic integration, while Parts III and IV treat, respectively, the cases of the developing economies and of Europe, both East and West. The reader will notice that there is no specific chapter dealing with the United States. In fact, the role of the American economy in shaping post-war effective demand features prominently in three of the essays presented in this volume. In Chapter 2, by analysing the dual role of the US dollar which emerged from the Bretton Woods agreements, Jan Kregel ties US domestic economic policies to the international setting. The role of the United States emerges also in Akyüz's study, Chapter 4, and in that of Halevi and Kriesler, Chapter 6.

PART I   THREE OVERVIEWS

The opening contribution by Amit Bhaduri explores the interconnections between the economic and political dimensions of the problem of mass unemployment. The author shows that the formation of unemployment cannot be sought in the working of the labour market but rather in the functioning of the product markets. In a Kaleckian–Keynesian fashion, Bhaduri analyses the two sided role of wages and of productivity growth. Wages are not just costs but represent spending power for the purchase of consumption goods. Hence depressing wages, rather than inducing labour market flexibility – not a sure thing even in a pure neoclassical framework – may stifle the expansion of the market and of employment. Likewise, productivity growth *per se* may emphasize the labour-saving character of technical progress which, ultimately, reduces the dynamics of consumption demand. In this context, the Keynesian theory of effective demand is considered to be valid for contemporary conditions. Yet, due to the greater internationalization of production and finance, Keynesian policies face much greater constraints than in the past. Internationalization of production implies a lesser degree of autonomy in the policy making capacity of the nation state. At the same time the globalization of financial flows makes the nation state significantly more sensitive to perceived balance of payments difficulties. As a consequence the authorities tend to opt for a conservative strategy aimed at obtaining foreign investment and at expanding exports. Globally such a strategy is not sustainable.

Chapter 2 by Jan Kregel provides the reader with a dense historical analysis of the factors that prevented successful demand stabilization policies. The Bretton Woods system is presented as based on a spurious compromise: the institutionalization of the international role of the American dollar on one hand and the scarce currency clause on the other. The United States became in this way the regulator of world demand, an acceptable situation as long as the USA were a net creditor. Yet the compromise assumed that the country supplying world currency would remain in a persistent external surplus position. When the United States moved into a deficit status the Triffin contradiction between a currency which is both national and international began to make itself felt. At the root of the Triffin contradiction lay Keynes's preoccupation – expressed in his alternative plan during the Bretton Woods negotiations – that asymmetric adjustments would impose the burden of adjustment on the deficit countries. The solution to this dilemma was sought in a system of floating exchange rates which, after 1971, ushered in the present period of instability. This meant competitive devaluations on one hand and, on the other, the financing of deficits by means of capital inflows involving upward movements in interest rates. Such a scenario typified the Reagan years, generating a very negative impact on the growth rates of the developing countries. Kregel points out that the dual function of the dollar as the international currency *par excellence* has enshrined the International Monetary Fund in its role as a debt collector rather than as a world institution with anti-deflationary objectives.

Renato Di Ruzza introduces in Chapter 3 the notion of a productive system and traces its constituent analytical elements both in a strand of the French *Régulation* school and in the writings of economists, such as Geoffrey Harcourt, Adolph Lowe and Luigi Pasinetti. In a nutshell, in all of these approaches sectoral and structural relations define the contours of the economic system. According to Di Ruzza, therefore, the framework for demand-stimulating policies must be sought in structurally coherent productive systems where the input–output relations at the sectoral level are sufficiently advanced so as not to give rise to major technological bottlenecks and to intractable balance of payments difficulties. Alongside sectoral relations, the consistency of a productive system is given also by its socio-institutional coherence. The norms defining and governing the use of labour in production are a crucial component in actually bringing separate economic areas into a single unified dimension. From this perspective Europe cannot be seen as yet forming a coherent *ensemble*. National economies are in Europe in a process of deep transformation without, however, a clear tendency towards the formation of a Continent-wide productive system. Hence, the author argues, the likelihood of a common European policy aimed at rehabilitating the dynamic role of demand is very scant indeed.

PART II   ECONOMIC INTEGRATION AND EFFECTIVE DEMAND

This section is concerned with aspects of the world economy which gained prominence from the 1970s onward: the international convergence towards deflationary policies in the wake of the second oil shock, the increased role of capital flows and the formation of an East Asian economic zone centred on Japan's productive power.

Chapter 4, by Yilmaz Akyüz, contains an analysis of the different stages of policy formulations in major industrialized countries. The study shows how, after the second oil shock, European economies converged towards a growth rate too low to prevent further and systemic increases in unemployment. Furthermore, for reasons already outlined by Jan Kregel, the United States growth rate was marked by stagnant and even declining real wages and by growing job insecurity. The study argues that the policy stance of central banks became mostly oriented to monitoring unemployment in relation to perceived inflationary risks. The fear of inflation led to a fear of a too high growth rate. Such a policy stance has tended to depress aggregate demand and with it profitability and investment. In effect a growing imbalance between the growth of the labour force and the accumulation of capital emerged accentuating the tendency for unemployment to rise. The attempt, for fear of inflation, to reduce the growth of potential output relative to the actual rate may become a self-fulfilling prophecy. The ensuing squeeze in profitability could be met through firms' restructuring which contributes to worsening the disequilibrium between capital accumulation and the growth of the labour force. Stagnation in domestic demand pushed firms to look for external markets. This phenomenon has resulted in an increase in the share of foreign trade in the economy, thereby making investment decisions increasingly dependent upon exchange rates and, consequently, upon their volatility. Along with financial deregulation this factor, Akyüz argues, has augmented the volatility of exports and imports increasing also investors' risk. The author concludes that the idea of seeking growth by expanding competitiveness among nations contains a neomercantilist flaw as it is not attainable for all the countries at the same time. Hence: 'Global demand deficiency is a recipe for an invitation to conflict among nations'.

The analysis of the significance of capital flows is carried out by Sunanda Sen in Chapter 5. The author begins her study by observing that in the post-war era the bulk of capital flows has originated from the industrialized world. It follows that without such flows the aggregate savings of the rich countries would have been underutilized leading to economic stagnation. The counterpart to capital flows is a stream of exports of goods and services – real resources – from the industrialized nations to the rest of the world. Therefore, at least in principle, capital flows can become an instrument for the revitalization of world effective demand. However, in the anti-growth scenario already described by by Akyüz, the financial sector developed a whole set of new forms of intermediations as a response to increased market uncertainty. The profitability of the financial sector depends on the expansion of debt by the other components of the economy. Yet, the slow growth context of the industrialized world meant that debt creation led to a debt explosion. The essay then proceeds to analyse capital flows by area, it outlines the conditions for the emerging financial fragility tying them to the Washington consensus about financial deregulation. Finally it ends by presenting a demand driven model where capital flows from the advanced to the developing countries can indeed act as a positive factor on overall growth.

The capitalist development of East Asia has been one of the major phenomena of the post-war period, so much so as to modify the economic geography of the industrial world. Most of the studies on the subject have emphasized the supply side aspects of the process. In Chapter 6 Joseph Halevi and Peter Kriesler suggest a different interpretation which is consistent with both Di Ruzza's and Kregel's overviews. It is argued that Japan could become the centre of industrialization because it followed a strategy of full range industrialization, to use a phrase coined by the Japanese economist Kyoshi Kojima. It is the coherence of the Japanese productive system which, eventually, enabled its corporations to transform East and Southeast Asia into the area generating the largest amount of Tokyo's current account surpluses. Without a corresponding market outlet in the USA these surpluses would have compelled an asymmetric adjustment on the East Asian economies. Japan's capacity to act as the industrial core depended crucially on a complex system of transfers engineered by Washington, and by American international public expenditure in the area set in motion by the Korean war. US spending during the Vietnam war had an even greater impact. It is then maintained that in the light of Japan's failure to act as a big spender and therefore as a buyer of the products of the region, and the declining willingness and ability of the United States to keep providing for markets and to clear the countries' external deficits, effective demand problems are bound to emerge in this growth area as well.

PART III FINANCE AND INVESTMENT IN THE CONTEXT OF UNDERDEVELOPMENT

Precisely because of the connection between the industrial completeness of Japan, its need to obtain an area of economic expansion and the overwhelming role of the United States as a market outlet and a source of public expenditure, the capitalist transformation of East Asia cannot be taken as a developmental paradigm. In their relations with the industrialized world many other developing countries fall within the analytical framework provided by Sunanda Sen and this is reinforced, albeit in a different form, by the essays presented in this part of the volume.

Victoria Chick takes up in Chapter 7 the issue of the link between investment and savings applying it in the context of developing economies. For the author, in a purely agricultural system savings did determine investment. With the consolidation of industry and the accompanying creation of a banking system, it is investment which became the determinant of savings. At this point Victoria Chick emphasizes the difference between the industrialization process taking place during the 19th century and that facing contemporary developing economies. The 19th century case is synthesized by the classical view where savings (profits) determined accumulation and investment. By contrast, contemporary developing countries have access to a sophisticated banking system. Their central problem is to find appropriate mechanisms for the funding and retirement of debt. The author then details the transformation of the ownership structure from sole proprietorship – where finance depended on savings which determined funding – to joint stock companies. It is in the latter case that savings and finance become a separate activity. Savings are important for funding development, not for financing it. Adequate finance can be obtained without difficulties from the banking system either domestically or internationally. The problem is whether there exist appropriate funding mechanisms, in particular in relation to indebtedness. It is then pointed out that the policy prescriptions put forward by the World Bank and the International Monetary Fund are faulty since they conflate, in a pre-Keynesian fashion, financing with funding.

The IMF-inspired policies are also criticized by Prabhat Patnaik in Chapter 8. The essay begins with a dense theoretical discussion of the limitations of traditional analysis and presents an alternative macroeconomic approach. A successful policy of financial liberalization may translate itself in accumulated reserves on account of capital inflows. If these financial surpluses are eliminated by means of greater imports, the market for the industries of the advanced countries would have expanded at the expense of the developing countries' use of productive capacity. This perverse outcome is due to the deflationary bias created by measures aimed at financial liberalization. The bias stems from the fact that to lure capital inflows it is necessary to ensure financial returns which may stifle real domestic investment. Such a situation opens the way for metropolitan financial interests to capture third world resources and assets. Indeed, as reserves are spent on imports, a confidence crisis may ensue leading to big devaluations in the selling price of third world countries' assets. Policies aimed at building up reserves can also limit the possibilities for demand stimulation since it would amount to a situation in which the country is borrowing short to invest long. The essay concludes by challenging the tenet that *free market* policies are needed because capital has become more mobile: 'What has become genuinely more mobile across countries is *capital-as-finance*, and in the case of such capital simply having more of it is not synonymous with having a higher rate of growth.'

The view that globalization involves first and foremost the mobility of capital as finance can be gathered also from the analysis presented by El Mouhoub Mouhoud in Chapter 9 dealing with the tendencies in foreign direct investment. The essay uses mostly microeconomic concepts such as economies of scope, learning processes, technological synergies and their links with the formation of comparative advantages. According to this study, low wage and labour abundant countries as well as those greatly endowed with natural resources are no longer the main recipients of foreign direct investment. The reversal of the flows back to the industrialized world is ascribed to the much greater uncertainty of the state of demand and to the consequent need of responding quickly to the volatility of demand conditions. According to Mouhoud, the new economic environment requires a more systemic utilization of the synergies made possible by the interconnectedness of the industrial structure of the developed world. Along with its sectoral completeness, the industrialized countries offer the possibility of advanced knowledge and skills represented by the high ratio of technicians, engineers and scientific workers over total employment. Hence, the high level of per capita demand, market proximity and sectoral and scientific interlinks provide a more solid environment than just the low wage structure of the less-developed countries, also known as the countries of the South. Those relocations to the South that are still occurring do not contain the conditions for sustained development. Indeed, they lack the complexities of advanced productive systems in an era in which demand, per capita and in the aggregate, is the guiding force of investment activity while being, at the same time, characterized by growing uncertainty.

PART IV   EFFECTIVE DEMAND IN EASTERN AND WESTERN EUROPE

The last section of the volume deals with effective demand problems in an area where it matters most: Europe. The Eastern part of Europe, including Russia which historically was always a major component of European polity, has suffered a veritable implosion of aggregate demand in its transition from a supply to a demand constrained system. For its part capitalist Europe is in a state of high unemployment at least since the early 1980s.

In this context it is important to point out that a linkage between the Eastern crisis and the prospects of recovery in Western Europe does exist, although it is seldom discussed. The crisis in the East clouds the political process of Western European unity with a great deal of uncertainty, having negative repercussions on the prospects of economic expansion in Western Europe. To put it simply, if Russia and the Ukraine could embark on a sustained process of recovery they would naturally gravitate towards Western Europe economically. Thus, in the constructive way described by Sunanda Sen, capital flows from Western Europe would be needed to expand and modernize Russia's productive capacity thereby generating demand for the splendid European machinery sectors. By contrast, a Russia in crisis generates the persistent fear of a Maelstrom, it brings no economic benefits and confines Western Europe to the status of a junior partner of the United States in overall European matters!

It follows that the problem of effective demand in Russia and Eastern Europe has a direct political connotation for the future of the continent as a whole. In this respect the first two chapters of Part IV are quite innovative since they are among the very first to look at the transitional economies of the former Soviet Union and Eastern Europe through the lenses of the question of effective demand.

The study by Louis Haddad in Chapter 10 begins by outlining the systemic factors which underpinned the working of Centrally Planned Economies. In the main, these factors are taut planning and the institutionalized orientation of those economies towards investment and production at the expense of consumption. As a consequence the Centrally Planned Economies were characterized by built-in shortages and forced savings, which were bound to evaporate with the abandonment of central planning. After detailing the fall in output which ensued the demise of central planning, the author argues that conventional macroeconomic stabilization policies are inadequate to deal with the specific conditions of economies in transition. Such polices failed 'to take into account the depressing effects on aggregate demand and output of the collapse of both central planning and CMEA trade'. The outcome of the macrostabilization policies was to restrict demand even further. They led to 'a vicious circle in which falling demand generated less supply and in turn falling supply created less demand'. The study goes on to discuss the possible measures aimed at rehabilitating the role of demand as a prerequiste for a successful transition to a market system. In this context it is pointed out that the implosion of demand and the deterioration of the social infrastructure has led to a situation where, instead of obtaining capital flows for productive purposes, Russia and also the other Eastern European economies have been characterized by the importation of luxury consumption goods and by net capital outflows.

In Chapter 11 Wladimir Andreff develops the effective demand theme further. The economies of Eastern Europe, he argues, still contain a component of inertial inflation. Under these circumstances, whatever the growth rate that might emerge, a strong exhilarationist pattern is likely to be displayed. The term 'exhilarating growth' was created by Bhaduri and Marglin to discuss the case in which growth occurs on the basis of increasing inequalities in income distribution. In essence, the creation of exhilarationist conditions are ascribed by Andreff to the IMF-inspired macrostabilization policies. In the context of the transitional economies exhilarationist growth implies a neglect of investment in the crucial productive sectors as well as in infrastructure. According to the study, the alternative to the traditional stabilization policies appears to rest upon the rehabilitation of demand provided the exhilarationist pattern is broken, otherwise the economies concerned will be exposed to a new wave of inflation. Thus: 'any demand oriented policy requires a supply policy as well. In the present analytical framework, the latter turns out to be essential for the stabilization of the inflation rate.' In other words, there must be an active policy of aggregate investment coupled with stimulating its appropriate composition: 'The restructuring of the latter acquires a much higher priority than privatization.' Without such an active investment policy, transitional economies risk being caught between stagnation and exhilarationist growth.

The last two chapters of the volume deal with the problem of stagnant demand in Western Europe and, in particular, in the European Union and in France. Jacques Mazier, in Chapter 12, discusses the hypotheses that led to an optimistic view about the formation of a single market and a single currency in Europe. Beginning with the Cecchini report in 1988 and ending with the Maastricht parameters, the economic criteria guiding the process of European unification are shown to be founded on a rather frail basis. In particular it is argued that

> satisfying the Maastricht criteria would exert devastating effects especially if one considers the high unemployment rate in EEC countries. Furthermore, there is little reason to expect that the fiscal evolution will allow relaxation of the monetary policy and bring rates of interest down, since they are determined by the Bundesbank. One must equally add that, when pursued simultaneously in closely interdependent countries, contractionary policies are quite ineffective. The cutback on public spending in each country lowers the growth rates both at home and in partner countries thus depressing the fiscal revenue all around. These policies eventually depress the rates of growth and push unemployment up without significantly improving the fiscal balances.

After this clear-cut assessment of the Maastricht scenario, the author develops a series of considerations regarding the possibilities of restoring the role of demand in the European Union. Past proposals for a common European reflationary policy did not succeed because many different national programmes required multiple levels of coordination. Instead, Mazier suggests a set of expansionary policies in which the European dimension would take over, thereby overcoming the coordination problem.

The evaluation of the policy choices facing Europe cannot be undertaken separately from the forces, social and intellectual, which brought about the process of European integration since the early days of the Common Market four decades ago. The formation of the EEC was crucially influenced by political and cultural factors, which often guided the economic objectives. This is so for the period of the long Christian Democratic rule in both West Germany and Italy in the first two decades after the end of the Second World War and for the formation of the Fifth Republic in France in 1958.

The last chapter by Alain Parguez links in a lucid Keynesian framework the political, the intellectual and the economic aspects of policy making in France since the birth of the Fifth Republic. The merit of Parguez's essay lies in highlighting the historical continuity, in matters of fiscal and monetary policies, of the views of the conservative elites which ruled over France independently of the political party actually in office. The lynchpin of the financial orthodoxy of France's élites is seen in the approach developed by Jacques Rueff which became institutionalized during de Gaulle's presidency. For Rueff the state budget ought to tend to zero. This means that the government's operating budgets – including those of the local authorities and of the Social Security – should be in surplus in order to pay interest on the national debt. The study shows how such an approach influenced the Gaullist presidencies as well as that of Mitterrand. It argues, in this context, that France's economic policies were among the most deflationary in the EEC. In fact it is shown that during the 1980s Germany had much greater structural deficits than France and on the whole the latter stuck to a much more rigid policy stance than Bonn. The author concludes that France's ruling classes are virtually deaf to Keynesian ideas and that the left tends to be ultra-Ricardian, seeing public deficits as inimical to investment and growth.

JOSEPH HALEVI AND JEAN-MARC FONTAINE

POST SCRIPTUM

The article of Jacques Mazier (Chapter 12) was ready for publication by the summer of 1996. As the reader will notice, his analysis contains the hypothesis that monetary unification in Europe would be slowed down because of the worsening unemployment situation. Such a state of affairs would have required the relaxation of the tight fiscal policies upon which monetary union is predicated. Indeed, in France two elections, the presidential one in 1995 and the parliamentary one in 1997, were fought with the successful parties advocating a redesign of the process of monetary unification. In reality they all capitulated to the most rigid interpretation of the Maastricht criteria as emphasized in the Dublin Summit of December 1996 and in the Amsterdam Treaty signed in 1997. In other words, the position of central bankers and financial institutions became the single criterion by which to gauge economic performance, jettisoning unemployment as an issue of concrete intervention. Europe today finds itself quite squarely within the pessimistic scenario hypothesized by Mazier as just a possible case. Hence the analytical underpinnings of the article are still valid.

PART I

Three Overviews

1. The problem of unemployment: its economic and political dimension

Amit Bhaduri

1. UNEMPLOYMENT AND THE LABOUR MARKET

The employment situation is deteriorating steadily in Europe. During the 1960s the main industrialized countries of Europe had an average unemployment rate of about 2 per cent, while it was somewhat higher at about 5 to 6 per cent in the USA and Canada. Throughout the 1970s unemployment rose in most of these countries, but it still remained relatively low, starting from the low rate of 3 per cent in 1970 in the 12 countries now constituting the European Union. However, a rising trend was visible. By the late 1980s the unemployment rate was in double figures in several industrialized countries, but in the USA after peaking at over 9 per cent in the mid-1980s, it decreased to about 6 per cent by the end of the decade. The problem now has assumed staggering social dimensions in Western Europe. The end of the tunnel is nowhere in sight. In contrast, however the unemployment problem has remained distinctly less acute in America, with a stable rate of around 5 to 6 per cent in the recent past.

The long-term decline in the employment situation in Western Europe is often considered *structural*, in the sense that it is viewed differently from the recessionary phase of a business cycle. Nevertheless, the word 'structural' is open to rather widely different interpretations. At the simplest level, it is an *arithmetical* concept. Given the rate of annual growth of labour productivity at around 2 per cent and the large stock of already unemployed, it is clear that even a sustained 3 per cent growth in output would hardly make any significant dent into the unemployment problem, after providing jobs for new entrants into the labour market. From this arithmetical point of view, it would then appear that unemployment would persist like a structural feature of these economies for a long time to come. However, this view is predicated on the assumption that the content of growth – both in terms of its output and employment composition – is a given datum.

Structural unemployment could also be interpreted in a *political* sense, extending Marx's notion of the reserve army of labour. As Kalecki (1971) noted, political business cycles may tend to become a structural feature of capitalist economies, in so far as sustained full employment over time through demand management policies undermines the authority of the captains of industry *vis-à-vis* the workers. Reinterpreted in its more modern version, the cost of losing jobs for workers needs to be kept sufficiently high in order to keep them disciplined. The cost of job loss also appears in a more oblique form in theories of efficiency wages. Suppose that workers in a firm are paid higher wages than they can earn elsewhere, for instance to keep them loyal to the firm-specific skills. This carrot of a high wage also implies the stick of the threat of job loss, because the worker cannot expect to find an equivalent job elsewhere. This keeps the employed 'insiders' loyal to the firms; but their higher wage also restricts artificially the demand for labour. As a result, a larger incidence of unemployment is borne by the outsiders who cannot bid down the high wages of insiders.

Efficiency wage and similar arguments are based fundamentally on the *microeconomic* neoclassical proposition that the wage rate is simply an element of cost to the employer. Thus a higher real wage reduces the demand for labour by the profit-maximizing firms who, according to textbooks, equate the marginal product of labour to the real wage rate. Note that, in its simplest form, the theory is perfectly symmetrical between an increase in money wage at constant price or a decrease in price at constant money wage. Because, the profit-maximizing assumption:

$$p/v = f'(L) \qquad (1.1)$$

yields immediately on manipulation:

$$[(v/L)(dL/v)]_{p=\bar{p}} = -[(p/L)(dL/dp)]_{v=\bar{v}} = (f'/Lf'') < 0 \qquad (1.2)$$

where,

v = money wage rate
p = price level
L = employment
$f(L)$ = short period labour utilization (or production) function, with $f' > 0$ and $f'' < 0$, which is also the second order condition for obtaining the comparative static result for profit maximization.

Continuing on this basis, it may be argued that high unemployment is the result of relatively high real wages in Western Europe. In turn, relatively high *real* wages may be seen as (mostly) the result of undisciplined, i.e. militant wage bargaining by trade unions who succeed in securing higher *real* wages for their members. Or, as is often the case these days, the blame is placed on the welfarism of the State – high unemployment benefit which raises the reservation price of labour, high employer's contribution which raises the cost of hiring labour, difficulty of firing workers and so forth. They are seen as structural rigidities in the labour market which directly or indirectly raise the cost of hiring labour to reduce employment through essentially the same route of high labour cost.

The high cost of labour in manufacturing in the industrialized West is also seen as an impediment not only to the short-term demand for labour, but also to the required direction of structural adjustments in these countries which tend to aggravate further the unemployment situation. OECD data for the G-7 countries between 1970 and 1990 reveal all-round decline in manufacturing employment. It declined in absolute terms in Germany and Italy, but as share of employment in all seven countries. In Germany and Italy the share of labour force employed in manufacturing declined by about 17 percentage points, by 10 percentage points in the USA, by about 6 percentage points in the UK, France and Canada, and even in Japan by about 3 percentage points. Consequently the extent to which the release of labour from traditional manufacturing could be absorbed by the service sector determined largely the overall employment performance of these economies. This is strikingly brought out by the fact that, over the same period 1970 to 1990, the US economy created nearly 38 million jobs mostly in low skilled and low paid service industries. In contrast, during the same period barely 10 million jobs were created in Europe. In effect, the United States maintained a low rate of unemployment by making some of the service workers accept wages which often kept them in poverty despite being employed. In the twenty-year period 1973 to date, the percentage of the US population in poverty rose from 11 to 14 per cent with nearly 50 per cent of American children living in poverty. More significantly, the proportion of full-time workers with earnings below the poverty line increased from 12 per cent in 1979 to 18 per cent in 1990 (Krugman, 1994). During the same period average real wages in the US remained nearly constant, but this hides an important fact. The real wage in low paid (like janitors') jobs fell quite sharply by about 15 per cent, whereas it increased by over 50 per cent at the other end of the spectrum for doctors and executives.

Despite the fashionable diagnosis of *Eurosclerosis* by economists like Lindbeck and Giersch who put the blame for high unemployment in

Europe on the rigidities of the labour market caused by an interventionist welfare state, two crucial questions arise in the light of the American experience. First, is the 'American way' any solution to the European unemployment problem, if it at times means wages so low as to keep even some full-time employed persons in poverty? Second, if the interventionist welfare state causing the labour market rigidities and high wages is identified as the central reason for European unemployment then a related question must be answered. Why did the unemployment rate remain so low in the 1960s and 1970s, despite similar interventions by the state then? To find any convincing answer to these questions, the ruling orthodoxy of *Eurosclerosis* must be examined more critically. In a nutshell, the *Eurosclerosis* view is unsatisfactory in so far as it focuses almost exclusively on the labour market. In contrast, the main cause of current unemployment in Europe needs to be located basically not in the labour market, but in the product market. It is this perspective and its implications which are developed in some detail in the next section.

2. UNEMPLOYMENT AND THE PRODUCT MARKET

Since the time Keynes and Kalecki attacked the orthodox remedy of wage-cuts as a solution to the massive unemployment problem in the 1930s, it has been well known that the labour market behaves in a fundamentally different way than the market for tomatoes or computers, owing to at least two important channels of macroeconomic feedback. First, any change in *money* wage rate would typically trigger off some changes in the price level in an industrial economy, where most important prices tend to be broadly cost-determined. Consequently, the *real* wage rate is an endogenous outcome of the system and not an exogenous policy variable to be operated upon. Essentially the same argument reappears in various modern versions of the augmented Phillips curve where the rate of money wage change is influenced not only by the level of unemployment but also by the past or expected price change. Going back to the basic neo-classical equations (1.1) and (1.2), this means that, in general, it is economically illegitimate to consider variations in the money wage rate, while holding the level of price constant (or the other way round). Instead, we have from simple manipulation of (1.1):

$$(v/L)\,(dL/dv) = [(1-n)f'/(Lf'')] \tag{1.3}$$

where: $(v/p)(dp/dv) = n > 0$, that is, the elasticity of price with respect to a variation in money wage.

It follows that for $n > 1$, an increase in money wage leads to a more than proportionate increase in the price level so that real wage falls, inducing profit maximizing firms to increase employment, that is, from (1.3) $dL/dv > 0$, if $n > 1$. Obversely, $dL/dv \leq 0$ if $n \leq 1$.

Note that the strength of this feedback between money wage and price, that is, the magnitude of (n), is a consequence of the interaction between the price-setting strategies of the firms in the product market as well as the money wage bargain by the workers in the labour market. As a result even under the strict neoclassical postulate of profit maximizing equilibrium, the comparative static results of money wage variations tend to be indeterminate, because the impact of a higher money wage on employment works through the interaction between the labour and the product market determining the real wage.

More explicitly in terms of Phillips curve-type formulation:

$$dv/v = H(u) = \alpha \, (dp/p), \; H'(u) < 0, \alpha > 0 \qquad (1.4)$$

where, u the unemployment rate. Equation (1.4) can be rewritten, using the notation of equation (1.3), as:

$$dp/p = n(1 - n\alpha)^{-1} H(u) \; \text{ and } \; dv/v = (1 - n\alpha)^{-1} H(u) \qquad (1.5)$$

both of which preserve the sign for the usual Phillips curve analysis so long as $n\alpha < 1$.

The second and more fundamental reason as to why the labour market is so different from all other markets, is the two-sided role of wages (unlike almost all other prices) in an industrial economy. At the *micro-level* wages usually constitute the most important element of (variable) cost to the firm or the individual industrialist. However, at the *macro-level* they are also usually the most important source of aggregate demand, determining the size of the market in a closed economy. Consequently, higher wages mean higher costs, but they also mean a larger market to sell output. This two-sided role of wages – a theme which should be familiar from Keynesian economics – again raises doubts that increasing labour market flexibility, for example by reducing wages, can be a potent macroeconomic solution to the current employment problems of Europe.

It is a recurring theme these days that individual firms and corporations would increase their competitiveness by raising labour productivity through shedding labour without a corresponding increase in wages. From the Keynesian point of view, the consequences of following such a strategy by the corporate sector may be most simply formalized in a closed economy through the usual multiplier mechanism. Assume all wages are consumed and a constant fraction s of profit is saved. If x is output per worker, i.e. labour productivity, then the investment savings equality yields:

$$I = S = s\,[x - (v/p)]L$$

so that employment determined from the multiplier mechanism becomes:

$$L = I/sx[1 - v/xp] \tag{1.6}$$

since θ v/xp is definitionally the share of wages, a positive fraction less than unity, the right-hand side of (1.4) can be rewritten as a convergent geometric series:

$$L = (I/sx)[1+\theta + \theta^2 + ...], \ 1 > \theta = v/xp \tag{1.7}$$

Given the level of investment I and a constant propensity to save out of profits, (1.7) shows how employment increases with higher wage share θ through the expansion of the size of the internal market – the crux of the underconsumptionist argument. Thus, for any given real wage or, for that matter, real wages rising more slowly than labour productivity in percentage terms, there would be a tendency for the size of the (internal) market to shrink. In turn, this would aggravate rather than alleviate the unemployment problem.

The implication for employment growth over time is seen more explicitly by logarithmic differentiation of (1.6) with respect to time to yield:

$$\lambda = m - \pi + [\theta/(1 - \theta)] \tag{1.8}$$

where λ is the rate of change of L, m is the rate of change of investment and π that of labour productivity.

Setting v as the rate of change of the money wage v, equation (1.8) can be rewritten as:

$$\lambda = m - (1+k)\pi + k(1 - n)v \tag{1.9}$$

where, $k = (\theta/1 - \theta)$ is the ratio of wages to profits in GDP.

The first term on the right-hand side of equations (1.8) or (1.9) shows employment generation through the multiplier; the second term captures the detrimental effect of labour productivity growth on employment, given the market size through the multiplier; whereas the third term on (1.8) implicitly and in (1.9) more explicitly shows the impact of labour market institutions on employment growth, but from the aggregate demand side. Note if $1 > n > 0$, then real wage rises with money wage to produce a positive demand impact on employment growth, while for $n > 1$, the employment impact of the money wage bargain is negative. Note also that this demand side impact of money-wage–real-wage relation is diametrically the opposite of the cost or supply side impact, as is evident from comparing (1.3) with (1.9).

It is not always explicitly stated, but often implicitly assumed, that the positive demand side impact of a higher wage share (rate) will be outweighed by its depressing effect on the profitability of investment so that aggregate demand would actually shrink. Analytically this argument is very different because the impact of a real wage reduction is worked out in this case through its effect on aggregate demand, that is, primarily in the product market and not in the labour market (Bhaduri and Marglin, 1990). This fundamental shift in focus from the labour to the product market is just another way of emphasizing the centrality of effective demand in *any* macroeconomic explanation of unemployment. It also indicates the two-sided role of labour productivity growth, parallel to real wage variation.

As equations (1.8) and (1.9) clearly indicate, labour productivity growth would also have an inhibiting effect on employment growth, similar to real wage reduction, from the demand side *unless* it is accompanied by a sufficiently strong growth in investment to expand the market through the multiplier mechanism. Note that during the period 1960–73 in OECD countries labour productivity grew at an average 4.4 per cent annum while high investment growth kept GDP growing an average 4.9 per cent per annum (Glyn and Gregg, 1994). During 1973–90 labour productivity growth slowed down to an average 1.9 per cent while GDP growth slowed down to 2.7 per cent, resulting in an arithmetic of growth in employment of comparable magnitudes. Neither labour market flexibility nor productivity growth *per se* can provide a solution to the unemployment problem for exactly the same reason: they raise microeconomic profitability and competitiveness at the enterprise or the firm level, but tend to depress the macroeconomic size of the internal market for selling products. At least from the policy point of view, it is not the microfoundations of macroeconomics which is at stake, but rather how to make micro-incentives compatible with Keynesian macro management of demand.

3. DEMAND MANAGEMENT: ITS SCOPE AND LIMITS

Despite the somewhat short-lived ascendancy of monetarism and supply-side economics of various descriptions in recent years the basic *theoretical* point of Keynesian economics remains valid. The solution to the serious unemployment problem of Europe does not lie solely or even primarily in a 'better' functioning labour market; instead it lies primarily in a sufficiently fast expansion of aggregate demand in the product market. However, while this *theoretical* point remains valid, wisdom can have more than one opinion about its *policy* implications.

Conservative economic policy could make its case by suggesting stimulation only of *private* investment through wage-cut and labour productivity growth by shedding labour in firms. This indeed seems the dominant view of business journalists these days although they do not always realize that they are using demand expansion policies, but only through a single route of expansion of private investment. The policy, if it succeeds, has much to recommend itself, but its success is bound to be limited to only a handful of countries, even within the OECD for a simple reason. Stimulation of private investment through higher profitability brought about by restraining real wages in relation to labour productivity growth, would tend to shrink the internal market owing to its income distribution effect (see equations (1.8) and (1.9)) and the outlet for domestic production has to be found in the *external* or export market. This not only means labour productivity growth or wage restraint has to be stronger in comparison to 'the rest of the world' of trade competitors, but even more absurdly, it means every country would need to have trade surplus to manage its aggregate demand. But as a matter of arithmetic, neither can all countries be in trade surplus (even within the OECD or the European Union), nor can all countries have a higher than average wage restraint or labour productivity growth! In short, mindless conservatism focusing *exclusively* on the stimulation of private investment pushes the industrialized economies towards a disastrous 'beggar my neighbour' policy resulting in a downward spiral. We need only add that competitive national tax reduction policies to stimulate corporate investment would have much the same effect.

In contrast to the Conservative perspective, the traditional Social Democratic view has been the economic interventionist role of the welfare state. It involves stimulation of public investment, if necessary through budget deficit, in the short run to counter serious cyclical unemployment. And, it also involves increasing real wages – either its private or its social component (i.e. public goods) or both – more or less in line with labour productivity growth to keep the expansion in productive capacity in line with growth in demand without serious distributive conflict in the longer run. These short- and long-run aspects of demand management envisaged by an ideology of 'reformed capitalism' can rightly take credit for much of the post-World War II prosperity in Europe. The attack on it in recent years can be classified under three different heads:

1. its implications in terms of public finance;
2. its consequences in terms of inflation;
3. its impact in terms of international trade, investment and finance.

The crux of the public finance argument is that continuous financing of public deficit by national or international borrowing would lead to an unsustainable burden of interest repayment on the state, reducing in turn the very flexibility of the pattern of public expenditure over time. The problem would compound as public borrowing can continue only at higher and higher rates of interest which in turn increases further the burden of interest repayment on the government budget. Since in the ultimate analysis, this is an argument about the credibility of the state as a borrower over time (otherwise, the state could always finance its repayment by borrowing more), it seems to suggest that continued public borrowing in itself must undermine confidence in the credibility of the state as a borrower. Even apart from the arithmetical truth noticed by Domar that the ability to repay depends on the rate of interest in relation to the rate of economic growth, the credibility of the state as a borrower depends critically on the overall performance of the economy: its growth, employment, balance of payments position, inflation rate and so on. Note that during the 1960s, the OECD governments also took recourse to large scale public borrowing (with a lower outstanding stock of public debt), but it was not intellectually fashionable then to speak of loss of government credibility on this count, mainly because the overall economic performances were considered satisfactory. In short, even large public debt *per se* does not generate a crisis of confidence in the government unless coupled with unsatisfactory economic performance. At worst, it can act as a catalytic agent to undermine the economic confidence of the public in the government, when economic performance is deemed to be unsatisfactory over a number of years. The Keynesian lesson again follows: expansionary fiscal policies supported by budget deficits could be used to improve the economic credibility of the state and its government provided that such policies improve economic performance. Otherwise, simply a balanced or even a surplus budget without improved economic performance has not been known to improve the economic credibility of the state.

The fear of inflation began to operate as a serious constraint on Keynesian demand expansionary policies, especially following the first oil crisis (1973). Concepts such as the 'natural rate' of unemployment and the 'Non-Accelerating Inflation Rate of Unemployment' (NAIRU) based upon the inflationary expectation-augmented reformulation of the Phillips curve proliferated in the literature.

The sacrifice of Keynesian demand expansionary policies even in the face of severe unemployment arising from the fear of (potential) inflation is based upon a fundamental analytical assumption. It presumes that any expansion of aggregate demand will lead almost entirely to upward price rather than quantity adjustment, despite the presence of unemployment and excess capacity. This assumption can make sense only if the economy is extremely prone to cost–push inflation, caused by sharp rises in money wages and prices following any demand expansion. It is doubtful that labour markets in the 1990s in Europe conform any longer to this description. But analytically even more important is the fact that (hidden by the augmented Phillips curve analysis) the economy's great tendency to cost–push inflation is essentially a manifestation of conflicting claims over distributive shares, when different groups have more or less equal bargaining power in the society (Bhaduri, 1986). Put bluntly, demand restraint policies are effective in combating inflation-proneness of the economy, only in so far as they weaken the bargaining power of the organized workers. However, it is not an unmixed blessing for the employers either, in so far as their price-setting power is also reduced in a market with lower demand and lower capacity utilization. Viewed this way, the fear of inflation as a constraint on macroeconomic policy appears as a contemporary version of the Kaleckian political business cycles.

Two further aspects of this fear of inflation argument should not go unnoticed either. First, in so far as investment fuels excess demand through the multiplier process, no logical case exists for stimulating private investment while curbing public investment. Both should be deemed inflationary. Even the (doubtful) argument that private investment is more 'efficient' cuts little ice. Because in the short run context of demand management, one is concerned primarily with the demand generating aspect of investment through the multiplier, not with its supply-generating aspect through efficiency (for example measured by the incremental output capital ratio).

Second, in its international aspect demand contraction in the OECD countries tends largely to shift the burden of adjustment of reducing inflation onto the poorer, primary producing countries. Thus, inflation is reduced, not so much by controlling money wage increases in the labour market, but by a sharp deterioration in the terms of trade against primary producers (recall oil price movements since 1973) whose prices are largely demand-determined with the main source of demand being in OECD countries (Beckerman and Jenkinson, 1986; Kaldor, 1976). It becomes easier to move towards a national consensus about the fear of inflation in OECD countries, largely because the cost of controlling inflation can be shifted internationally to the primary commodity exporters, mostly from the third world.

However, there is almost an irony in this view that the costs of adjustment can be shifted internationally to solve domestic problems, because internationalization or globalization of trade, investment and finance has gradually undermined the autonomy of the nation state itself in conducting economic policies. And, it is precisely here that the fundamental limitation of Keynesian economic *policy*, but not of Keynesian economic *theory*, needs to be located.

The assumption of a closed economy implies considerable independence of the nation state in pursuing domestic fiscal and monetary policies. The rapid globalization of international trade, investment and finance called into question the applicability of this model. For example, the deliberate process of European integration can no longer attribute (even legally) the same degree of autonomy to the nation-state.

Underlying the process of globalization, there are two distinct tendencies. First, there is the tendency towards globalization of production, where the centre of gravity shifts steadily in favour of the multinational enterprises. The tendency has been worldwide. It is estimated that during the last two decades (since the early 1970s) the number of multinational firms increased fourfold, with approximately 37 000 multinationals having 170 000 subsidiaries around the world, who now own about one third of the productive capital across different countries (Beer, 1992). This has also resulted in a rapid growth in sector-specific and intrafirm trade as a proportion of total international trade with the important consequence that much of the international transactions in goods and services no longer need to pass directly through the tax net or the fiscal system of the national government. As a result, an implicit zero-sum game among national governments, even with the European Union, let alone the third world countries has come into play. Each nation state seems increasingly more interested in attracting or retaining multinational activities and investments within its national boundaries by offering more liberal and deregulated economic policies. This has also provided a strong impetus towards economic liberalization, which reflects the increasingly powerful role of the multinational enterprises *vis-à-vis* the nation states.

Ironically this tendency is accentuated in times of persisting economic recession and severe unemployment as national governments look upon the multinationals as possible providers of jobs at home in order to counteract unemployment. The case of Germany, probably the most significant economic player in the EU, can be taken as an example. Towards the end of the 1980s the seven largest German multinational firms had approximately 1 million employees at home in Germany compared to nearly 1.6 million employees abroad in its worldwide subsidiaries. This ratio of home to foreign employees and investment may tend to be highly sensitive to national taxation and labour market policies, compelling the national government to be competitively more liberal in pursuing economic policies. Thus deregulation of national policies is driven by the increasing significance of the multinationals as dominating players in determining employment patterns.

The other tendency towards globalization has been in the area of international finance. The deregulation of international restrictions on currency transactions has seen the phenomenal growth of transactions in the foreign exchange markets. In the light of the fact that the daily turnover of foreign exchange tends to exceed foreign exchange reserves held by central banks (Scholtens, 1992), it is evident that central bank policies in any individual country have become extremely vulnerable to private trading in the foreign exchange markets. Central banks can mostly follow rather than lead the market in the event of a sudden change in market expectations against a particular currency. The deregulation of international financial markets has meant that market interventions by a central bank are extremely costly in terms of loss of foreign exchange reserves. The intervention of the central bank is unlikely to succeed when the market sentiments are pitted against such an intervention.

This has resulted in a kind of paralysis of caution in monetary and fiscal policies by national governments, because of the fear of generating unfavourable market reactions. Thus, expansionary fiscal policies threaten to be highly counterproductive in so far as they carry the danger of stimulating speculative capital flight following a possible deterioration in the current account balance. National monetary policies, especially regarding the levels of the interest rates, have at the same time lost autonomy because interest rate differentials can also cause massive speculative capital flights in a cumulative manner. In short, both the globalization of production evidenced by the growing importance of multinational enterprises and the globalization of finance resulting from the overwhelming importance of private transactions in the foreign exchange markets have steadily eroded the autonomy of national fiscal and monetary policies.

With respect to both multinational investments and production decisions as well as to private foreign exchange transactions, national governments have been forced to follow a highly market-friendly and cautious approach, because they are now dominated – some may say, even paralysed – by the power of the market. Naturally, the compulsion under these circumstances has been to go along with competitive liberalization to attract foreign investment within national borders by restraining wages, maintaining competitively high interest rates and following tight money policies against borrowing by the government but in favour of borrowing by the private corporate sector. Although macroeconomic variables like the level of employment and economic activity and the state of the balance of payments remain responsibilities of the national government, in the globalized context these national targets of economic policy have been set against one another.

It is convenient for our argument to reclassify the balance of payments in terms of the private and the official sector, involving all transactions in the current and capital account. The balance of private sector transactions requiring official (central bank) settlement or BOS (balance for official settlement) involves both current account and capital account surplus (or deficit) created by private transactions on the international dealings. It is legitimate to assume that the current account component tends to be negatively related to the level of economic activity (employment) because higher domestic demand spills over partly into import from the foreign market. The capital account component on the other hand, is related positively to the higher domestic interest rate (i) margin compared to the foreign interest rate (i_f), given the degree of substitutability between domestic and foreign assets, i.e.

$$B = BOS = [E - M(Y)] + \Phi\,(i - i_f) \qquad (1.10)$$

implying, for any given level of $B = \bar{B}\,(= 0$ in long-run equilibrium):

$$dY/d_i = \Phi_i/M_y > 0,\ \Phi_i > 0,\ M_y > 0 \qquad (1.11)$$

The main policy implication of the positive relation between economic activity and interest rate captured by (1.11) is to show that for individual nation states the monetary and the fiscal policy would tend to contradict each other. Thus, in contrast to the Keynesian national setting where a cheap monetary policy could complement an expansionary fiscal policy, any fiscal expansion raising domestic economic activity level (Y) would tend to lead to deterioration of current trade balance which would, in turn, need to be compensated by capital inflows attracted through higher domestic interest rate (i). A contractionary monetary policy would thus neutralize partly or wholly an expansionary fiscal policy, raising doubts about Keynesian demand management.

It should be stressed however, that this opposition between monetary and fiscal policy is quite asymmetrical, because it operates usually in the case of a deficit, but not so automatically in the case of a surplus on the current account. Thus, when the level of economic activity is low resulting in low domestic purchasing power and low import, a trade surplus may result. But an expansionary monetary policy lowering the interest rates may not still be pursued to stimulate domestic activity due to the fear of either inflation or speculative capital flight leading to forced depreciation of the domestic currency. This asymmetry stems from the fact that no central bank could be confident of acting unilaterally to lower the interest rates drastically in the face of the quantitatively overwhelming importance of private and speculative transactions in the foreign exchange markets described earlier. The high mobility of international financial capital (for example, portfolio investments) has not only reduced sharply the autonomy of national macroeconomic policies, it has also introduced asymmetries between contractionary and expansionary monetary policy through the interest rates with a built-in bias towards economic depression.

4. CONCLUSIONS

Deficiency in aggregate demand is still the central mechanism through which unemployment and economic depression are precipitated. Nevertheless, while that theoretical understanding is still correct, management of demand is no longer an easy policy option for national governments in the increasingly globalized market of production and finance. And, precisely to turn attention away from the inconvenient political questions regarding the role of the nation state under globalization, monetarism and various microeconomic supply-side solutions have been made respectable by both politicians and economists.

REFERENCES

Beckerman, W. and T. Jenkinson (1986), 'What stopped the inflation? Unemployment or commodity prices', *Economic Journal*, **96** (381), 39–54.
Beer, E. (1992), 'Globalisierung der Wirtschaft', *Information uber Multinational Konzerne*, (4).
Bhaduri, A. (1986), *Macroeconomics: The Dynamics of Commodity Production*, London: Macmillan.
Bhaduri, A. and S. Marglin (1990), 'Unemployment and the real wage: the economic basis for contesting political ideologies', *Cambridge Journal of Economics*, **14** (4), 375–93.
Glyn, A. and P. Gregg (1994), 'Employment in the developed market economies', unpublished paper.
Kaldor, N. (1976), 'Inflation and recession in the world economy', *Economic Journal*, **86** (344), 703–14.
Kalecki, M. (1971), *Selected Essays on the Dynamics of the Capitalist Economy*, Cambridge: Cambridge University Press.
Krugman, P. (1994), 'Europe jobless, America penniless', *Foreign Policy*, (95), 19–34.
Scholtens, L. (1992), 'Centralization in international financial intermediation: theory, practice and evidence for the European Community', *Banca Nazionale del Lavoro Quarterly Review*, (182), 255–304.

2. The myth of economic policy independence: some reflections on the failure of post-war schemes for stabilization of global demand in the post-war period

Jan A. Kregel[1]

So what can the IMF do? It doesn't have the funds to provide more support itself. The banks are unwilling. So you have to propose rather tough adjustment programs. Today the feeling is, I think correctly, that this adjustment has often been too painful and too tough. But what can the fund do? Neither the commercial banks nor governments are willing to provide more financing. *That* is the main difficulty, that the main industrial countries have been unwilling to provide, in some way, additional finances. (J. Witteveen, 1988)

1. INTRODUCTION

Most of the anniversary assessments of the Bretton Woods System have evaluated it as an attempt to provide a durable international monetary system to replace the gold standard. Most seem to have overlooked its origin in 1940 as part of a British propaganda programme to counter German broadcasts exalting the benefits of Dr Funk's 'New Order' which awaited the citizens of the Allied countries after Germany's ultimate victory. Keynes's ideas, which eventually took the form of a proposal for the reconstruction of post-war monetary arrangements through an International Clearing Union, were motivated by other concerns. Of major importance, in Keynes's view, was the necessity of combining the short-term realities of post-war economic reconstruction with an international monetary system which would alleviate the difficulties of sustained depression which had characterized the inter-war period and created the environment in which Fascist and Socialist solutions had flourished. Although many recent commentators have suggested that the system which emerged from Bretton

Woods was born of Keynes's ideas, or under his influence, this is not precise with respect to the necessity of resolving these two requirements. The failure of the Bretton Woods Agreements to deal with either the short-term problem of reconstruction or the longer-term problem of ensuring global demand was sufficient to employ available resources is one of the main reasons for its downfall. The lack of financing, noted in the opening quotation above, reflects this failure, which could have been resolved by following Keynes's recommendations. This chapter outlines the process which led to the failure of the Bretton Woods Agreements to deal with these problems, and then argues that the inability to resolve the long-term problem remains a major explanation of the current instability in the global economy.

1.2 The Origins of the Post-war International Monetary System

Keynes's original proposal for the post-war system was designed to produce 'the least possible interference with internal national policies . . . [to] operate not only to the general advantage but also to the individual advantage of each of the participants, . . . No participant must be asked to do or offer anything which is not in his own true long-term interest'. The proposal 'must be capable of application, irrespective of the type and principle of government and economic policy existing in the prospective member states' (IMF, 1969, pp. 19–20).

The proposal was in the tradition of Adam Smith, defending national sovereignty and building on the premise that it would be voluntarily adhered to only if it could be shown to provide benefits for its individual participants as well as for some abstract conception of the international community. Perhaps the most striking point about the proposal, given the current exclusive reliance on exchange rate adjustment caused by the inability to attain formal international policy coordination, is the clear recognition that 'the Clearing Union must also seek to discourage creditor countries from leaving unused large liquid balances which ought to be devoted to some positive purpose. For excessive credit balances necessarily create excessive debit balances for some other party. In recognising that the creditor as well as the debtor may be responsible for a want of balance, the proposed institution would be breaking new ground' (ibid., p. 20).

As in most of his practical policy proposals, Keynes does not attempt to create an institution which will directly control specific activities of individuals or nations, rather he seeks to construct an institutional framework which will direct individuals to actions which allow them to achieve their desired goals in a manner consistent with satisfying the goals of other individuals. Thus the novel aspect of the Clearing Union, the sharing of the burden of adjustment to international payments imbalances between creditor and debtor countries, was based on the introduction of an extremely simple institutional framework, the extension to the international sphere of the 'essential principle of banking as it is exhibited within any closed system' (ibid., p. 22).

2. THE CRUCIAL ELEMENT FOR SUCCESS OF THE NEW INTERNATIONAL SYSTEM

It was the application of this essential principle that provided the possibility of satisfying both the short- and the long-term requirements of the new international system. Of course, the short-term adjustment was the major concern of the European countries and Japan. Their devastated economies required imports of both capital and consumption goods from the US, without any prospect of being able to balance them with exports or asset sales.

Although the British economy had not sustained the physical damage of the continental economies, it had used all of its overseas assets to finance war expenditures. Since income from overseas investments had more than offset the traditional deficit on merchandise trade from 1850 to 1914, the post-war prospect was of serious balance of payments deficits, and a structural adjustment of the industrial sector which would require both time and financing, if Britain were to retain its position as an international financial centre and a global economic power. Thus although the character of Britain's need for restructuring was different from that of the other European economies, Britain was similar in facing the prospect of substantial imbalances on foreign account, and a constraint on its ability to make the required changes which was linked to the international monetary regime adopted for the post-war world. A group of countries facing prolonged structural payments deficits thus confronted the United States, which was considered to be the country with the counterpart structural surplus. Short-term payments balance and reconstruction were competing goals; economic survival and reconstruction could only be achieved if the US agreed to finance the deficits the Europeans would contract through their imports of US goods.

The logic of Keynes's plan was to make the financing of trade deficits, which would include those linked to the process of industrial reconstruction, virtually automatic through a supra-national entity, independent of any political conditions imposed by the lender as to the economic policies adopted in reconstruction or to the political complexion of the government. Of course, there was another motivation behind this proposal which referred to the behaviour of the system once reconstruction had been achieved (which was generally anticipated to be around twenty years). This was to prevent the process of adjustment to international payments imbalances from exercising downward pressure on the level of world aggregate demand and to avoid the return of the slump of the 1930s. This was the basic condition for a durable international monetary system.

Adjustment to payments imbalances would exercise a negative impact on demand whenever deficit countries were forced to restrict domestic expenditures in order to reduce imports and increase domestic savings in response to problems which were caused by other countries operating at levels of demand which were deficient to produce full employment. The automatic extension of financing to deficit countries, and the sharing of the burden of adjustment by increasing demand in the demand deficient countries and reducing it in the excess demand countries, was meant to allow adjustment to take place without reducing the overall level of demand and employment.

3. THE FEAR OF INFLATION

However, the key to a durable new international monetary system, the automatic financing of deficits by creditor countries to produce automatic sharing of the adjustment burden, was expressly excluded from the final Bretton Woods Agreements. One of the major objections to this idea was the belief that it would introduce an inflationary bias into the system. But Keynes's proposal was simply an attempt to restore an aspect which had already existed in the operation of the gold standard by

> putting some part of the responsibility for adjustment on the creditor country as well as on the debtor. This is an attempt to recover one of the advantages which were enjoyed in the nineteenth century, when a flow of gold due to a favourable balance in favour of London or Paris, which were then the main creditor centres, immediately produced an expansionist pressure and increased foreign lending in those markets, but which has been lost since New York succeeded to the position of main creditor, as a result of gold movements failing in their effect, of the breakdown of international borrowing and of frequent flight of loose funds from one depository to another. The object is that the creditor should not be allowed to remain entirely passive. For if he is, an intolerably heavy task may be laid on the debtor country, which is already for that very reason in the weaker position. (IMF, 1969, p. 28)

Since the gold standard was generally considered as providing a defence against inflation, the fear that Keynes's proposal would have an inflationary bias does not seem credible.

Further, in order to deal with the potential for inflation, Keynes's proposals imposed restraints on the debit position of any individual country.

Individual countries' quotas in the Union were to be limited to 75 per cent of the average of their imports and exports over a three year pre-war sample period and revised at fixed intervals. Debit balances could not increase by more than a quarter of a country's quota in a year, and collateral in the form of foreign exchange or gold would be required for up to half the quota. Upon exceeding three-quarters of its quota for over a year, or if borrowing increased unacceptably, further credit could be denied. A 1 per cent penalty on average debit or credit balances in excess of a quarter, and a further 1 per cent on balances in excess of a half, of the country's quota acted as incentives to return to a balanced position.

Finally, the proposals suggested that during the transition the use of the facilities of the Union would be limited to the amount of gold committed in the event that 'liberal and comprehensive' resources were available from outside the Union for reconstruction, given that 'The expansionist tendency of the plan ... might be a danger in the early days of a sellers' market and an excess of demand over supply.' But, the proposal also warns that 'We must not be over-cautious. A rapid economic restoration may lighten the tasks of ... the restoration of social order. ... We cannot afford to wait too long for this, and we must not allow excessive caution to condemn us to perdition' (IMF, 1969, p. 35).

These restraints would have limited the creation of money to that necessary to produce non-inflationary reconstruction and after that to what was required to support global full employment; the intermediary function of the Clearing Union was to assure that the global money supply would be held, whatever its composition in terms of domestic monies. Inflationary potential does not seem to have been a real threat.

3.1 An Imperfect Substitute: The Scarce Currency Clause

The only recognition of Keynes's major concern, the sharing of the burden of adjustment to payment imbalances, which survived in the final Agreement was the 'scarce currency clause':

> when it becomes evident to the Fund that the demand for a member country's currency may soon exhaust the Fund's holdings of that currency, the Fund shall so inform member countries and propose an equitable method of apportioning the scarce currency. When a currency is thus declared scarce, the Fund shall issue a report embodying the causes of the scarcity and containing recommendations designed to bring it to an end. A decision by the Fund to apportion a scarce currency shall operate as an authorization to a member country, after consultation with the Fund, temporarily to restrict the freedom of exchange operations in the affected currency and, in determining the manner of restricting the demand and rationing the limited supply amongst its nationals, the member country shall have complete jurisdiction. (IMF, 1969, p. 134 of the Joint Statement by Experts)

Since the USA was expected to be a surplus country permanently, it was presumed that the US dollar would be the only candidate for 'scarce' currency. The necessity of a formal report, proposing remedies for the imbalance (White's proposal gave the scarce currency country automatic membership on the committee drafting the report), gave the USA some control over the direct lending it might be required to make to finance other countries' deficits.

At the same time the clause substituted exchange controls and trade restrictions by debtor countries for creditor country expansion or lending in support of restructuring of the payments of the debtor country as the basic remedy. Such restrictive actions by debtors were clearly contrary to the support of global demand which Keynes had intended.

It was also clear that the clause was only an expedient to meet the trade imbalances foreseen for the post-war reconstruction; for example, it could not even operate when no country was indebted with respect to any other to a degree necessary to invoke the scare currency clause. But, the final Agreements went further in eliminating any automatic financing, stating explicitly that the 'Fund is not intended to provide facilities for relief or reconstruction or to deal with international indebtedness arising out of the war' (IMF, 1969, p. 135). To this end it exempted countries from current account convertibility for a five-year period. After the experience with the British Loan, this limit was relaxed and it was only in 1958–59 that the convertibility provision was satisfied by the European countries.

4. THE ROLE OF CAPITAL CONTROLS – A SHORT OR LONG-TERM ASPECT OF THE SYSTEM?

In all likelihood the acceptance of controls on capital flows which was included in the joint statement was meant to emphasize the point that Fund resources would not be available for short-term reconstruction purposes, rather than indicating that such controls were to be considered as 'a permanent feature of the post-war system' (IMF, 1969, p. 31) as had been the case in the Clearing Union proposal. These controls can be seen as a counterpart to the power given to countries 'temporarily to restrict the freedom of exchange operations in the affected currency and, in determining the manner of restricting the demand and rationing the limited supply amongst it nationals' provided in the scarce currency clause.

While the White Plan had permitted the use of borrowing from the Fund to 'facilitate a transfer of capital . . . desirable from the point of view of the general economic situation' (IMF, 1969, p. 90) as long as the Fund's holdings of the country's currency remained below 150 per cent of the quota, the joint statement expressly forbade the use of Fund resources for a 'large or sustained outflow of capital' such as might have been necessary to finance the imports required for reconstruction, permitting capital transfers only 'of reasonable amount required for the expansion of exports or in the ordinary course of trade, banking and other business' (IMF, 1969, pp. 133–4).

This substitution for Keynes's proposed device of automatic lending in support of global demand thus left the problem of how to deal with the immediate problems of financing post-war reconstruction in the hands of the US and its willingness to allow the scarce currency clause to be invoked. This failure to deal explicitly with the immediate problems of reconstruction had been the chief motivation of the 'French Plan' and J.H. Williams's 'central countries' approach. Both suggested that the most important aspect of any new system was that 'it must be applicable as soon as hostilities are over and even earlier whenever possible' (IMF, 1969, p. 97) for 'If the international monetary system is so ambitious that it cannot become of general use until political and economic conditions are peacefully settled in the whole world, it may have to wait a long while'. It was these concerns that led Williams to suggest starting the new system in 'piecemeal' fashion, first attempting to gain stability in the dollar–sterling exchange rate, extending arrangements to European currencies after the period of reconstruction (IMF, 1969, p. 126).

Thus the short-term problem was isolated from the design of the post-war international monetary system, and its solution was eventually provided independently of the scarce currency clause by the Marshall Plan. This gave the USA direct control over the amount of funds to be committed, as well as the particular uses to which these funds were put and the types of policies adopted by governments to administer them. This was clearly not a solution in which participation was 'irrespective of the type and principle of government and economic policy existing in the prospective member states'.

5. THE USA AS REGULATOR OF GLOBAL DEMAND

More importantly, this solution meant that the USA became the major regulator of the level of global demand through its willingness to finance foreign growth through its foreign balance. Robert Triffin eventually diagnosed a basic incompatibility in the framework of the Bretton Woods System's use of the US dollar, in place of gold, as the basis for international reserves, and the use of the dollar as the US national currency. However, there was a more basic problem linked to the willingness of the US economy to provide a level of internal demand compatible with financing global full employment.

As long as the USA remained the dominant creditor economy, the problem which Keynes had attempted to remedy in his Clearing Union did not arise; the USA supported global demand, at least for reasons of political expediency, first through the Marshall Plan, and then through outflows of funds on what might be called 'political capital' account, allowing reconstruction to proceed unhindered by financing constraints. Because the flow of dollars was adequate to finance payments' imbalances, the 'scarce currency' clause was never invoked. Indeed, it was the USA which suffered problems of unsatisfactory demand in the period, exception taken for the Korean War period.

Yet, it was the failure to provide an integrated solution to the short- and long-term problems which delayed recognition of the essential flaw in the Bretton Woods compromise: the failure to resolve the problem of the destabilizing nature on global demand of asymmetric adjustments by creditor and debtor countries to disequilibrium. This short-term solution also effectively masked the deflationary impact of the IMF itself, for Marshall Plan participants were precluded from access to IMF funds as long as they participated, and the time limits on return to convertibility were virtually eliminated. The Fund thus was never called upon to play any active role in payments adjustment in the early period of reconstruction.

In the absence of implementation of the scarce currency clause, the only role which remained to the IMF was that of international bill collector for surplus countries whose funds it started to lend to debtors on a short-term basis after the introduction of convertibility. Its major concern was not sustaining growth in the deficit countries, or in the global economy, but simply to ensure that it recovered the funds it lent to member countries. To do this it set out a series of measures, including devaluation of the currency and domestic fiscal restriction, which countries had to satisfy to receive support. These conditions more resemble those which a liquidator sent in to salvage a company facing a liquidity shortage might impose, rather than a plan to restore growth.

6. FROM DOLLAR SCARCITY TO DOLLAR GLUT

The decision to rely on a practical solution to post-war reconstruction masked the problem of asymmetric adjustment behind the increasing deficits on the overall US balance of payments. To meet the dollar outflows, US gold stocks fell continuously from the record post-war high of around 60 per cent of total world stocks. The combination of the sustained dollar expenditures in support of cold war commitments, and the rapid recovery of industrial competitivity and equilibrium in the trade accounts of the major Western European countries that had participated in the Marshall Plan turned dollar 'scarcity' into a 'dollar glut'.

The institution of a European Common Market, virtually simultaneously with the declaration of currency convertibility by most European countries in 1959, attracted substantial US direct investment to the European economies and aggravated the US dollar outflows. As a result the price of gold peaked above $40 an ounce in October 1960. This was outside its permitted fluctuation band around the official parity of $35. This was not a typical balance of payments crisis for the USA, for the trade balance remained in surplus; the deficit was primarily composed of foreign direct investment and such politically motivated expenditures as foreign aid and military transfers. None the less, it signalled that the basic hypothesis upon which the Bretton Woods system had been founded, the USA as a substantial international creditor country with an unconstrained ability to support global demand, was no longer valid.

7. THE TRIFFIN DILEMMA AND ASYMMETRIC ADJUSTMENT

As already noted, the first diagnosis of the problem facing the system was known as the 'Triffin dilemma', linked to the opposed needs of a national currency serving as both domestic and international means of payments and store of value. While overall payments deficits are required to supply international reserves, the larger the deficits, the lower the confidence in the currency as an international store of value. This conflict is aggravated if, as in the case of Bretton Woods, the value of the currency is pegged to gold and the outstanding foreign official balances of the currency exceed the gold stock of the country issuing the currency. This was already the case for the US dollar by 1964. There was thus an inherent conflict between meeting all demands for dollar liquidity by foreign holders and keeping the credibility of the fixed, constant gold price.

This conflict was further aggravated by the US stagflation of 1958–60, which along with the birth of the 'ICBM (intercontinental ballistic missile) gap', gave currency to the 'GNP gap' and Kennedy's campaign promise to eliminate it by expansionary economic policy at the same time as he pledged to financial markets that he would defend the dollar price of gold. But, the support of the gold value of the dollar required contractionary fiscal policy and tight monetary policy, in direct conflict with the electoral promise to expand the economy to eliminate the GNP gap.

A series of measures were introduced from 1960 to try to bridge this conflict, starting with 'payments offsets' for countries receiving US military aid, the creation of the General Agreements to Borrow and the informal Group of Ten (G-10), outside the official structure of the IMF.

These stopgap measures were reinforced by a series of more creative policy devices. The best known was 'Operation Twist', which attempted to invert the yield curve and provide low long-term interest rates in support of domestic expenditures compatible with high short-term rates to attract foreign demand for the dollar and reduce the redemption of dollars into gold. The 'interest equalization tax' was also an attempt to create synthetically a dampening impact of higher interest rates on capital outflows without actually having to tighten domestic monetary policy and domestic investment expenditures.

It was the same concern for the conflict between domestic and foreign equilibrium which tipped the balance in favour of tax reduction, rather than increased government expenditure, becoming the centrepiece of the expansionary fiscal policy designed to eliminate the GNP gap. Kennedy's mainstream Keynesian economic advisers argued that lower taxes coupled with investment incentives would raise the level of productivity, reduce domestic production costs and make US exports more competitive, thus reinforcing the external position of the dollar. Increasing government expenditure, it was argued, would have the opposite effect because it would increase imports, cause the trade balance to deteriorate, and cause companies to shift investment and production abroad.

However, by the time the tax reduction was approved (under President Johnson) in late 1964, the increased public expenditure it was to make unnecessary was taking place in the form of Vietnam war expenditures and Great Society spending programmes. The GNP gap quickly disappeared and the increased tax yields caused the government budget to move back towards balance, but the combination of tax reductions and increased government expenditures now suggested that fiscal restraint would be required to keep the economy from exceeding its productive potential and producing inflationary conditions.

8. RECONCILING DOMESTIC AND INTERNATIONAL POLICY

The failure to cut government expenditures or increase taxes as war spending and economic expansion accelerated, finally led the Federal Reserve to step in to substitute for the absent fiscal restraint, tightening monetary policy at the end of 1965. This decision was taken against the backdrop of the need to bolster the international payments position, strengthening the voluntary restraints on foreign lending by banks and corporations.

This tightening nearly produced a collapse of financial markets; banks lost substantial amounts of deposit funds and were forced to take losses as they sold securities to raise funds to meet existing lending commitments to regular borrowers. Overall lending collapsed. This episode, which has come to be known as the 'credit crunch', had international as well as domestic implications. Recurrent balance of payments difficulties brought the decision to make the voluntary lending restraints obligatory and the interest equalization tax at about the same time. The combination of these two factors sharply reduced bank earnings and reinforced the banks' move into the Eurodollar markets to seek alternative sources of funding in the event of another credit crunch.

When the Federal Reserve was again forced to substitute monetary for absent fiscal restraint in the payments crisis of late 1968 the money centre banks were now well established in the Euromarkets. They offset their decline in domestic funding by increasing their borrowing of funds from the Eurodollar market. This first caused the dollar to strengthen, but when the flow was reversed as rates fell back in 1970–71 the result was increased instability in international capital flows and massive pressure on European central banks, in particular the Bundesbank. Dollar holdings in German banks increased by over 400 per cent and the decision was finally taken to float the Deutschmark. These movements were interpreted by the Nixon Administration as an unsustainable permanent outflow and the final argument for the August 15 decision to abandon gold convertibility, which effectively ended the Bretton Woods system. The response of the banking system to the use of monetary policy to substitute for asymmetric adjustment and coordination of fiscal policy on the global level thus eventually led to the breakdown of the Bretton Woods System.

In retrospect, the primary cause of these difficulties was not simply the Triffin dilemma, it was the problem Keynes had originally placed at the centre of his Clearing Union proposal – the deflationary impact of asymmetric adjustment. The problem reappeared in the 1960s because the USA had ceased to be the dominant surplus country. In contrast to the basic premise of the Bretton Woods system and the scarce currency clause, the balance of payments surpluses were in Europe and Japan. These countries had completed their reconstruction process, and thus the factors which had produced an independent source of support for global demand were declining. The USA thus went from being the relatively slow growing economy, to the relatively fast growing economy, and the policies which were being put forward to produce an acceptable rate of growth in the US economy became subject to international constraints.

Throughout the decade of the 1960s the USA fruitlessly tried to convince surplus countries to expand their economies sufficiently rapidly to allow the USA to avoid having to sacrifice domestic growth and employment to the defence of the gold value of the dollar. Ironically, the USA was no more successful in convincing the European countries to cede their advantage than Keynes had been in trying to convince the USA at Bretton Woods 20 years earlier that an automatic mechanism to solve such problems would be necessary. The expedients which the USA was forced to adopt in order to try to avoid domestic demand restriction set into action a series of forces which eventually destroyed the Bretton Woods system itself. It was thus the failure to resolve the problem of asymmetric adjustment that led to the acceptance of more or less freely flexible exchange rates as an alternative solution. But the introduction of flexible exchange rates simply transformed the problem into one of competitive devaluations.

The fundamental weakness of the scarce currency clause as a remedy for global demand failure thus became evident in the 1960s, for it was based on the assumption that the country supplying the international currency would also be a surplus and creditor country. It was clearly not intended to apply to a number of individual members' currencies, none of which played a major role in international reserves or as an international means of payment. Consideration was never even given to invoking the scarce currency clause for surplus countries such as Germany in the 1960s. The nearest equivalent, the General Agreements to Borrow, which gave rise to the Group of Ten, and the semi-official Central Bank swap arrangements, were all informal attempts, outside the official channels of the IMF, to remedy the deficiencies of the scarce currency clause.

9. THE RETURN OF ADJUSTMENT DIFFICULTIES WITH FLEXIBLE EXCHANGE RATES IN THE 1980s

But by the end of the 1970s the problems of international payments adjustment had re-emerged. The response in the 1980s aggravated conditions by turning the positive benefits of developing countries' demand into a negative impact. The Federal Reserve chose to substitute tight monetary policy for absent fiscal policy as the Reagan administration sought to reduce individual and corporate taxes in the 1981 tax bill. The reduction in tax rates was meant to threaten Congress with such a large deficit that they would approve reductions in spending appropriations. A budget deficit was expressly engineered in order to force Congress into reducing the role of government in the economy.

In contrast to the experience of the 1966 Kennedy–Johnson tax cut, the dollar was floating and the Federal Reserve attempt to fix monetary aggregates produced double digit interest rates which were highly variable and extremely high relative to rates abroad. The brief 1983 expansion produced a deterioration in the current account, while the high rates attracted large capital inflows which caused a sharp appreciation of the dollar. The output expansion due to the reduced corporate tax rates never produced the expected rise in fiscal revenues, while the increase in the deficit had little effect in forcing Congress to cut government expenditures; the result was an increase in the trade and government deficits.

This also acted to reverse the positive impact on global demand of the expansion of the developing countries in the 1970s. As a result of the appreciation of the dollar and interest rates on LDC debt, developing countries entered a period of asymmetric adjustment which saw a sharp collapse in primary product prices, imports and growth as they introduced IMF-inspired structural adjustment policies to bring their payments into balance. These programmes were not intended to defend exchange rate convertibility, and only a small amount of official international lending was involved. The IMF nevertheless continued to play the role of debt collector, now for the private banks, who made it a condition of continued lending that the Fund approve adjustment programmes and lending on normal repayment conditions in the hope that this would improve the probability of repayment. In contrast to the policies applied by the IMF during the fixed exchange rate period, in addition to devaluation and restrictions on government expenditures, stabilization programmes now also included reference to 'structural adjustments'. This usually meant shifting to export oriented policies and privatization of provision of most government services and state enterprises. Here the IMF once again contravened a basic assumption of the Clearing Union, national autonomy in deciding employment and growth strategies. The more important point, however, is that none of these recommendations recognized the negative impact of these policies on the level of global demand and tended to aggravate the problems of asymmetric adjustment by exhorting the entire developing world to operate simultaneously with balance of payments surpluses. All this while the United States continued to be the main deficit country without any stabilization policy.

By 1985 the impact of high interest rates and dollar appreciation convinced the US Administration that the operation of the market in conditions of flexible exchange rates would not eliminate the trade deficit. The policy introduced in September 1985 at the Plaza was intended to bring about a controlled 10–12 per cent depreciation of the dollar which, in an abrupt change of direction, the administration suddenly considered to be overvalued. In little over a year the dollar depreciated by four times that much, while the trade balance continued to deteriorate. The Louvre conference was called to attempt a coordinated effort to stem the fall of the dollar. Nearly a decade after Plaza, with the

Yen periodically breaking the 80 Yen to the dollar level, the basic problem still had not changed. The US is still trying to convince its trading partners to take measures to increase their domestic growth rates and threatening continued depreciation of the dollar if they don't. This is, of course, just another repetition of the problem of asymmetric international adjustment which plagued the original Bretton Woods negotiations, but now, in conditions of flexible exchange rates, relative price adjustment has been substituted for aggregate demand adjustment in an attempt to force the latter.

Much as the Marshall Plan overcame the problem of the asymmetric distribution of world demand in the 1940s, and the recycling of OPEC surpluses to support demand for developed country exports by developing countries in the 1970s, in the second half of the 1980s the decision to create a single European market, and then the decision to proceed to rapid German unification, provided the boost to European demand required to bring about both domestic expansion and an increase in US exports. European expansion based on unification produced an offset to the flagging US economy from 1987–88 until 1990. But Britain had already entered a downturn by the end of that period and the investment and modernization generated by the expectation of the unified European market had started to wane by 1990, replaced by the strong expansion in Germany of more than 3 per cent per annum from 1988–91 linked to unification. As German government expenditures and inflation rates rose, the Bundesbank increased interest rates; growth fell to 1.5 per cent in 1992 and –2 per cent in 1993. The EMS transmitted the higher German interest rates to the rest of Europe and created a recession that eliminated the positive external impact of European expansion on US demand.

In addition, the decision to proceed to Monetary Union in Europe via the provisions of the Maastricht Treaty implied convergence of various economic indicators, such as government deficits, outstanding government indebtedness as a proportion of GDP, inflation and interest rates. Since a majority of countries did not meet the minimum requirements for deficits and debt, and others such as Germany, the UK and France which had met the conditions when the Treaty was drafted, found their positions deteriorating rapidly for reasons of domestic weakness or exceptional factors such as German integration. The result was a generalized introduction of contractionary fiscal policies to satisfy the Maastricht requirements. Fiscal contraction induced by monetary union thus joined the restrictive monetary policies required to keep currencies within permitted fluctuation bands relative to the German Mark, buoyed by the high German interest rates.

Japan had also exercised a positive impact on the US external position after 1985, as a result of a policy of extremely low interest rates which produced a substantial increase in asset prices; this was eventually reversed by extremely tight monetary policy. The policy produced a collapse in asset prices in 1990 and has substantially eliminated growth in the Japanese economy since.

10. FAILURE TO DEAL WITH ASYMMETRIC ADJUSTMENT AND THE 1990s SLUMP

Much of the disappointing growth performance in first half of the 1990s is due to asymmetric international adjustment as the USA comes to depend increasingly on expansion in Europe and Japan, while Europe is counting on US recovery to bring it out of recession, and both depend on expansion in their exports to developing countries. It is not surprising that efforts at economic policy coordination have again broken down as fiscal policies in all countries are directed to reducing government debt and expenditures, while monetary policies are being used to counteract what is considered to be insufficient domestic fiscal retrenchment. It thus becomes impossible for monetary policy to be coordinated internationally; indeed, international coordination becomes impossible, as the conditions in the foreign exchange markets demonstrated during in the summer of 1993.

11. CONCLUSIONS

The global economy thus faces the impact of a number of factors which lead to declining levels of demand, the postponed post-war reduction in defence spending, the presumed necessity to reduce government indebtedness through reductions in current deficits produced by increasing taxation and decreasing domestic expenditures. But, the 1990s appear to be most like the 1930s in the increased role that international factors will play on domestic demand. Resolving the problem that Keynes raised over fifty years ago of creating an automatic mechanism to defuse the natural tendency of the international system to produce a deficient level of global demand is thus even more important.

NOTES

1   This paper draws on my contribution to the 11th Keynes Seminar sponsored by Keynes College, University of Kent, November 1993, 'The slump of the early 1990s – a post Keynesian explanation'. I am indebted to Jean-Marc Fontaine for extensive comments which have improved the argument and extended it to the developing countries.

REFERENCES

References to the various post-war plans and the Joint Statement are from:

(IMF) (1969), *The International Monetary Fund 1945–1965: Twenty Years of International Monetary Cooperation*, Volume III, Documents, Washington, D.C.: International Monetary Fund.

Witteveen, Johannes (1988) Interview in *The Way It Was: An Oral History of Finance 1967–87*, The Editors of *Institutional Investor*, New York: William Morrow, pp. 225–38.

3. Effective demand and productive systems

Renato Di Ruzza

1. PRODUCTIVE SYSTEMS: AN OVERVIEW

In the *General Theory* Keynes took pains to define the basic time unit of his analysis. Yet, he said nothing about the spatial dimension to which the *General Theory* was supposed to apply. On balance, it appears that the nation state constitutes the referential framework of Keynes's approach. It must be pointed out that, indirectly, Keynes did refer to elements which may be used to specify the space within which his theory would hold. The most important of them is the idea of 'community', thereby hinting at a certain homogeneity as to the domain of application of the theory. Furthermore, in Chapter 19 of the *General Theory* we find the suggestion that the principle of effective demand can be best made operational in an economy where foreign trade is relatively small. Nevertheless, the absence of a clearly defined spatial unit in Keynes's approach emerged implicitly during the 1970s, when the failure of expansionary policies – as it was the case in France with both Chirac's 1976 and Mauroy's 1982 reflations – was taken as the proof of the inapplicability of Keynesian demand management.[1]

In this context the purpose of the paper is to argue that the spatial dimension of Keynes's monetary economy of production is defined by the notion of a *productive system*. In the post-war period demand oriented policies have been successful as long as they were within the limits of national economies, which constituted the main referential point for the strategies of both corporations and labour organizations.

The notion of *productive systems* originates with the Grenoble branch of the French School of the *Régulation* (GRREC, 1983, 1989). According to this component of this *Régulation* School, production must undergo a process of valorization in the Marxian sense. The objective of capitalist production is to start with a certain amount of value in order to set in motion the elements of the labour process with the purpose of obtaining

33

a higher mass of value. In an interconnected sectoral framework, each production process depends upon the working of all the others. When the whole set of sectors involved is capable of reproducing itself, the system is then structurally coherent. This requires that the physical composition of production be such that the labour process is reconstituted from one period to the next and that capitalists obtain a rate of profit enabling them to continue on an expanded basis.

Models like those of Von Neumann and Sraffa are simplified versions of a productive system. The economy produces a physical surplus product made of basic commodities (circularity of production) which ensures both a positive rate of profit and the continuation of the process of production. More recently the reproduction schema developed by Adolph Lowe (1976), identify the capacity to renew and expand the stock of capital in a special machine tools sector, called sector 1a, capable of providing equipment for all the branches producing non shiftable capital. In Lowe a dearth of capital in sector 1a would eventually prevent the normal replacement of worn out equipment, thereby causing a decay of the productive system. Finally, the work of Luigi Pasinetti (1981) has shown that the evolution of effective demand has an impact on the structure of production itself and not just on the quantity produced.[2]

It is clear that in the models I have used to describe the notion of a productive system, there is nothing which would confine this concept exclusively to the national sphere. A productive system may encompass a number of countries which together will form the spatial unit within which the principle of effective demand can be rendered operational. The areas forming a productive system are organized hierarchically. A typical example is provided by the era of classical imperialism in which productive systems were structured around a core country with a definite economic periphery.

The nature of monetary relations prevailing in and among productive systems can be summarized as follows (Di Ruzza, 1983; GRREC, 1989). Each system is characterized by one currency and economic relations within it are entirely of a monetary nature. By contrast, relations between different productive systems are of a quasi barter nature. This view stems from the consideration that money is a social convention and must, therefore, reflect the norms, in particular those pertaining to the labour process, which regulate economic activity. These norms differ between productive systems so that their mutual exchange relations must take the form of monetary flows mediated by a real commodity like gold. It can be argued that this was indeed the case during the stability phase of the post-war period when the US dollar was formally exchangeable into gold. Hence, the monetary instability which followed the end of the convertibility of the US dollar may be seen as reflecting non-reversible changes in the nature of productive systems. In this context, the phase of structural instability which has set in since the end of the 1960s is also a crisis affecting the very spatial configuration of capitalism and, in particular, the role of the nation state (Calvet, 1994).

2. THE CRISIS

The various branches of the *Régulation* School seem to agree on the point that the origin of crises is to be found within each productive system (Borrelly, 1990; Di Ruzza and Fontanel, 1994). The world economic disorder does not spring from the world but rather from ruptures occurring within the productive systems. Yet the international dimension has a particular role to play in the evolution of the crisis because, if anything, every productive system attempts to dispose of its own problems via the world market. Thus it might be useful to start from the international monetary system. Its functioning must be based on a set of consistent procedures so as to enable exchanges to flow smoothly between productive systems. For over two decades after the end of the Second World War the required rules were provided by the Bretton Woods agreements.

As often has been the case in history, the present crisis begins with a series of monetary turbulences at the international level. The first signs of the dislocation and eventual demise of Bretton Woods appeared in 1966 with the devaluation of the British pound, followed by the statement of the President of the United States that the US government would cease exchanging gold against dollars held by foreign central banks. The evolution of the structure of international trade, by altering the composition of output within the productive systems led, by the mid 1970s, to the abandonment of the procedures and rules devised at Bretton Woods. In less than a decade the number of countries whose currency was linked to the US dollar fell from 62 to 31. Furthermore, the British pound lost its own area so that no currency was any longer linked to it. The same observation holds for the Spanish Peseta, while 10 countries attached theirs to the Special Drawing Rights and 26 chose a trade weighted index. It is in this monetary framework, leading to persistent balance of payments disequilibria, that the exchange rate and the rate of interest have become the main instruments of economic policies. As a consequence the management of effective demand has given way to policies aimed at disinflation and at structural adjustments.

These two types of interventions (disinflation and structural adjustments) are subject to the same logic: they are rooted in the international setting, being in a sense *imposed* by the opening up of the national economies (Treillet, 1994). By using interest and exchange rate policies governments attempt to attain a quite large number of objectives, curiously of both short- and long-run nature. The aim is to control inflation, to stimulate exports and to reduce both external and internal deficits. These policies invariably postulate a reduction of domestic demand, to be recouped only in the long run, and a type of structural adjustment operating exclusively from the supply side, such as deregulation and greater opening to international competition. Their outcomes are never evaluated in terms of absolute levels, such as the full employment level of investment, but in terms of worldwide comparative performances related purely to indicators of competitiveness.

Two observations follow from the description made above. First, in the context of a slow growing world demand, the normal consequence of policies aimed at curbing the expansion of domestic markets in each country consists in that an increase in the share of world's trade by a given set of countries tends to generate an absolute loss of foreign trade by another set. This sort of competitive law of the market cannot but reinforce the international disequilibria which those policies were supposed to cure in the first place. Second, looking at the matter from the angle of the single nation there seems to be no real alternative to those restrictive interventions. The integration of each country in the world economy is subject to conditions, and if a country refuses to play by the rules it will suffer losses, unless a large number of countries decide not to play which is tantamount to a plan of world recovery, unthinkable in today's political relations. As a consequence any form of demand rehabilitation at the national level appears to be most problematical.

3. MULTIPLE FORMS OF ECONOMIC SPACES

The crisis has brought about a profound transformation of the national productive systems which emerged after the Second World War. This factor has caused the world economy to acquire a configuration which terms like globalization and internationalization capture only marginally. In effect we are witnessing the formation of economic spaces which often overlap and whose dynamic tendencies are difficult to apprehend.

The world as a whole constitutes the playground of the large firms, in terms of markets, production and finance. This is the terrain of their strategies, of the networks which they establish and the type of information they use and generate. The world as a single economic space is also the reference point for the other economic units mostly because these are subject to the mercantile and commodification effects stemming from the action of the large firms. National entities, however, still form the area where political and juridical power is explicitly exercised. Social relations, such as activities by the trade unions, wage determination, working conditions, are largely, although no longer entirely, defined at the national level. Between the world as a single economic space and the national spaces there exist intermediate zones which are either in the process of being formed or of being undone, displaying very different dynamic tendencies. We notice, for instance, the rekindling of multinational regionalism expressed by the acceleration of the process of European unification, as well as the formation of the North American Free Trade Agreement (NAFTA) and of MERCOSUR, the trade pact between Argentina, Brazil, Uruguay, Paraguay, Chile and Bolivia.

The heterogeneity of these three forms of intersecting spaces – the global, the national and the intermediate – raises a number of questions concerning both their mutual coexistence and their evolution. Essentially these different but sometimes criss-crossing areas have non-commensurable norms. Even the European Union cannot yet be considered as a single productive system, as shown by the obstacles encountered by the major European firms to negotiate with their workers on a continental rather national basis. Historically the national space has been the territory with which the trade unions are most familiar. For the labour movement the nation still represents the terrain of social struggle and of new institutional gains. Labour organizations are definitely ill at ease in this undefined space intersecting both the national and the global dimension. Analytically we should also question whether the evolution of the new forms of economic spaces foreshadows a novel system of regulation and, consequently, is heralding the emergence of new productive systems (Attali, 1991; Gerbier, 1995). In this context, it is clear that any discussion about the rehabilitation of demand must take into account the spatial structure of the world economy. In policy terms, for demand rehabilitation measures to be successful, it is necessary to define and actually constitute the appropriate spatial units to which policies may be applied.

4. OBSTACLES TO THE REHABILITATION OF DEMAND

The history of the European Union is a good example of the hindrances to the construction of an economic space suitable to demand rehabilitation policies. It must be pointed out at the outset that the long duration of crisis has changed the very nature of the process of European unification. The political forces which brought about the Treaty of Rome in 1957 thought of an economic union attainable independently from the practice of specific economic actors. This conception of European unification stemmed from the ideology of supranationality which considered integration as equivalent to an even and smooth merger. Instead national productive systems resisted and benefited from the formation of the EEC for a number of reasons. The modalities, social as well as technological, of the high growth patterns which accompanied the creation of the Common Market were based on a preference for national structures. Private firms, whose main domain of action was the national economy, used the EEC to expand exports and to acquire a larger variety of industrial inputs, but never to 'Europeanize' themselves.

The crisis, which began with the monetary turbulences of the late 1960s, by causing a systematic weakening of the autonomy of national economies, has changed the course of the unification process in Europe. Given the present state of intercompenetration, Europe might appear to have become the space on which to build a new productive system. It is with this view in mind that, from the mid 1970s, a number of political leaders decided to revitalize the construction of a united Europe. The difficulty in achieving this objective lies, however, in the fact that firms, in particular those leading the processes of structural transformations, have not become today more European than they were at the beginning of the formation of the EEC. Before the crisis they were anchored to national productive systems which served them well in terms of expansion of markets and exports. With the crisis the same set of firms has tended to go transnational and develop global strategies.

The present modalities of European unification belong to the realm of the autonomy of politics relative to economics. Implicitly such modalities aim at compelling leading firms to focus on Europe as a whole entity. This strategy is being implemented by completing the disarticulation of national productive systems in order to make national solutions impossible. Furthermore, the target of a single currency would guarantee to those firms a large area characterized by perfect monetary stability. Yet there is no solid indication that the waning of the national dimension is leading towards the formation of a consistent European productive system.[3] It follows that attempts to rehabilitate expansionary demand policies in a substantial way are bound to hit serious barriers.

5. CONCLUSIONS

In some ways the observations made in this paper tend to a quite pessimistic view as to the possibility of rehabilitating demand. In order for demand-oriented programmes to be minimally successful, they will have to be consistent with a spatially structured set of internally coherent (homogeneous) productive systems which, as a consequence of the crisis, no longer exist. Just the same, demand policies seem to be urgently needed especially if devised to counter the tendencies of the present situation. But, the formulation of this sort of policy is likely to be very problematical unless two preliminary issues are tackled at once. The first deals with the character of international economic relations, whereas the second relates to the role of protectionism.

Up to what point is it possible to envisage a reconstitution of the world economy into relatively autonomous productive systems, each internally consistent and homogeneous? This question concerns simultaneously all the economic areas of the planet. Let us take Europe as an example. If the European Union is to constitute itself into a coherent productive system (something which at present appears to be rather unlikely), it is conceivable that a number of developing areas will gravitate towards and around it. At this point we should also bring into the picture the nature of the possible relations between the European Union and the areas over which it is likely to exercise a gravitational influence. With Europe acting as a core, will these relations imply a new form of imperialism, or will it be feasible to think in terms of productive systems specific to the outlying areas? If yes, then what kind of national groupings will they require, what norms of trade relations with Europe?

The analysis of the role of protectionism has always been a complex task. From an ideological standpoint those who raise it are *ipso facto* branded as retrogrades, while in practice tendencies in its favour periodically reassert themselves. It is absolutely legitimate to consider a scenario in which the dissolution of national productive systems may lead to a reaction from nations which refuse to decompose themselves into the magma of a global economy. Moreover, the quest for protectionism may appear as a solution of the last resort in the event of a further deterioration of the crisis. Under these circumstances protectionism is usually combined with dangerous forms of nationalism. Yet, from the intellectual point of view, it is equally dangerous to believe actively in the processes of globalization which, as such, would prevent the formulation of any idea running against the tenets of economic orthodoxy.

NOTES

1. Exceptions to this view were, among others, Paul Davidson (1978), Sheila Dow (1984 a, b) and, in France, Alain Parguez (1984, 1985).
2. In the Post-Keynesian literature Harcourt (1963, 1965) and Pasinetti (1965, 1981) must be credited for being among the first economists to stress the link between the structure

of production, employment and effective demand. Harcourt's approach was then applied to a Lowe three sector model by Joseph Halevi (1984).

3. A study by C. Bourry (1994) has shown that, between 1980 and 1990 at the three digit level of the Standard Industrial Trade Classification (SITC), the degree of penetration of the European Union's external trade has systematically increased accompanied by a decline in the ratio of exports to imports. These findings suggest a loss of autonomy and mutual consistency among the productive structures of the EU countries.

REFERENCES

Attali, J. (1991), *Lignes d' horizon*, Paris: Fayard.

Borrelly, R. (1990), 'L'articulation du national et de l'international. Concepts et analyses', *Economies et Sociétés*, **24** (12), 67–96.

Bourry, C. (1994), *Existe-t-il une industrie européenne? Etude à partir du commerce extérieur de l'Union européenne*, Paris: Iseres.

Calvet, J. (1994), 'Un débat unilatéral: l'espace économique', in R. Di Ruzza, and J. Fontanel (eds) *Dix débats en économique politique, Grenoble: Presses Universitaires de Grenoble*.

Davidson, P. (1978), *Money and the Real World*, London: Macmillan.

Di Ruzza, R. (1983), 'Monnaie et système productif', in GRREC, *Crise et régulation I*, Grenoble: Université Pierre Mendès-France.

Di Ruzza, R. and J. Fontanel (1994), *Dix débats en économie politique*, Grenoble: Presses Universitaires de Grenoble.

Dow, S. (1984a), *Methodology and Macroeconomics*, Oxford: Basil Blackwell.

Dow, S. (1984b), 'Methodology and the analysis of a monetary economy', *Economies et Sociétés*, **18** (4), 7–35.

Gerbier, B. (1995), 'Globalisation ou regionalisation?', *Economies et sociétés*, **29** (11), 29–55.

GRREC (1983), *Crise et régulation I*, Grenoble: Université Pierre Mendès-France.

GRREC (1989), *Crise et régulation II*, Grenoble: Université Pierre Mendès-France.

Halevi, J. (1984), 'Structure économique et demande effective', *Economie appliquée*, **37** (1), 201–13.

Harcourt, G.C. (1963), 'A critique of Mr Kaldor's model of income distribution and growth', *Australian Economic Papers*, **2** (1), 20–36.

Harcourt, G.C. (1965), 'A two sector model of the distribution of income and the level of employment in the short run', *Economic Records*, **41** (93), 103–17.

Lowe, A. (1976), *The Path of Economic Growth*, Cambridge: Cambridge University Press.

Parguez, A. (1984), 'La dynamique de la monnaie', *Economies et sociétés*, **18** (4), 83–118.

Parguez, A. (1985), '*La Théorie générale*: la révolution inachevée dans la théorie du capital et de la monnaie', in A. Barrère (ed.), *Keynes aujourd'hui: théories et politiques*, Paris: Economica.

Pasinetti, L. (1965), *A New Theoretical Approach to the Problem of Economic Growth*, Vatican City: Pontificia Scientiarum Scripta Varia, no. 28.

Pasinetti, L. (1981), *Structural Change and Economic Growth*, Cambridge: Cambridge University Press)

Treillet, S. (1994), 'Une nouvelle norme de développement?', *Economies et sociétés*, **28** (12), 117–43.

PART II

Economic Integration and Effective Demand

4. Inflation paranoia and growth phobia in the major industrial countries

Yilmaz Akyüz[1]

1. INTRODUCTION

The importance of aggregate demand as a crucial determinant of growth and employment was clearly recognized by the architects of the post-war system at Bretton Woods. All participants agreed on the need to avoid a repetition, even on a smaller scale, of the experience of the Great Depression of the inter-war years. However, neither the Bretton Woods arrangements nor the floating exchange rate system that took its place in the 1970s were properly equipped to ensure that the major economies pursued macroeconomic policies that yielded an adequate pace of global demand expansion.

In the 1950s and 1960s governments generally sought high levels of employment and capacity utilization, and there was no need for concerted global action to generate an adequate pace of demand expansion. The 1970s were characterized by substantial differences in national policy responses to the first oil price shock; while some countries continued to pursue policies to support employment and income growth, others sought to defeat cost-push inflation by restrictive macroeconomic policy. It was expected that exchange rate adjustments would serve to make these diverse policy choices compatible internationally.

National policies were more uniform after the second oil price shock. In this period the need for demand management to stabilize employment and output was by and large denied owing to a perception that the inflationary threat was uppermost and a growing belief that it was best tackled by each country 'putting its house in order' by means of restrictive monetary and fiscal policies and liberalization and deregulation aimed at the supply side of the economy. None the less, diversity remained as Europe decided to return to a system of fixed exchange rates, while the United States shifted to a policy of targeting monetary aggregates, leaving interest and exchange rates free to fluctuate.

This policy shift in the 1980s has produced acute instability in the world economy, with adverse consequences for all countries, in particular developing countries, as well as a legacy for the 1990s that continues to present serious difficulties for policy-makers everywhere. Insufficiency of the overall level of demand has proved once again to be a major impediment to sustained growth while disparities in demand creation have been a prime source of tensions in international trade. These twin phenomena have been responsible for problems that have increasingly become structural, such as unemployment, government debt and deficits, and trade imbalances.

2. FROM GOLDEN AGE TO MASS UNEMPLOYMENT

The prosperity and stability enjoyed by the major industrial countries during the early post-war period stands out as a standard of economic performance. During this period, which has been dubbed a 'Golden Age' (Marglin and Schor, 1989; Maddison, 1989), all the major industrial economies grew faster than they had ever done before, with output expanding nearly 5 per cent per annum. Labour productivity rose rapidly, while demand grew sufficiently to offset the employment-reducing effects of productivity growth, so that unemployment remained low. Indeed, in countries such as the United Kingdom sectors with the highest productivity growth expanded so fast that they became leaders in job creation. On the other hand, rising productivity made it possible for real wages to rise while keeping inflation at tolerable levels.

Opinions differ on the extent to which active aggregate demand management contributed to the steadiness of aggregate expenditures in this period. But there was a policy stance, shared by parties across the political spectrum, that was clearly in favour of growth and employment. Policy-makers had a balanced attitude towards the two objectives of price stability and full employment, with recognition of the trade-off; accordingly, full employment was not defined in relation to price stability, but was treated as a separate objective (Maddison, 1982; Sargent, 1995; Boltho and Glyn, 1995). The commitment by governments to full employment, and the general conviction that they would act to sustain aggregate demand, fostered expectations of strong demand growth, and thereby encouraged investment.

The first oil price shock caused dislocations in the OECD economies, involving a slowdown of investment and growth. The declines in output in the mid-1970s were attributed to the failure of wages to absorb the effects of the oil price increases. It was also held that the labour market itself, as well as excessive taxation for social spending since the 1960s, had cut into profits, caused wage–price spirals, and reduced the incentives for investment. These perceptions led to a change of government priorities after the first oil price shock. After the recovery in the later 1970s, investment and growth again declined in 1980–82, this time under the influence of disinflationary policies.

The existing policy consensus unravelled when high employment and low inflation were no longer seen as compatible goals; during the 1980s most governments accorded priority to combating inflation, arguing that it was necessary for the resumption of economic growth. There has certainly been success on the inflation front; its rate for the G-7 economies since the mid-1980s has been comparable to that achieved during the Golden Age. However, this success has not produced a return to the growth rates of that time. More strikingly, it has coincided with rates of unemployment that would have been unthinkable only a few years earlier. During 1983–94 the unemployment rate continued to exceed the levels experienced during the 1980–82 recession in every G-7 country other than the United States. There has been a tendency to converge around a growth rate too low to reverse Europe's high and persistent levels of unemployment, to prevent Japan's historically high levels of the 1990s from climbing even further, or to address growing wage inequality as well as the deep insecurities that have accompanied job growth in the United States.

The main objective of the new policy was to restore growth based on private initiative. Supply-side measures such as lower taxes, financial deregulation and greater labour market flexibility were to help correct relative prices, boost profits and thereby create the incentives for investment, output, employment and productivity growth.

Tax policies, labour market policies and the decline in commodity prices in the first half of the 1980s did indeed help restore profit margins, and by the middle of the decade the share of profits in manufacturing value added in the major industrialized countries exceeded the 1972 level (UNCTAD, 1987). In the second half of the 1980s, net profit ratios (ratio of profit, net of depreciation, taxes and interest payments, to turnover) and financial profitability (net profit in relation to equity capital) in manufacturing increased (European Commission, 1995), and profits as a share of GNP also showed the normal cyclical upturn in this period (Uctum, 1995). Nevertheless, the expected rise in private investment failed to materialize and unemployment mounted.

3. THE ROLE OF MONETARY AND FINANCIAL POLICY

Although inflation in most OECD countries was brought down by 1985 to levels comparable to those of 1960–73, central banks have continued to steer monetary policy according to the perceived risks of inflation. Initially most central banks, particularly the Federal Reserve, adopted the monetarist strategy of targeting money supply in order to control credit expansion and inflation. Although some monetary authorities (like the Bundesbank) continued to adhere to money supply targets, others, notably the Federal Reserve and the Bank of England, returned to reliance on interest rates to fine-tune the economy as the stability of money demand necessary for monetary targeting deteriorated. They have conducted monetary policy by monitoring the evolution of unemployment in relation to NAIRU and/or actual GDP growth in relation to its estimated potential growth. The merits of these strategies are evaluated on the criterion of how far the inflation rate can be reduced, not only to discourage inflationary expectations, but also to leave a safety margin for exogenous shocks on prices.

With such a policy stance, the deflationary bias of discretionary monetary policy has turned out to be stronger than even the bias which a monetarist fixed rule for monetary expansion would entail. It has resulted in declines in potential growth by depressing investment. It has also created a fundamental imbalance between the growth of the labour force and the accumulation of capital, thereby accentuating the tendency for unemployment at given capacity utilization rates in OECD countries to rise (Elmeskov, 1993).

The major influence of policy on capital accumulation is through the level of economic activity. Since profits depend critically on sales, the higher the average level of capacity utilization, the greater will be the willingness of firms to invest to enlarge potential output. When capacity is regularly underutilized investment is adversely affected, which in turn reduces the growth of potential output. The interaction between actual output and investment can thus give rise to a *low-growth hysteresis* whereby the tendency for actual output to fall short of potential output is corrected by reducing the growth of the latter, resulting in higher structural unemployment and NAIRU. Restrictive macroeconomic policies can therefore be self-validating: if demand growth is checked too much on the grounds that potential output is not sufficient to satisfy it, the growth of potential output will be held back.

Potential output estimates obtained on the basis of past trends, and macroeconomic policy based on these estimates, are thus liable to generate a low-growth hysteresis in potential output: a period of low growth would pull down the trend, and policies giving priority to preventing GDP growth from exceeding potential output so determined would eventually serve to lower the trend still further. Calculating potential output from production functions also suffers from a similar inherent bias in so far as these estimates are based on NAIRU, since the latter too is subject to hysteresis, as in the method now favoured by OECD (Giorno *et al.*, 1995). Macroeconomic management based on such estimates consequently ends up disregarding a growing proportion of unemployment in the economy.

The growth targets set by policy-makers according to indicators that they take as given (such as a 2.5 per cent growth rate, obtained from potential growth estimates) have thus determined, and continue to determine, the pace of capital accumulation and the trends of employment and unemployment. The fact that policy aimed at preventing growth from exceeding such rates (except temporarily, at times of recovery from recession) has effectively imposed limits on capacity and job creation in the private sector.

All industrialized countries have experienced these effects of slower investment on employment over the last two decades. Measured potential output growth has slowed down because of the slower growth of fixed capital formation after 1973 (Economic Commission for Europe, 1995). The cumulative effects of lower rates of capital accumulation since the early 1970s explain much of the rising structural unemployment. According to one study, if the capital stock in European countries had grown by a modest one percentage point faster since 1973 than it actually did (which would still be below the rate prevailing in 1960–73), the capital stock by 1992 would have been 23.4 per cent greater than it actually was, making room for an extra 3.9 million jobs in manufacturing and 4.1 million in services (Rowthorn, 1995, p. 33).

A faster pace of accumulation could not be possible with monetary policy pushing interest rates to exorbitantly high levels. Real long-term rates in recent years have been higher than in almost any similar period since the last century. They were exceeded only in the Great Depression years 1930–32, and they are three times as high as those during the subsequent recovery of 1933–39 and in the Golden Age.

Increased financial instability due to the deregulation of financial activities and the conduct of monetary policy has also contributed to the rise in interest rates. Financial deregulation, by easing access to credit, lifting restrictions on the transactions of financial intermediaries and encouraging increased competition among them, led to excessive risk taking and speculation. Intermediaries have thus become more vulnerable to shocks, transmitting financial instability among money, exchange and stock markets. Systemic risk of the financial system has consequently increased, creating greater uncertainty in the economy.

The shift in monetary policy to targeting monetary aggregates, implied allowing interest rates, exchange rates and other asset prices to fluctuate more widely. Instability did not diminish when central banks shifted to using interest rates to fine-tune the economy. For instance the lowering of United States short-term rates in seven discrete steps from November 1990 to August 1992, and the subsequent seven rises in rates since February 1994, have created confusion and instability in financial markets. Thus, the policies of managing monetary aggregates and fine-tuning the economy through interest rates were both implemented at the cost of interest rate stability.

At times readjustments in monetary policy have been forced upon central banks by turmoil in currency markets. Growing and volatile international capital flows have heightened exchange rate fluctuations and necessitated counteraction through interest rate adjustments. The result has generally been a tendency for interest rates to rise, particularly since the burden of corrective action, essentially through monetary policy, has fallen primarily on deficit countries (or countries with weak currencies). This was most clearly visible during the EMS crisis in 1992.

The growing instability of key financial prices has placed a higher premium on liquidity. This increase in liquidity preference is clearly evident from the term structure of interest rates and changes in the sensitivity of long-term rates to short-term ones. For example, in the United States long-term rates have risen much more than short-term rates; the average yield gap was 2.3 percentage points in 1983–93, compared to 0.6 in the 1960s.

Increasingly volatile interest rates, together with the shortening of maturities, have made the long-term costs of borrowing for the corporate sector less predictable, as the rates on short-term loans being rolled over became liable to change more frequently. Greater uncertainty over the costs of borrowing has raised the rate of return required to undertake investment projects. The requisite rate of return has also been raised by increased borrower's risk arising from two other sources of instability: greater fluctuation in exchange rates and in aggregate demand.

With the slowdown in domestic demand growth, firms have tended to look for markets abroad and the share of foreign trade in the economy has risen. This has increased the influence of the exchange rate on investment decisions. Exchange rate movements have thus produced considerable uncertainty regarding prospective yields on investment, and, like volatile interest rates, have raised the average return required for investment projects.

Financial deregulation has also made aggregate demand more unstable by increasing the volatility of consumption expenditures, exports and imports. Easier access to credit has enabled consumers to spend more freely, but their accumulated debt has made their current expenditure more vulnerable to changes in interest rates. Furthermore, it also became easier for households to use their savings for investment in high-risk assets. This, together with the increased frequency and intensity of booms and busts in real estate markets, has made the value of household wealth more unstable. The consequent fluctuations in household net wealth and debt-servicing obligations have reduced the stability of consumption expenditure. Export and import volatilities have also increased because of sharp changes in competitiveness brought about by exchange rate fluctuations and because of swings in economic activity. The net result of all these movements has been to increase investors' risks.

Cuts in public investment have not made way for greater private investment because of complementarity between the two. The profitability of private investment tends to be influenced positively by public investment, especially in infrastructure. According to one study of the United States economy, each percentage point increase in public investment is associated with a 0.4–0.6 percentage point increase in private investment in equipment. On this basis it has been estimated that if the rate of growth of the stock of public capital had continued unchanged in 1966–87 from its average in 1947–65 (instead of declining by 10 percentage points), the annual growth of investment in equipment in the private sector would have been 4–6 points above the actual rate (Erenburg, 1993, pp. 15–16). Taking into account the strong linkage that has been observed between GDP growth and equipment investment (De Long and Summers, 1991), it has thus been concluded that annual GDP growth in the United States could have been 1.3–1.9 percentage points higher had public infrastructure investment been sustained (Erenburg, 1993).

In sum, private investment has been adversely influenced by a combination of factors closely linked to the policies pursued by the major industrial countries during the past two decades. Slow demand growth and deteriorating public infrastructure have lowered the expected rates of return to investment projects, while high interest rates have raised the feasibility threshold rate of return and increased the opportunity cost of devoting funds to investment. Greater demand instability and exchange rate volatility have increased borrowers' risk for investment projects, again raising the required rate of return on projects.

This new environment, while inimical to new investment to expand capacity, has forced the business sector in industrialized countries to cut costs through restructuring. Firms in most countries reduced their overall indebtedness ratios in the 1980s in order to diminish their exposure to high interest rates (European Commission, 1995). They have also downsized and restructured their operations so as to reduce costs and boost profitability, competitiveness and market shares; stagnation in markets has made enlarging market share or obtaining quick capital gains through mergers and acquisitions more attractive than new investment. As increased uncertainty has shortened firms' time horizons, they have tended to prefer short-term trading activities with large financial components to long-term investment in physical assets. Such activities have been facilitated by financial deregulation, which has made it easier to borrow in order to acquire existing assets.

4. POLICY OPTIONS FOR FULL EMPLOYMENT

A faster pace of capital investment is unlikely to occur without a substantial improvement in business expectations regarding future sales and the level and volatility of key determinants of the costs of and return on investment such as interest rates and exchange rates. This requires policies designed to bring about a faster expansion of demand and greater financial stability.

The official view is that, rather than lift growth and reduce unemployment, expansionary policies would only fuel inflation. On this view, monetary policy designed to lower short-term interest rates would instead lead to faster inflation, and hence to higher long-term interest rates, thereby restraining rather than promoting investment and output growth. Furthermore, expansionary fiscal policies would create pressures not only in product markets, leading to faster inflation, but also in financial markets, resulting in higher real interest rates, thereby crowding out private investment. These views are particularly widespread in financial markets, not least because *rentiers* are most concerned about the possible impact of policies on the real value of their financial wealth.

The concern that faster demand expansion would only lead to faster inflation is unjustified in current economic conditions. Not only is there a considerable slack in the labour market, but also the institutional changes that have been introduced since the beginning of the past decade have made it much more difficult for a wage–price spiral to emerge. Given the reduced bargaining power of the unions and increased competition in the labour market, workers are wary of pricing themselves out of the market. There is also a greater realization that in today's environment of increased global competition, workers' jobs depend on the profitability of their companies. This has been a major factor in establishing a closer link between productivity and compensation. Indeed, one of the most significant features of the current recovery is the tendency for unit labour costs in manufacturing to fall and profit margins to rise, even in countries which have had substantial currency depreciations. Inflation rates have continued to fall in the United States and Europe throughout the recovery, while in Japan the price level has actually been falling. Clearly, labour markets may tighten somewhat as the slack is reduced, but on the other hand productivity will rise as new investments come on stream.

Besides, the reduced costs of undertaking international transactions and greater and faster dissemination of information have weakened considerably the quasi-monopolistic positions enjoyed by local firms. Hence the probability that greater demand will result in higher prices and profits rather than higher output and sales is now much smaller, and firms attempting to raise prices and profits run the risk of losing business.

4.1 Removing the debt overhang

With the exception of Japan, fiscal policy has not generally been used for macroeconomic management since the beginning of the last decade. Systematic resort to fiscal policy tools for counter-cyclical purposes has been eschewed in the belief that, once deregulated and freed from high taxes, the economy would not need management of this sort, since the private sector would generate the requisite level of demand. This thinking held sway, for instance, in the United States where, despite its financial orthodoxy and anti-Keynesian rhetoric, the supply-side experiment beginning in the early 1980s has left a legacy of a large public debt and large budget deficits.

In Europe an important component of the medium-term financial strategy in the early 1980s was convergence of fiscal and monetary policy in order to better control inflation, and a reduction of government borrowing and debt to lessen the crowding-out of private investment. These objectives were formalized in the Maastricht Treaty fiscal convergence criteria: the deficit/GDP ratio set at 3 per cent, and the debt/GDP ratio set at 60 per cent. However, budget deficits and government debt have continued to rise. At the end of 1994, Luxembourg and Germany were the only EU members to have met both of these criteria.

For the G-7 countries their combined recorded and structural deficits were higher during the first half of the 1990s than in the 1980s. The same period has also witnessed a rate of accumulation of government debt that is unprecedented since the Second World War. As a proportion of GDP, government debt increased by some 50 per cent from 1978–82 to 1991–94 for the G-7 countries as a whole.

The rapid accumulation of government debt has been due to a combination of slower growth, increased unemployment, and high interest rates. While cyclical downswings widened deficits considerably, upswings have been less vigorous. Economic upturns have been quickly reined in by monetary tightening, adding to interest payments on government debt, while downturns have often been left to self-adjusting forces which have worked only slowly if at all. This behaviour of policy has also contributed to persistently higher budget deficits by raising expenditures on unemployment benefits and other forms of income support. Total expenditures on unemployment compensation have increased considerably in a number of countries despite the cutback in benefits, and pension funds have suffered losses as employment declined and claims exceeded contributions.

Precise quantitative estimates of these effects are extremely difficult to make. OECD's cyclical fiscal deficit adjustment model shows that the estimated effect of the slowdown in potential growth on budget deficits is subject to considerable margins of error and uncertainty that vary considerably across countries (Chouraqui *et al.*, 1990). According to a rough estimate, with the structure of revenues and expenditures prevailing in the late 1980s, a 1 per cent drop of actual output below the trend (or potential) level of output could raise public sector deficits in the major industrial countries taken together by as much as 0.5 percentage points of GDP. In short, the fiscal deficits incurred in the 1980s and 1990s would have been considerably smaller had employment and growth been more buoyant.

More importantly, much of the recorded and structural deficits in recent years has been due to interest payments on outstanding government debt. In the G-7 countries taken together, such payments now account for almost the entire budget deficit, which means that the primary budget has been in balance (in respect of both the recorded and the structural budget positions). With the exception of Japan and the United Kingdom, government interest payments stand at much higher levels than in the late 1970s and early 1980s; in the United Kingdom both deficits and debt have started to rise again with the slowdown in privatization.

By pushing up the interest rate and depressing growth, tight monetary policy has raised the nominal rate of interest on government debt above the rate of growth of nominal income (i.e. the real rate of interest above the real growth rate). In such a situation, the ratio of debt to GDP will rise unless there is an offsetting primary budget surplus. This disparity between real interest rates and real growth rates first appeared in the 1980s, when monetary policy was directed single-mindedly to combating inflationary tendencies, but it now seems to have become a feature of the industrial economies even in the absence of inflation. The persistence of high real interest rates has meant that in most major industrial countries the driving force behind government budget imbalances is the interest on government debt rather than discretionary spending and tax policies. Thus, monetary policy has resulted in a major transformation in the nature of fiscal imbalances; they are structural rather than cyclical.

The logic of this situation suggests that the only way to regain the ability to use fiscal policy for overall economic management is to reduce the outstanding stock of debt. The combination of increased public debt with reduced public investment during the past two decades suggests that this debt does not correspond to an equivalent build-up of productive capacity; it would not be possible to service it without incurring additional debt in a Ponzi-type financing process. Nor is it possible to reduce it by creating primary surpluses; this would lead to a serious deterioration of public services and introduce a self-defeating deflationary force that would dampen government revenues and raise unemployment- and poverty-related spending.

A reduction of the real value of debt will eventually be needed. In the past this has been achieved through inflation; recent and current efforts to eliminate inflation go precisely in the opposite direction. Accordingly, as Keynes (1971, pp. 53–5) pointed out, a once-and-for-all capital levy designed to bring the stock of government debt down to a sustainable level represents the most sensible solution (UNCTAD, 1993). It is also one that is much more equitable – and hence politically more feasible – than meeting the claims of bondholders year after year by increasing and inventing new kinds of taxation on incomes or transactions, and/or cutting welfare spending and thus adding to social problems that are already serious, not least because of mounting unemployment and inequality in earnings.

4.2 Redirecting monetary policy

Even if governments were able to overcome their fiscal paralysis, little would be achieved unless the goal of monetary policy were widened to include growth and employment objectives. In particular, it needs to be aimed at reestablishing low and stable interest rates, which would also help reduce government deficits.

The changes needed in fiscal and monetary policy are thus complementary. If fiscal policy could be and were used for counter-cyclical purposes, the burden on monetary policy would be considerably lighter. Using fiscal rather than monetary policy to smooth business cycles would avoid the disturbances that sharp swings in interest rates inflict on the balance sheets of both banks and business corporations. Fiscal tightening rather than interest rate hikes should be used to cool an overheating economy in order not to discourage private investment, and to slow down demand without changing its composition at the expense of investment. Should the need arise, it might be desirable to allow inflation rather than interest rates to vary over the course of the business cycle, provided that such variations remain within relatively narrow limits (say 2–5 per cent) and inflation shows no tendency to accelerate.

Even if central banks were willing to use monetary policy to keep interest rates low and stable, they may not be able to do so because they can only influence short-term intervention rates directly; the expectations of investors in the bond markets may move long-term interest rates independently of policy intentions. Thus, even if there are no real grounds for believing that a monetary policy more appropriate to increasing employment would generate an acceleration of inflation, bond markets may react perversely to such a policy. If long-term interest rates rise as a result of an increased inflation premium, there would be no gain to economic activity from monetary policy. The possibility of joint action by the central bank and the treasury to influence the bond market and engineer a durable decline in long-term interest rates is limited because of the sheer size of government debt. This problem has also been aggravated by the increasingly speculative character of trading in long-term government securities.

It should be noted that this rapid growth of the bond and securities markets is closely linked to the increased government indebtedness. Consequently, the constraints placed on monetary policy by those markets would also be greatly reduced if monetary policy were reoriented and the stock of government debt reduced in the ways suggested above. The consequent reduction of the size of the bond market and of government deficits, together with low interest rates, would slow the rate of growth of the securities markets relative to investment, GDP and the money market. This, in turn, would widen the scope for using monetary policy to influence asset prices, interest rates and economic activity.

On a number of occasions the bond market has failed to respond to monetary relaxation, and long-term interest rates have remained high. This steepening of the yield curve is usually explained as reflecting expectations of faster inflation. However, such a reaction can also reflect an expectation that short-term interest rates will be quickly raised again as soon as the economy begins to recover. This has indeed been the case on a number of occasions since the beginning of the 1980s, particularly in the United States. A return to a policy of stabilizing short-term interest rates can thus have a strong influence on the behaviour of the bond market and long-term interest rates. It can also narrow the yield gap by reducing the risk and the liquidity premium entailed by the increased instability of interest rates and asset prices.

4.3 Full employment in one country

A single country seeking to attain full employment is apt to be constrained by its balance of payments. Indeed, this was a major concern of the architects of the Bretton Woods system, who realized that with fixed exchange rates a country which ran persistent trade surpluses might prevent other countries from pursuing a policy of full employment. Floating exchange rates tend to facilitate balance of payments adjustment, but at the cost of increasing the trade-off between full employment and price stability.

When domestic demand in one country grows faster than in others, demand tends to spill over abroad; output and employment grow more slowly than domestic demand, and the balance of payments deteriorates. If a potentially inflationary currency depreciation is to be avoided, it is consequently necessary for interest rates to rise sufficiently to generate the additional capital inflows required to finance the additional imports. However, a higher rate of interest may be inimical to full employment. Thus, while a depreciation can help to reconcile full employment with external payments equilibrium, it can result in strong pressures on the price level.

A country that pursues expansionary policies on its own thus tends to export jobs, as well as create them at home, and import inflation. Attempts to check the leakage of jobs through depreciations will tend to increase the import of inflation, whereas greater emphasis on exchange rate and price stability will tend to make it more difficult to generate domestic employment without resorting to protectionism. The consequence is that, unless strong inflation is feared, there may be a tendency to resort to beggar-my-neighbour devaluations. However, if many countries opted for this approach, the outcome would be competitive devaluations with consequences disastrous for international trade and payments – a danger that the Bretton Woods system was designed to avert. Despite mounting unemployment and social pressures, competitive currency devaluations have so far been avoided because concerns over inflation have been stronger than those over unemployment. The large global deflationary gap in the 1980s did not give rise to serious conflicts among the major industrial countries, in large part because the United States was willing to act as a locomotive for the rest of the world. Furthermore, while this was clearly giving rise to serious trade imbalances and undermining the international economic position of the United States, its freedom of manoeuvre *vis-à-vis* other industrial countries was constrained by the political imperatives of the Cold War. With the collapse of communism in the late 1980s, and with international trade and finance producing an increasing impact on domestic conditions, the United States now seems to be poised to correct these imbalances and defend and strengthen its international economic position.

Moreover, now that inflation is negligible, the risks of deflation are becoming more evident for the first time since the collapse of the Bretton Woods system. Furthermore, there have been substantial changes in real

exchange rates and consequently sharp shifts in international competitiveness, which have hurt producers in countries with appreciating
currencies and have revived memories of the competitive devaluations of
the inter-war period. Tensions are high not only in the framework discus-
sions between Japan and the United States, arising partly from the
'benign neglect' of the recent depreciation of the dollar by the United
States: in France and Germany, for example, there are suggestions that
producers in Spain, the United Kingdom and Italy have been the unfair
beneficiaries of the large exchange rate movements which have taken
place over the last two years. Again proposals have been made in the
United States Congress that Chile should be admitted to NAFTA only
on the promise that it would not devalue the peso. These are perhaps the
first serious signs of potential exchange rate conflicts.

The difficulties faced by a single country in attaining full employment,
and the potential for trade and exchange rate conflicts point to the need
for international policy coordination to make it possible for all to do so.
Such a coordination should aim at a global expansion of demand while
at the same time altering the pattern of demand generation among the
major industrial countries so as to reduce trade imbalances and conflicts.
Domestic demand generation in Europe and Japan needs to expand relative to the United States. However, while both Europe and the United
States need to maintain a high pace of investment, consumer as well as
government spending need to lead growth in Japan.

This has almost become inevitable following the recent success of the
United States in restoring its competitiveness via its first investment-led
recovery since the breakdown of the Bretton Woods system. The recovery
beginning in 1992 has given rise to productivity increases at rates not
experienced since the 1960s and sharply improved international competitiveness, particularly in manufacturing, where the United States had a
structural trade surplus until the early 1980s. The continued weakness of
the dollar has served to reinforce this process.

Japan has found adjustment to this situation far more difficult than the
earlier adjustment to the two oil crises and the Plaza Agreement, and has
experienced its most severe downturn since the war, as loss of competitiveness made redundant much of the additional capacity from the
investment boom of the 1980s. Clearly, relocation of production to countries in Southeast Asia with lower labour costs compounds the difficulties
facing the Japanese economy. The repatriation of Japanese funds from
the United States needed for balance sheet restructuring in the corporate
sector tends to appreciate the yen *vis-à-vis* the dollar, thereby further
squeezing profit margins and stimulating further resiting abroad.
Unemployment has already breached the traditional barrier of 3 per cent

and may rise to 5–6 per cent in the near future if demand deficiency due to underconsumption is not addressed, primarily by redistributing income from profits to wages (UNCTAD, 1994).

Clearly, macroeconomic policy coordination designed to avoid large trade imbalances and to secure low and stable interest rates will be an important step in attaining stability of capital flows and exchange rates. However, given the size and mobility of international capital, and the tendency of currency markets to amplify the effects of policy shocks and to generate disturbances on their own, exchange rate stability requires more than macroeconomic policy coordination and concerted intervention in currency markets. The experience of the European Monetary System shows that even a multilateral commitment to exchange rate stability combined with convergence of macroeconomic policies and performance is not enough to cure currency turmoil.

Since neither fixed nor flexible exchange rates achieve the desired results, one way out is for interested countries to establish a monetary union, as is the intention in the EU. However, the convergence process laid down in the Maastricht Treaty needs to be reconsidered so as to remove some of the restrictions on policy and deal with the overhang of excess debt through a once-and-for-all capital levy.

Serious consideration should be given to possible ways and means of reducing the scope of currency markets for generating disruptions and instability, for instance through an internationally agreed tax on foreign exchange transactions (Tobin, 1978). Banks should also be discouraged from holding open positions in foreign exchange via non-interest-bearing reserve requirements or capital charges. These practices are analogous to those already proposed as part of the current initiative of the Basle Committee concerning standards for the supervision of banks' market risks for prudential reasons (Akyüz and Cornford, 1995).

More direct controls may also have to be introduced, since market-based and prudential measures may still leave considerable leeway for speculation. The consequences of excessive risk taking and speculation are not confined to those engaged in such activities; they have serious repercussions on other actors and institutions over a whole range of financial markets and countries. Direct restrictions may therefore be warranted on the acquisition and issuance of financial assets and liabilities.

5. CONCLUSION

Over the past decade, the performance of the major industrial economies, and *pro tanto* of the world economy, has been seriously impaired by problems of demand. The degree of global demand deficiency has not been constant; indeed, fluctuations in the pace of demand creation have been only too evident. Nevertheless, a deficiency of demand has been the general rule. It is largely because of that deficiency that the basic factors of production – labour and raw materials – have been in excess supply globally, with unemployment rates in the major industrialized countries rising to extremely high levels and, conversely, primary commodity prices falling to record lows. Similarly, the large imbalances among the major market economies have also to an important extent been a reflection of the success with which some countries have been able to increase their share of global demand at the expense of others.

Increasingly, surpluses are again being valued not only as a means of accumulating national wealth, but also as a prop to economic activity at home, while deficits are once again deplored not only because of their implications for indebtedness but also, and even more so, because of their impact on jobs and profits. The mercantilist notion that countries should seek growth by improving their overall competitiveness *vis-à-vis* other countries is fast becoming accepted as an axiom, but it is very largely a mistaken one. Competitiveness is a relative concept. While one country can improve its international competitiveness (and thus, perhaps, its growth performance), that is not possible for all countries at the same time. Global demand deficiency is a recipe for an invitation to conflict among nations.

NOTES

1. I am grateful to Jan Kregel and Cem Somel for comments and suggestions at various stages of this work. However, the opinions expressed in this chapter do not necessarily reflect the views of UNCTAD, and the author assumes full responsibility for analysis and interpretation.

REFERENCES

Akyüz, Y. and A. Cornford (1995), 'International capital movements: some proposals for reform', in J. Mitchie and J.G. Smith (eds), *Managing The Global Economy*, Oxford: Oxford University Press.
Boltho A. and A. Glyn (1995), 'Macroeconomic policies, public spending and employment', *International Labour Review*, **134** (4–5), 451–70.
Chouraqui, J.-C., R.P. Hagemann and N. Sartor (1990), 'Indicators of fiscal policy: a reassessment', *OECD Department of Economics and Statistics Working Paper*, no. 78.
De Long, J.B. and L.H. Summers (1991), 'Equipment investment and economic growth', *Quarterly Journal of Economics*, **106** (2), 445–502.

Elmeskov, J. (1993), 'High and persistent unemployment: assessment of the problem and its causes', *OECD Economics Department Working Paper*, no.132.

Economic Commission for Europe (ECE) (1995), *Economic Survey of Europe in 1994–1995*, Geneva: United Nations.

Erenburg, S.J. (1993), 'The relation between public and private investment', Washington University in St. Louis, The Jerome Levy Economics Institute of Baird College, New York, *Working Paper*, no. 85, February.

European Commission (EC) (1995), *European Economy, Supplement A*, no. 2, February.

Giorno, C., P. Richardson, D. Roseveare and P. van den Noord (1995), 'Estimating potential output, output gaps and structural budget balances', *OECD Economics Department Working Paper*, no. 152.

Keynes, J.M. (1971), 'Public finance and changes in the value of money', ch. 2 of *A Tract on Monetary Reform* in *The Collected Writings of John Maynard Keynes*, vol. IV, Cambridge: Cambridge University Press.

Maddison, A. (1989), *The World Economy in the 20th Century*, Paris: OECD Development Centre.

Maddison, A. (1982), *Phases of Capitalist Development*, Oxford: Oxford University Press.

Marglin, S. and J. Schor (eds) (1989), *The Golden Age of Capitalism: Reinterpreting the Postwar Experience*, Oxford: Clarendon Press.

Rowthorn, R. (1995), 'Capital formation and unemployment', *Oxford Review of Economic Policy*, **11** (1), 26–39.

Sargent, J.R. (1995), 'Roads to full employment', *National Institute Economic Review*, **151** (February), 74–89.

Tobin, J. (1978), 'A proposal for international monetary reform', *Eastern Economic Journal*, **4**, 153–9.

Uctum, M. (1995), 'The evolution and determinants of corporate profits: an international comparison', *Federal Reserve Bank of New York Research Paper*, no. 9502, March.

UNCTAD (1987–94), *Trade and Development Report*, Geneva: United Nations.

5. International capital flows and global demand

Sunanda Sen

1. INTRODUCTION

Flows of capital across international boundaries can arise because of two underlying possibilities in the capital-exporting countries; the flows may reflect tendencies of over-savings in the capital exporting nations, which are related to a deficiency of demand relative to savings in their respective domestic economies. Alternatively such capital flows may reflect a tendency on the part of domestic capital in the capital exporting countries to prefer opportunities for investments overseas. Movements of capital related to the latter factor reflect a structural problem in the area of domestic utilization of potential credit lines.

Flows of international capital over the last few decades mostly had their origin in the rich industrialized nations of the OECD, reflecting the large volume of credit potential available with well advanced financial institutions which seek out profit opportunities by means of financial intermediation. In the absence of international openings, the savings-rich countries are thus prone to slide back to a path of stagnation in their domestic economies, a problem which typically recurs in the mature capitalist economies. Considering the OECD which, as a group, has been lending internationally on a net basis over the past few decades, international financial flows from the OECD countries to the rest of the world warrant an equivalent flow of real exports from these countries. This process can also be viewed as one of an equivalent transfer of real resources to the borrowers. The flow, if put to productive use, is capable of generating output and demand in the receiving economies. International flows of capital can thus generate and revive global demand, an aspect which merits special attention.

This paper analyses the demand-generating role of international capital flows, laying emphasis on the typical pattern of credit generation and its use in the industrial areas and also the lost opportunities of reviving demand in the management of the third world debt during the last decade. Section 2 provides the background in terms of the realities relating to the volume and the direction of international capital flows. It is of concern that despite the steady increases in the magnitude of the cross-border flows of finance within the OECD, real growth has failed to pick up in the area. The observed pattern of financial flows and their impact indicate that recycling of finance within the OECD has rather generated speculation, with demand for activities in the finance-related services. The process has thus been responsible for contributing to financial fragility rather than real growth in the rich industrial areas. As a contrast one looks at the experiences of the developing countries, with the region's share in international capital inflows dropping sharply with the onset of the debt crisis in the early 1980s. While these countries received a much smaller proportion of the net flow of bank credit which itself has shrunk in the international capital market, the boom in international security transactions had little or no effect on the flow of finance to the majority of the developing countries, most of whom had little or no access to the security sector.

It is pointed out that international capital flows, when directed to the developing countries on a net basis (that is, at end of investment income payments and amortization) had generated demand for imports of goods rather than for the sophisticated services from the rest of the world. Indeed, the non-oil developing countries have been exporting services on a net basis (if debt services are excluded). This fact is a pointer that net flows of finance, if directed to the developing countries, are capable of generating global demand for goods (which these countries import on a net basis) rather than services (other than those which are debt-related). Alternatively, when these international capital flows circulate within the confines of the industrialized countries, international demand is generated for services rather than goods, a situation which in the past has proved incapable of reviving real demand.

A brief account of the direction of international capital flows and the composition of net international demand from different regions lends credence to the above arguments. Attention is drawn to the play of 'fictitious' capital and the related financial fragility in the 'post-industrial' societies of the advanced economies with booming service sectors. The latter had very little impact on the continuing real stagnation in these economies, as indicated in the statistics relating to their GDP variations. One can contrast the diminishing and even negative flows of international capital in the direction of the developing area as a whole, many economies within which are still experiencing the deflationary consequences of debt management policies.

Section 3 builds up the analytical theme, providing the central thesis of the paper on links between international capital flows and global demand. It highlights the contents of the received doctrines which dictate the policies of international and private financial institutions. Arguments provided in this section offer a critique of the current policies and a plea for a revived flow of finance in the direction of the developing countries in the interest of global demand and real growth. Section 4 provides the conclusion, drawing attention to the limiting aspects of the prevailing approaches to global financial management. Evidently, such policies have not been able to remove either the real stagnation or the financial upheavals in their own economies, an aspect which provides a direction to possible policy reforms.

2. THE BACKGROUND TO INTERNATIONAL CAPITAL FLOWS

2.1 The Magnitude

During the 1970s private flows of international credit increased significantly, reaching out to the developing country borrowers; this provided a ready market for recycling the OPEC surpluses deposited with the international banks. The pattern changed by the early 1980s with industrial countries absorbing most of it, leaving a small margin of residual flows for the developing country borrowers, many of whom were servicing their huge debts with difficulty. By the mid-1980s syndicated bank credit flows which had a booming business during the 1970s had already been substantially replaced by securities of various categories which constituted the main instrument of financial intermediation in the international capital markets. Developing countries, having very little or no access to the security market for international borrowings were unable to reach out to these emerging markets till the early 1990s when a handful of them had some degrees of access. Net flow of bank credit to the developing countries, adjusted for exchange rate variations, declined from an annual average of $28 billion during 1979–82 to –$19 billion and –$44.7 billion respectively during 1983–86 and 1987–90 (Turner, 1991). It is not difficult to anticipate the fact that net financial and real flows in the direction of most of the developing countries were rather small or even negative.

2.2 Tendencies for Financial Fragility

It may be relevant, at this point, to draw attention to the qualitative transformations in the international credit market and its deleterious impact on the stability of the financial system. With large doses of deregulation in the banking industry, bank assets and the sources of their profits are no longer confined to inter-bank and/or industrial activities alone. Banks of late have been lending more to the non-financial institutions, as is indicated by the large proportion of financial assets the banks held with non-banks.

As a consequence, non-bank sources of profits have become important to the banks, as is indicated by the rising proportion of non-bank sources in gross banking income for the major OECD countries. Income earned from a range of bank activities, earned as fees, commissions, brokerages and so on, rose from 24 per cent of annual gross banking income in USA in 1981 to 32.8 per cent in 1988.[1] However, bank loans to the non-financial institutions and the increased bank earnings from non-interest sources did not imply that these additional bank lendings generated industrial activities, a fact which can be ascertained from the large flows of bank loans on real estates and also from the financing of mergers and acquisitions, both in the financial and in the non-financial sectors in OECD countries (Bank for International Settlements, 1992; OECD, 1992; Gart, 1989). Off-balance sheet activities of banks, which had their origin in the national tax regulations of the different OECD countries, were as common as the use of the derivative financial instruments or the over-the-counter (OTC) operations on the part of the banks. Use was made of warrants and asset- (including mortgage-) based securities, against motor car advances, credit cards and so on. The practice continued despite the reluctance of governments, say in the USA, to back mortgage- and consumer-finance-related securities.

It was common to see successful 'financial boutiques', with small high-powered expertise with contacts at the top level which avoided the organizational problems of big investment banks. According to the Bank for International Settlements (BIS), a combination of excess liquidity with the banks and the rather low transaction costs together played a role in diverting funds to the future market. Off-balance sheet activities of US banks exceeded 700 per cent of their on-balance assets at the end of 1990. For the BIS banks as a whole, steep increases were observed in their off-balance activities. Banks in the industrial countries were also advancing money to finance real estate transactions and also to arrange mergers and acquisitions for the corporate sector. Both activities had special reasons for multiplying in these countries. Off-balance sheet activities and use of the derivative OTC type of instruments, including warrants, asset-based securities (ABS) and so forth were widely practised by banks (Bank for International Settlements, 1992).[2] In fact the bankers actually claimed that these operations were no less risky than the ordinary credit business in the

1980s. Clearly, the ordinary (or traditional) functioning of banks, which had closer links with the real sector, have of late failed to keep pace with the emerging pattern of non-conventional banking. Consumer credit, advanced against purchases of durables as well as investments in real estates often provided additional demand, thus reducing the pressure on unutilized savings (Magdoff and Sweezy, 1985, 1986).

It is interesting to point out that these new forms of intermediations by banks and other agencies including the security houses, were in essence a response to the increasing market uncertainties, especially in the financial sector. The outcome was a paradox where finance survived through its own turbulence and not because of growth in these economies (Sen, 1996). As in the rest of the market economies, the survival of the financial sector as a sub-system of the economy usually rests on the realization of profits. Thus financial intermediation has to dwell on the creation of debt by the other sectors. With a rather unimpressive record of real growth in the industrial economies, financial activities have been instrumental for a 'debt explosion' which often is not backed by real transactions. In terms of data released in the Flow of Funds Account of the US Federal Reserve, the index of total debt, based on the year 1965, was at 742.5 in 1985 in the US economy. Of this, maximum expansion was accounted for by financial business, followed by consumer debt, which also acted as a dynamic force. While gross savings have averaged around 21–22 per cent of GDP in most countries, Japan as well as Germany experienced even higher rates. Evidently, it was a major problem. However, this component of consumption tends to reinforce the cyclical pattern of changes in output and employment, since changes in borrowed consumption are always influenced by the expected changes in disposable income. As for the ability of the corporate sector to borrow from the market, limits were set by the compulsion to maintain safe debt to equity margins. The other major borrowing agent, the government, is pre- committed in its expenditure programme towards pension benefits, which in effect supplement household savings. In fact the current demographic trends in the advanced economies warrant an increasing proportion of government expenditure in the form of these superannuation benefits. It is not difficult to see that such expenses reduce the effective role of governments in these economies to borrow on a net basis the savings from the household sector. With problems experienced by the domestic corporate sector both in the advanced economies and in the rest of the world (as well as the lending agencies in the advanced economies) in trying not to exceed the safe limits to debt, it is not surprising that these countries were led to a path of stagnation and unemployment.

Table 5.1 Balance of international accounts 1986–92 ($ billions)

	CAB	MB	SB	IIB	of which DII	of which DIIR	of which OII	CAB less IIB	CAB less SB	SB less IIB
	(1)	(2)	(3)	(4)	(5)	(6)	(7)	(8=1–4)	(9=1–3)	(10=3–4)
A. Industrial countries										
1986	–30.2	–11.4	26.5	4.1	7.9	–19.6	15.8	–34.4	–56.7	22.4
1987	–59.2	–30.0	21.9	4.3	7.8	–29.4	25.9	–63.5	–81.1	17.6
1988	–54.5	–8.4	6.8	7.5	14.9	–34.8	27.4	–62.0	–61.3	–0.7
1989	–79.8	–34.3	9.5	8.7	18.3	–46.6	37.0	–88.5	–89.3	0.8
1990	–112.6	–37.6	12.1	–2.2	8.1	–62.0	51.7	–110.4	–124.7	14.3
1991	–28.4	10.1	24.8	–9.0	16.1	–70.7	45.7	–19.4	–53.2	33.8
1992	–46.5	43.7	20.5	–20.5	19.5	–76.9	36.9	–35.5	–67.0	41.0
B. Non-oil developing countries										
1986	–12.7	4.8	0.8	–57.4	–5.3	–2.2	–49.9	44.7	–13.5	58.2
1987	11.8	22.7	3.6	–58.6	–6.1	–2.5	–50.0	70.4	8.2	62.2
1988	9.1	21.5	3.6	–60.4	–6.8	–2.9	–50.7	69.5	5.5	64.0
1989	–4.7	8.9	0.9	–62.3	–10.6	–3.0	–48.7	57.6	–3.8	63.2
1990	–22.7	–17.2	2.1	–62.8	–11.9	–2.3	–48.6	40.1	–20.6	64.9
1991	–25.7	–27.1	5.0	–57.4	–10.1	–2.8	–44.5	31.7	–20.7	62.4
1992	–42.8	–51.5	8.2	–57.7	–11.8	–3.3	–42.6	14.9	–34.6	65.9

Notes:

CAB:	Current account balance	MB:	Merchandise balance
IIB:	Investment income balance	SB:	Services balance
DII:	Direct investment incomes	OII:	Other investment income
DIIRA:	Direct investment income reinvested abroad		

Source: IMF, *Balance of Payments Statistics Year Book*, New York, 1993

2.3 The Flow of Goods and Services: The OECD and the Non-oil Developing Area

We have provided (see column 8 of Table 5.1) the statistics on the net flow of real transfers – the flow of goods and services – defined, at current dollar prices, as the current account balance less net investment income flows. The balance, if negative, indicates an equivalent inflow of financial and real resources to the country. The sum for the respective areas of the OECD and the non-oil developing areas, however, has been arrived at by adding up the country totals, the sum thus including the intra-regional flows. Contrary to what is expected of the relatively prosperous areas in the world economy, industrial countries as a whole seem to have been receiving net inflows of real transfers, with the negative sum peaking up to $110.4 billion in 1990.

The opposite seems to be the case for the non-oil developing economies which have been providing steady net outflows of real transfers over most of the period, with a positive sum as large as $70 billion during 1991–92. Analysing the flow of services which includes both factor income (investment income) and non-factor income payments, industrial countries as a group seem to be net exporters of services, as is indicated by the positive entries in column 3. The latter, however, includes large flows of direct investment income retained and re-invested abroad, a sum which was as large as –$62.0 billion in 1990. If the net flow of services excludes the investment income payments, net exports of (non-factor) services by the industrialized countries turn out to be even larger than net service flows as a whole, as can be seen by comparing entries in columns 3 and 10. With their merchandise balance consistently negative during 1986–90, the industrial area emerges as a net exporter of services and net importer of goods during most of these years, a picture which may shed some light on the current debates relating to their on-going domestic stagnation. As for the non-oil developing countries, the net flow of real resource transfers, as indicated by the positive entries in column 8, were consistently negative. A positive merchandise balance during 1986–89 confirms the above. The developing countries, many of them large debtors, were paying out large sums as investment income payments on their past borrowings. Disregarding imports of these services (as related to capital flows from abroad), the non-oil developing area as a whole emerge as net exporters of services other than investment income payments, as can be witnessed from the entries in column 10.

However, during the 1990s the area as a whole seems to have been able to finance net imports of merchandise with the help of a return flow of capital to a selected number of countries, an aspect which resulted in a substantial drop in the value of real transfers from the area. Observations such as above can be used to arrive at the following generalizations:

1. In recent years the industrialized countries have mostly been importing merchandise on a net basis. Thus the external sector has not been contributing to domestic demand in these economies during recent years.
2. However, net exports from these industrial countries consisted of services including investment income and other flows, the magnitude of which seems to be even larger as the flow of investment income reinvested abroad is excluded. Evidently it has been the services sector in their domestic economies which got a fillip from external trade in the industrial countries, as can be judged by the net flow of services exports from these regions.

3. Trade has failed to obtain for the non-oil developing countries substantial transfers of real resources from abroad. This is indicated by the surpluses in their merchandise balance during 1986–89 (column 2) and positive sums recorded for the current account balance less investment income payments for the entire period 1986–92 (column 8). This reflects the diminishing flow of net finance in the direction of these countries, as remained after meeting the debt charges. Merchandise imports for the developing areas as a whole revived by 1990 when some developing nations experienced a return flow of private capital. However the fact that net service flows, excluding payments of investment income, continued to be positive signifies an observed propensity, on part of the developing nations, to import goods rather than non-factor services.

4. To dwell a little further on the more recent pattern of the international capital flows as during the 1990s, the recent strengthening of the borrowing capacity of some developing countries can partly be explained by the fact that government or corporate borrowers in these countries can now raise funds from the international bond market and even to a restricted degree, from international banks. The above, along with a drop in the real interest rates in the international credit market has been responsible for the declining real transfers from these non-oil developing countries since 1991.

As can be seen from Table 5.2, the distribution of net financial flows to the developing countries as a whole (including the oil-exporting countries of West Asia) was rather uneven during 1991–93, with West Asia and Latin America appropriating most of the resources while Africa as a whole and Other Asia experienced negative financial (and real) transfers during 1991 and 1992 (the former during 1993 as well). It is interesting to note that of the total sum of $30.6 billion of net financial transfers which were received by the developing countries during 1991–93, West Asia's share, at $95.1 billion, was nearly two-thirds of the total. The second group of countries which also were net recipients of these transfers included Latin America and the Caribbean, receiving roughly one-tenth of the net transfers during 1991–93. To be precise, Latin America started receiving financial transfers on a net basis only from 1992.

A major factor behind this new wave of financial flows to Latin America was the restructuring of debt by the lender institutions which realised that very little of these sums could be recovered. Also some countries in Latin America received substantial inflows of the return of flight capital, based on some positive perceptions on the economic performances in these economies.

Table 5.2 Net transfer of financial resources 1986–93 ($ billions)*

	All countries	USA	Germany	UK	Japan	Others
A. Industrial Countries						
1986	−5.6	144.3	−44.9	5.0	−78.4	−31.6
1987	18.5	157.5	−54.6	8.8	−74.0	−19.2
1988	12.7	120.6	−59.4	31.1	−62.7	−16.9
1989	35.5	96.8	−59.9	35.0	−37.8	1.3
1990	37.4	84.0	−47.5	26.0	−18.2	−6.9
1991	−23.7	35.2	5.9	11.8	−58.7	−17.9
1992	−54.8	47.0	8.7	16.9	−86.0	−41.4
1993	−113.9	83.9	0.4	−18.3	−96.1	−83.8
	All countries	Latin America	West Asia	Other Asia	Africa	
B. All Developing Countries						
1986	5.2	−11.8	26.9	−11.6	1.9	
1987	−33.7	−17.9	18.3	−30.1	−3.2	
1988	−20.3	−21.4	19.2	−17.2	3.7	
1989	−27.7	−28.5	10.1	−10.1	0.8	
1990	−31.3	−25.8	−2.0	−3.0	−10.6	
1991	−32.9	−7.2	41.9	−2.6	−6.9	
1992	−43.7	12.2	32.2	−1.4	−4.5	
1993	54.0	18.9	21.0	6.7	−0.2	

Notes: * Net transfers are arrived at on an expenditure basis, as the negative of balance of payments on goods, services and private transfers excluding investment income.

Source: UN (1994, pp. 97, 286–7)

5. It is possible to relate the pattern of international capital flows since the mid-1980s to the changing portfolio decisions in countries with surplus finances. Portfolio investment rather than bank lending regained popularity in countries with surplus savings during the period. In addition, the superior growth performance (compared to what it was in the industrial countries) made the developing countries relatively invest-ment-worthy, especially for the institutional fund managers who were in control of vast amounts of household savings. Funds raised from the market, mostly as bond finance which have restored the positive net flows since the year 1990, were actually restricted to specific countries in Latin America (United Nations, 1994).

6. Slow growth or stagnation of output as well as high rates of unemployment in the industrial countries seem to have continued over the past decade, as is indicated by an annual average of 1.1 per cent rate of output growth in the industrial areas during 1991–93. This has been the recent pattern despite the relative boom in finance and in the services sectors in these economies. Of the different services, the finance related services did relatively better, as can be expected from the wide-ranging deregulation in the financial sector and its dynamics in terms of integrating the international capital markets in the OECD. A rather anomalous picture, which arises from the prevailing UN System of National Accounts (SNA), relates to the exclusion of the value of services offered by the financial intermediation industry from final demand. Thus a large part of the income originating in this booming sector gets unrecorded for national income statistics. While resolving these issues opens up serious methodological problems in the area of national accounts, one feels the necessity of separating out the transitory and speculatory financial gains and losses from final demand which is linked to generation of output in an economy. On the whole the prevailing pattern of capital flows in the international capital markets, the major part of which tend to remain confined within the OECD, has clearly failed to generate a proportionate pace of real growth in these economies.

7. Attempts to control stagflation in the industrial economies resulted in a tight control over the growth of high powered money in their respective domestic economies. A high rate of interest which resulted was accepted, in terms of the received doctrines of monetarism, as an effective device to curb stagflation. However, these policies had little impact on the supply of (bank) credit financed money which often was channelled to the speculatory financial activities, with financial intermediation by private financial agencies. Involvement of the latter in third world debt was resolved by means of debt management policies which ended up by reducing not only the stock of debt but also the net flow of credit in the direction of the developing countries. Debt management policies have often been guided by the interests of the most active partner in the debt process, viz., the private financial institutions in the lending countries. Even official agencies, both national and multilateral (which are often dominated by the creditor governmets), seem to have displayed a disproportionate concern for finance. A major factor behind such tendencies has been the reality that finance has for some time been the main conduit of profit generation in these economies. Efforts to avoid a collapse of the international banks has often led to a refinancing of loans, a debt–equity swap or loan–loss

provisioning. In none of these cases could new credit be advanced to the debtor nations since the gross credit advanced was actually compensating for the shortfalls in debt charges due from the borrowers. Possibilities of a pick up in the volume of gross advances at a scale which could ensure positive net flows after meeting the debt charges seemed to be rather remote, as can be confirmed from Table 5.3. Recent increases in direct foreign investment in the developing areas, which have drawn much attention in the literature, have so far been inadequate to ensure a rise in the net flow of finance to most of the developing countries.

Table 5.3 Developing countries: transfer of financial resources 1983–93 ($ billions)

	Net transfer of financial resources	Net IMF lending	Funds raised in international credit markets	Total external debt*	Official reschedulings
	(1)	(2)	(3)	(4)	(5)
1983	16.2	10.6	36.6	871.5	8.6
1984	−23.0	4.3	34.4	894.1	3.7
1985	15.0	0.3	30.1	977.0	6.4
1986	−5.2	−2.4	22.2	1071.8	12.1
1987	−33.7	−5.2	27.8	1210.5	19.9
1988	−20.3	−4.7	26.9	1198.4	9.3
1989	−27.7	−1.9	22.7	1208.8	18.6
1990	−31.3	−2.3	28.9	1292.1	6.0
1991	32.9	1.0	42.2	1356.3	44.3
1992	43.7	−0.2	37.5	1398.6	12.5
1993	54.0	−0.4	71.3	1489.7	3.3

Notes: * Debt of 122 economies, drawn from the data reporting system of the World Bank (107 countries). For non-reporting countries data are drawn from the Creditor Reporting System of the OECD (15 economies) excluding non-guaranteed bank debt of offshore financial centres.

Source: UN (1994, pp. 288–304)

As a consequence the developing countries have been forced to adjust downwards their real expenditure which in turn also did reduce real growth in these areas. The global implications of these adjustments have been harmful, not only for the developing countries but also for the industrialized countries which have lost, as a consequence, the opportunities of an expanding market in these areas. The dominance of finance in the world economy is thus manifest in the policies adopted to manage third world debt, resulting in a widening gap between the performance of finance and the real sectors in the world economy.

2.4 Financial Opening, Monetarism and Financial Fragility

In the advanced economies, policies concerning money and credit were influenced heavily by the received doctrines of monetarism, the central messages of which embodied the interest of finance in these economies. Characterized as the 'Washington Consensus' in the literature, policy has been geared to a liberalization of financial markets, both to achieve higher growth rates of output by means of efficiency gains and also to allow the rate of interest to be determined by market forces. The latter, if higher, would generate savings which in turn would make for additional investment, as is implicit in terms of an 'enabling assumption'. In general, control over domestic monetary variables is expected to generate domestic growth with price stability and exchange rate equilibrium under financial opening and exchange rate floating.

In recent years the principles of monetarist doctrines have been qualified in the New Keynesian models which rely on asymmetric information and heterogeneity of bank assets (with differential risks), to explain the widely prevalent phenomenon of credit rationing in the financial markets. Thus lendings and borrowings as well as acts of default or their absence are explained as optimal decisions based on rational choices. Tinkering with the market as, for example, with deposit insurance or with the Central Bank acting as lenders of last resort, is disapproved of in these models as causing moral hazard problems with distortions. Problems with both the mainstream neoclassical as well as the New-Keynesian analysis with the reliance placed in the latter on the notion of the 'risk-adjusted rates of returns' have been criticized as improbable and unreal. At a more fundamental level, it has been argued that neoclassical theory fails to recognize the crucial role of both internal savings and of liquidity (credit) advanced by the banking system as sources of finance for investment. The latter involves liability management on the part of the banks, an aspect which is lost sight of, even by the new-Keynesians who emphasize the importance of differentiated assets.

Liability management provides the requisite elasticity to the credit system, an aspect which reduces the effectiveness of monetary policy to control credit by regulating high powered money. Thus the ability of banks to extend credit is self-fulfilling as loans in turn create deposits with the banking system. Innovation in liability management allows banks to seek off-balance sheet fundings as well as loan commitments, an aspect which often leads to pro-cyclical variations in money and credit supply. The Central Bank is clearly inadequate to control these sources of 'inside money' (Moore, 1989). With their access to liability management, especially with the wholesale loan markets acting as provider as well as a repository of banks' discretionary funds, it was no longer necessary for banks to seek a cover under deposit insurance (Wolfson, 1990). Liability management by banks also creates an endogenous source of financial crisis at the peak of a cycle when debt is high in relation to equity. As a consequence monetary policy often aggravates the tendencies for financial fragility, for example, with high interest rates affecting genuine demand from less creditworthy but productive borrowers. A social construction of credit thus reveals its different use in an economy with financial volatility, much of which is linked with high-risk speculatory ventures.

While credit sets the liquidity constraint for growth the sources of credit money are endogenous and cannot be controlled by monetary policy. Ultimately, in a monetary economy, where 'money matters', that is money is never neutral, it is liquidity constraint and never an income (or savings) constraint that limits expansion before full employment. Urge to invest is thus not necessarily restrained by a high rate on investment. Thus, '[finance] is best treated along with the animal spirits of the firms, as an element in the propensity to accumulate in the economy' (Robinson, 1962, p. 43). The analysis provided above can now be used to interpret the scenario relating to the flow of capital across nations, and especially between the advanced and the developing economies.

3. INTERNATIONAL CAPITAL FLOWS AND GLOBAL DEMAND

3.1 Some Conceptual Issues

Let us consider a group of advanced industrial economies, each of which exports capital on a net or a gross basis. With net exports of capital from these areas, the process warrants an equivalent outflow of real resources, the magnitude of which is measured by the current account surplus of the region less net investment income therein from abroad. The above process provides the possibility of utilizing their surplus savings by means of demand generated overseas, an outcome which is captured by the following set of equations.

$$X = S - (I + G) = (Y - C) - (I + G) \tag{5.1}$$

where X, S, I, G and C respectively indicate net exports, household savings, domestic investment, government borrowings and household consumption.

For simplicity it is assumed that all savings are made by households and all investments are made by the corporate sector. Let household consumption be partly financed by consumer credit. Net household consumption (C_n) by households is arrived at by deducting borrowed consumption (C_b) from gross household consumption (C). Again, the government in these countries is assumed to be spending on pension-related superannuation benefits (G_p). The latter effectively supplements household savings (Steindl, 1990), thus reducing net borrowings by government to G_n $(= G - G_p)$. We can now rewrite equation (5.1) as follows:

$$X = [Y - (C_n + C_b)] - [I + G - G_p] \tag{5.2}$$

Abstracting from the problems of oversavings as are caused by C_b and G_p, we get back to net exports (X) in equation (5.1) which can, from the angle of balance of payments, be viewed as follows:

$$\dot{D} = X + iD \tag{5.3}$$

where D is the stock of international debt (or assets for lending countries) on which a rate of interest 'i' is charged. For simplicity we assume that investment income flows are the only form of service transactions. Equation (5.3) captures what can be described as the '*rentier*' and 'trade' effects of the flow of overseas investments for capital exporting countries (Sen, 1991). While the *rentier* effect relates to the flow of investment income or services (iD in equation (5.3) above) the trade effect is indicated by net exports of goods (X in equation (5.3)). The trade-creating effect (α) of D on X can be spelt out as

$$X = \beta + \alpha \dot{D} \tag{5.4}$$

From (5.3) and (5.4), when $\beta = 0$

$$\alpha = 1 - i/r \tag{5.5}$$

where 'r' is the growth rate of gross capital exports D while equation (5.5) captures the conflicting *rentier* and trade interests in capital exporting countries. Conflicts in the capital exporting countries make it interesting to enquire whether exports of capital from the lender nations furthers trade/*rentier* interests in the domestic economy.

$$\text{Let } \dot{D} = (\Theta_1 + \Theta_2)\dot{D} \tag{5.6}$$

where Θ_1 and Θ_2 are the respective shares of capital flow $\dot{D}$ which goes to country groups 1 and 2. It is further assumed that country group 1 consists of the rich industrialized borrowers with higher propensities of importing services (consisting of investment income payments) while the country group 2 includes the developing borrowers having a propensity to import goods rather than services.

$$\text{Let } \alpha = A + \dot{D}(\Theta_1/\Theta_2) \tag{5.7}$$

where A is a constant and $\dot{D} < 0$. Substituting the value of α from equation (5.5) and rearranging:

$$i = r[(1 - A) - \dot{D}(\Theta_1/\Theta_2)] \text{ or } i = r[K - \dot{D}(\Theta_1/\Theta_2)] \tag{5.8}$$

where $K = (1 - A)$ is also a constant.

Now $di/[d(\Theta_1/\Theta_2)] = -r.\dot{D} > 0$. It is evident from the above that a distribution of international capital flows which favours the group 1 of rich industrial country borrowers would, in the lending areas, further the *rentier* interests and hence harm (or at least be neutral to) the trader interests. The opposite would be the case when group 2, consisting of the developing country borrowers, gets a larger share of international capital flows.

It is now possible to see how a link can be forged between the traders' interests in capital exporting countries and the interests of the borrowers of the developing country which has a natural propensity to import goods rather than services. We introduce here a notion of real transfer (RT) which is measured by the import surplus in goods alone. (This definition of real transfer deviates from the definition provided earlier since we are now assuming that net flow of all services is zero.)

$$\text{Thus } RT = M - X = I - S \text{ or } RT = (kg - s) Y \tag{5.9}$$

or

$$g = [(RT/Y) + s] / k \tag{5.10}$$

k, g and s in the two equations respectively indicate the capital–output ratio, GDP growth rate and savings rates in the economy receiving inflows of real transfers RT. Equation (5.10) makes it evident that countries as above are supply constrained and hence dependent on net capital imports from overseas for their domestic growth. Simultaneously, the process instils a harmonious pattern of growth in the world economy, one where the trading interests (the real sector) in lender countries grow along with borrowing economies creating a market space for goods from the former. It is not far-fetched to argue that the above opens up a plea for diversion of capital flows in the direction of the developing country borrowers.

4. CONCLUSION

This chapter, with its brief reference to the strategies followed by the lending agencies in the industrialized countries on the one hand and the experiences of the borrowing countries in the developing regions, indicates some of the failures of the current pattern of international capital flows to generate growth in either the developing or in the lending areas. The chapter also looks into the pattern of trade as is typical for the two types of countries, with the developing countries offering a potential market for goods rather than services, especially if the compulsive invisible payments in the form of investment income are ignored. This makes the case for a transfer of net finance in the direction of the developing countries, both for generating global demand for real activities and for an end to financial fragility.

NOTES

1. Bank for International Settlement, *Annual Reports*, Basel, various years.
2. See also: *Euromoney* 1989; *The Financial Times*, 16 October 1986; *The Financial Times*, 24 June 1988.

REFERENCES

Bank for International Settlements (1992), *Special Papers on International Monetary and Financial Market Developments*, May.
Gart, A. (1989), *An Analysis of the New Financial Institutions: Changing Technologies, Financial Structures Distribution Systems and Deregulation*, Westport, Conn.: Greenwood Press.
Magdoff, H. and P. Sweezy (1985), 'The financial explosion', *Monthly Review*, **37** (December), 1–10.
Magdoff, H. and P. Sweezy (1986), 'The logic of stagnation', *Monthly Review*, **38** (October), 1–19.

Moore, B. (1989), 'A simple model of bank intermediation', *Journal of Post-Keynesian Economics*, **12** (1), 10–28.

OECD (1992), *Banks under Stress*, Paris: OECD.

Robinson, J. (1962), *Essays in the Theory of Economic Growth*, Cambridge: Cambridge University Press.

Sen, S. (1991), 'Swings and paradoxes in international capital markets: a theoretical note', *Cambridge Journal of Economics*, **15** (2), 79–98.

Sen, S. (1996), 'On financial fragility and its global implications', in S. Sen, (ed.), *Financial Fragility, Debt and Economic Reforms*, London: Macmillan.

Steindl, J. (1990), *Economic Papers*, London: Macmillan.

Turner, P. (1991), 'Capital flows in the 1980s: a survey of the major trends', *BIS Economic Papers*, **30**, April.

United Nations (1994), *World Economic and Social Survey*, New York: United Nations.

Wolfson, M. (1990), 'The causes of financial instability', *Journal of Post-Keynesian Economics*, **12** (3), 335–55.

6. History, politics and effective demand in Asia

Joseph Halevi and Peter Kriesler

1. INTRODUCTION

Most of the literature on the growth of the Japanese economy as well as on the transformation of Northeast and Southeast Asia is centred on supply conditions, ignoring the fundamental role played by demand. In fact, it is possible to detect a remarkable conceptual convergence between those who claim that accumulation and growth were oriented to, and driven by, market forces (Hughes, 1988) and those who stress the role played by the State (Amsden, 1989). Both concentrate on supply factors, arguing about the sources of improved productivity in the area. However, this perspective ignores the important question of where demand for the output of the area originated. It overlooked the fact that the question of markets is a crucial one in understanding the development of the region, which is the main concern of this paper. However, as argued below, the issue of markets cannot be understood in purely economic terms, as the underlying forces are political in nature.

In historical terms the dichotomy drawn between market driven and state driven forces is of little importance as it fails to grasp the international political dimension of the process. Historians, rather than economists, have provided the best work on the area. Their studies have succeeded in producing a genuine political economy of Japanese and East Asian growth. The dialectical relationship between economic liberalism and institutionally guided interventions is well captured in the conclusions of an excellent study on Southeast Asian post war history:

> Most ironic was the American determination that the production and protection of Southeast Asia were of such paramount importance to the ultimate success of liberal capitalism that the tactics temporarily used to attain these goals might themselves be illiberal or protectionist. (Rotter, 1987, p. 220).

This article will maintain that the industrial transformation which has engulfed the Eastern part of Asia cannot be separated from US sponsored international arrangements which, more than anywhere else, enabled the area to find market outlets, hence ensuring adequate demand for their output. Interestingly enough, the non-orthodox approaches focusing on the role of the state seldom, if ever, raise this issue. It is simply taken for granted that the ingenuity of industrialization policies has overcome the question of the market.

The first and crucial step towards an all-pervasive role for the United States was the Kennan–Forrestal line elaborated in the wake of the British currency crisis of 1947. As documented by Michael Schaller in his definitive study on the American occupation of Japan, the crisis had direct and swift repercussions on the US government's conception of the post-war capitalist order (Schaller, 1985). From that moment onward, Kennan and Forrestal, the two major foreign policy-makers in Washington, saw the future of the capitalist world as based on the United States, flanked by two growth poles: West Germany in Europe and Japan in the Far East. That Europe was to provide the economic space of German capital was obvious, the hurdle being only of a political nature concerning the elimination of the sources of the Franco-German conflict. It was Japan which represented the most severe economic difficulties since it had no economic space left, unless it was allowed to gravitate towards China. By the very end of the 1940s the United States identified an economic space for Japan, nicknamed the Asian Crescent, stretching from the archipelago to India via Vietnam. The problem with that vision was that since such a space did not exist, it had to be structured.

The implementation of the Kennan–Forrestal approach was made possible by three factors. The first was the closure by the US government of any open option towards the People's Republic of China (Blum, 1982). Drawing the line against China implied a very strong commitment to the economic viability of Japan, which boiled down to a search for markets for its industry. Eventually, these markets were found, not in Asia, but in the United States itself. Just the same, Washington's protracted involvement in Asia created a Japanese economic zone but only in so far as the latter became import dependent upon Japan and export dependent upon the North American market. This, as we shall see, is the crux of the problem of effective demand in Japanese and East Asian post-war accumulation. The second factor was the Korean War, the economic aspects of which will be discussed in the second and third sections of the paper. The third, and perhaps the most significant, factor was France's defeat in Vietnam, since it permitted Washington to tie together the two components of the strategy. According to Rotter's detailed archival study:

For nearly ten years American policy makers had tried to convince the French to fight on in Vietnam; in that way, the departure of the French and the breathtaking ease with which the United States assumed the burdens of battle suggested that the policy had failed and foretold grave danger. But the Eisenhower administration, like its predecessor, understood that the approach of French withdrawal created at last an opportunity to rearm West Germany. (Rotter, 1987, p. 217)

The transfer, in 1956, of South Vietnam to American influence seemed to vindicate the strategy which saw in the preservation of Southeast Asia from third world independist movements the essential condition for the economic recovery of Japan. It also gave renewed importance to the position of South Korea. Within the American establishment the developmentalist current, represented by Walt Rostow, argued that the United States should tackle directly the two critical points of the confrontation in Asia: economic growth and the armament race. Its implementation required, in effect, the normalization of relations between South Korea and Japan. It took, however, the Vietnam War to create the momentum for such a normalization and for putting an initially very reluctant Seoul regime firmly onto an export-led growth path. The industrialization of South Korea on an export basis constituted the formation of a Japanese economic zone in East Asia. The extension of the zone to other countries during and after the Vietnam war has not altered its basic features: structural dependency *vis-à-vis* Japan and, therefore, a compelling necessity to expand exports outside the area itself.

Japan began to reenter Asia only in the early 1960s. Yet, the Japanese economic zone, brought about essentially by the Vietnam war and the collateral activities of the United States, such as the formation of the Association of South East Asian Nations (ASEAN), turned out to be very different from the vision of Kennan and Forrestal, for whom West Germany, with Europe, and Japan (with a still to be defined Asia) were supposed to act as regional powers, each dominating a relatively coherent region. In Asia American intervention has led to the formation of an area virtually glued to the United States, thereby making Washington the catalyst of its own problems.

2. FROM THE PRE-WAR TO THE POST-WAR PERIOD

In his seminal study on the role of the Ministry of International Trade and Industry (MITI) in Japan's post-war growth Chalmers Johnson observed that the structural foundations of that growth were laid down in the 1930s with the rise of heavy industry paralleled by the formation of the main guiding institution: the Ministry of Munitions which later was to be transformed into the well-known MITI (Johnson, 1982). The Japanese economist Kiyoshi Kojima coined the term *full range industrialization* to define a strategy aimed at building all the fundamental sectors of the economy (Kojima, 1979). This definition lacks, however, a dynamic dimension. It is the concept of *vertical integration*, developed by Luigi Pasinetti, which allows us to see the links between the structure of the economy and the composition of demand (Pasinetti, 1973; 1981; 1993). A country is in a position to develop all the sectors as it grows, when the benefits of technical change are retained within the country itself. This requires that productivity gains be systematically translated into higher overall real wages so that the ensuing changes in the composition of per capita demand determine a more advanced composition of output.

There is nothing automatic in this process. Situations may arise in which the country cannot retain the fruits of technical progress within its own system. After 1945 and especially after 1953, the whole web of political and financial institutional relations created by the United States *vis-à-vis* Japan enabled the latter to proceed through its full range industrialization strategy, combining productivity gains with the rise in domestic demand and the consolidation of a powerful oligopolistic bloc, stretching from industry to the whole political spectrum (Johnson, 1995).

In the pre-war period, the Great Depression highlighted the disproportion between the economic objectives of Japan's fledgling capitalism and the still too limited scope of its imperialism. The solution sought through the war against China, that is, through an extra-economic factor, was the complete integration between markets and raw materials on one hand, and the creation of a large enough yen trading area on the other, so as to compel the dollar and sterling areas to trade with it. The yen area was supposed, in the end, to clear Japan's balance of payments deficits with the advanced capitalist countries. In spite of the expansion of chemical and heavy industries, the developmental strategy ran into difficulties well before the war against the United States. Japan consistently realized a trade surplus with its exploited areas, but experienced growing difficulties with the rest of the world. Trade with its areas was in yens, whereas Tokyo had to pay its deficit with third parties in gold or in foreign currencies. As a consequence, the problem was not alleviated even when the surplus with the yen bloc surpassed the deficit with the rest of the world (Nakamura, 1983). During the 1930s the share of exports over Japan's GDP was much higher than that prevailing in the first two decades of the post-war period (18 per cent against 10 per cent, Itoh, 1990). Tokyo failed to establish a system of trade relations capable of sustaining long-term accumulation in the core country.

The necessity to find an anchor for Japan was a priority the US authorities were fully aware of even before the end of the Second World War. As Schaller has so convincingly argued in his definitive study, the issue was not just one of rebuilding but rather of creating an American alliance in Asia within which the Japanese recovery 'appeared to rest on the reconstruction of a highly centralized, regionally predominant economy'. Thus, 'conservative political forces within Japan joined with their American sponsors to rebuild a nation in ways that bore an uncanny resemblance to the pre-war order' (Schaller, 1985, p. 55). Imperialism failed to consolidate a productive space for Japanese capital, and the plans worked out by the United States occupation authorities did not, as such, provide the thrust needed to attain the objectives expressed hitherto.

Until the Korean War, the United States directed its action towards a revival of Japanese trade with East and Southeast Asia with rather ingenious means. Washington distributed dollars against yens to Japan so that the latter could purchase industrial goods from the United States. Meanwhile, the useless yens obtained by Washington were distributed as grants to the countries of the area so that they could spend them on Japanese commodities (Nester, 1990).This tended to push the Japanese economy towards non-dollar-based imports. By contrast, the new role assigned to Japan required a massive capacity to import from the United States in order to modernize its industrial system relative to the pre-war structure. The inconsistent trade strategy was coupled by the domestic crisis induced by the anti-inflationary stabilization plan enforced by Dodge (Yamamura, 1967). What, initially, got the Japanese economy out of the crisis is the special demand engendered by the Korean War. Its aftermath proved still more significant. Thus, on two crucial occasions, in 1931 and in 1950, the forces which led to a drastic transformation of Japan's economic structure were not economic but socio-political.

3. THE INTERNATIONAL FRAMEWORK OF JAPAN'S SHELTERED GROWTH

The importance of the Korean War in Japan's post-war history is not disputed (Kosai, 1986). However, its significance tends to be treated just as a quantitative, albeit very important, impulse. The Korean War had long-term effects and widespread ramifications from an institutional point of view. By 1952 it was already clear that the impulse of the war was not sufficient to guarantee Japan's growth. Thus the crucial problem for Tokyo was how to restart trade with the People's Republic of China. It was this preoccupation that led the American authorities to renew, after

1953, their drive for an Asian Crescent stretching from Japan westward encompassing Vietnam (Rotter, 1987).

During the decade separating the Korean from the Vietnam War, the United States created the financial and diplomatic conditions for the opening up of an economic space for Japan. Washington initiated a form of international public expenditure aimed at Japan as well as at other East and Southeast Asian countries. US transfer payments to Tokyo lasted well into the 1960s enabling Japan to cover the trade deficits stemming from its high growth policies. The most important form of transfer was the Special Procurements programme devised at the onset of the Korean conflict. From the end of the war till the end of the 1950s, Special Procurements expenditures lifted Japan's import ceiling by nearly 80 per cent (Nakamura, 1981). The US transfer programme allowed Japan to get over the fall in demand caused by the end of the Korean War precisely when business and government were undertaking two major rationalization plans in the steel and heavy industry, both requiring large amounts of imports (Kosai, 1986). Special procurement transfers had also an important structural implication. They insulated the economy from international competition, allowing higher prices to be set consistently with the aim of developing a capital goods producing economy. The significant relief obtained in relation to the search for outside markets, coupled with the price protection effect, meant that the Japanese economy could retain domestically a much greater share of its own productivity gains than would have otherwise been the case (Pasinetti, 1981). The breathing space given to the Japanese economy empowered the larger Japanese corporations to 'normalize' labour relations, so that, by 1960 these were firmly secured within the institutional framework of company unions. The loss of autonomy by the Japanese labour movement should be seen as the main factor accounting for the systemic faster growth in productivity relative to real wages.

Internationally, the United States acted as the main sponsor of the interests of the Japanese system. Even before the end of the occupation, the US administration allowed the retention of the laws restricting foreign investment. In this context, the case of the automobile industry is particularly illuminating. Until the early 1930s the Japanese domestic market was supplied overwhelmingly by foreign companies, the largest share accruing to American producers. The Americans were shut out in the second half of the 1930s and this state of affairs was *de facto* institutionalized when, in the wake of the Korean War, the automobile industry received a new boost. Thus, by 1954, when Japan was applying to join GATT, Tokyo drastically curtailed the allocation of foreign exchange for the importation of vehicles, virtually closing its domestic market to foreign cars. Furthermore, during the negotiations leading to Japan's membership of GATT, in order to stem the opposition to Tokyo's import restrictions, Washington signed 14 trilateral agreements on the basis of which third countries were given greater access to the American market provided they accepted Japanese exports (Nester, 1990; 1991). Lastly, the Korean War gave birth to a regional form of American public expenditure. Until Washington's war against Vietnam, the United States covered more than 70 per cent of South Korean and Taiwanese trade deficits, indirectly susbsidizing Japan's exports to these countries.

Under these circumstances, and with the ability to exercise total control over their own productive strategies Japan's corporations – in conjunction with the bureaucratic apparatus – could concentrate first and foremost on the internal process of accumulation, while expanding exports by means of industrial targeting. Thus, compared to the inter-war period, a remarkable change occurred in Japan's pattern of growth. The current account balance lost its connotation of being a structural constraint becoming, instead, a matter of cyclical concern. The United States absolved Japan from the preoccupation of finding an area of economic influence, which had contributed so significantly to its outward and imperialist orientation during the 1930s.

The inward-oriented character of the process of accumulation in the first two decades of the post-war period (Itoh, 1990) gave to the oligopolistic bloc several important permanent features. In industry a dual structure exists, the pinnacle of which is represented by a limited number of large industrial groups (*Keiretsu*). The Japanese system favours the formation of cartels according to specific economic circumstances. These can be formed for rationalization purposes, because of recessionary conditions, or for the promotion of exports including agreements aimed at ensuring favourable input prices (Yamamura, 1967). In branches where cartel policies could not be implemented because of excessive fragmentation, such as in the machine-tool industry, the state, through MITI, identified market niches and, through its licensing powers, tried to obtain the best agreements in relation to the transfer of technology (Nester, 1991). These policies continued during the 1980s, becoming part of the normal working of the system.

The period of sheltered growth permitted a smooth functioning of the dual structure of the economy. In particular, the method of subcontracting gave rise to a system called 'ordering externally on unequal terms' so that in adverse conditions large firms 'would drop subcontractors and postpone payments on their accounts, while in good times [they] would increase subcontracting. Then, citing the need for rationalization among subcontractors, they would beat down prices to low levels' (Nakamura,

1981, p. 175). By the same token, the labour market acquired the characteristics of a buyer's market for the large firms, which could force
unfavourable conditions on their temporary workforce while the workers
in the small units experienced significant wage differentials *vis-à-vis* the
tenured workers of the large companies. During the *era of high speed
growth*, the gap between productivity and wages, translated into rising
industrial profits, financed investment projects leading to large economies
of scale at home. These allowed companies to plan expansion into export
markets. Thus, the era of high speed growth was based mostly on the
domestic retention of productivity gains.

Companies could flexibly organize their strategies of competition and
collusion among themselves, as well implementing policies of cooperation and rationalization *vis-à-vis* the small business sector. In sectoral
terms, export growth has often been obtained through industrial targeting which implied a phase of market flooding to break entry barriers, and
a subsequent phase of voluntary restraints. This sort of strategy requires
a strict link between markup policies at home and the barrier breaking
price to be charged externally, as well as the ability to prevent the reentry
into Japan of the low priced exported goods. Such a strategy is conceivable only if the export policies of Japanese firms included a target market
share, which was made to appear as resulting from voluntary restraints
(Nester, 1991). It must be pointed out that there is a profound conceptual
and concrete difference between Japanese industrial targeting of foreign
markets and similar policies followed in other East and Southeast Asian
countries in the last two decades. *Full range industrialization*, and its necessary corollary represented by the internal retention of productivity
gains, always remained the central pillar of Tokyo's growth policies.
Other countries, by contrast, by relying heavily on the importation of
Japanese technology and capital goods, had to make industrialization a
strict function of external growth and, as a consequence, their pricing
policy, on the surface similar to Japan's, implied that part of their own
productivity gains were leaked abroad.

Japan could implement its export strategies, because, in addition to the
role played by its institutions, the political relations established by
Washington towards Tokyo gave access to the American market without
equivalent reciprocity. At the same time it would be misleading to conclude that the policies eliminated macroeconomic Keynesian uncertainty
as to the prospects of future investment. Macroeconomic uncertainty sur-
faced strongly in the first half of the 1960s when the results of the income
doubling plan became clearer, and Tokyo's export policies began to
encounter severe external criticism. The fear was allayed by other, mostly
external, forces. As noted by Calder, 'Japanese growth of the postwar

period, particularly in the 1950s and 1960s, typically came in surges. Many of these volatile surges were totally unanticipated, arising as they did from sudden overseas stimulus. . . . growth was strongly stimulated by American offshore procurements to support wars in Korea and Vietnam whose scale and substantial economic benefits to Japan were previously unanticipated' (Calder, 1988, p. 52). The American role was therefore that of providing a covering shield, an umbrella under which Tokyo could organize both its domestic expansion and its export plans. In the rest of Asia, such as in South Korea, the picture would turn out to be quite different. The United States would provide markets, financial coverage and salvation from extreme crisis, but in structural terms output and investment had to be determined first by export priorities, which, in their turn, were governed by the structural dependency *vis-à-vis* Japan.

4. JAPAN'S REENTRY INTO SOUTHEAST ASIA: THE ROLE OF SOUTH KOREA

The expansion of Japanese exports and, later, of direct investment into East Asia was not entirely a natural process nor was it just a consequence of deliberate policies. According to the historian Michael Schaller '[t]he Japanese, at least through the 1960s, were far more interested in commerce with China and with the West (for which they needed hard currencies) than in barterlike arrangements Washington hoped to foster with Southeast Asia. To assuage Japanese resentment and meet their dollar needs, the United States had to continue a variety of expensive military procurement programs for many years' (Schaller, 1985, p. 297).

The role played by the economies of the area until the early 1960s is evidenced by the type of trade flows that prevailed between Japan and South Korea and Taiwan. For these countries Japan was, then, the major export market while the United States was the principal source of imports. The situation changed, almost abruptly, from the early 1960s onward when Tokyo became the dominant source of import and the USA the most important area of destination of exports. This change had its root cause in the fact that 'America's huge escalation of the Vietnam War . . . actually helped Japan reenter the Southeast Asian economy' (ibid., p. 298).

The strategic objectives pursued by Washington gave rise, alongside the military intervention, to the approach called 'the double hegemony' which assigned to Japan the dominant economic role, while the United States provided military and financial coverage and access to North American markets (Woo, 1991). In this context, South Korea became the linchpin of the double hegemony theory requiring a tight integration with American foreign policy, expressed by Seoul's participation in the Vietnam War. The export-oriented policies of South Korean industrialization, were also the product of American thinking which feared that a domestic growth strategy would involve persistent US aid. The diplomatic document which formalized the content of the links between Seoul and Washington was the 1966 Brown Memorandum, named after the US Ambassador to South Korea. The memorandum connected Seoul's participation in the Vietnam War with Washington's commitment to promote South Korean exports (Landsberg, 1993). Furthermore, the 1969 Nixon–Sato communiqué institutionalized Seoul's position within the framework of US–Japanese relations. Thus, in the case of Northeast Asian industrialization, the diplomacy of 'security' has become, more than in Europe, a codeword for economic policies and for social restructuring.

At the productive level, the Vietnam War, financed by American public expenditure, generated a hot-house effect for those industries which were to gain dominance in the subsequent decade. By 1967, the share of South Korean exports, as a share of total exports by sector, going to South Vietnam was 94.29 per cent in steel (72.48 per cent for Taiwan), 51.75 per cent in transport equipment (Taiwan: 36.5 per cent), non electrical machinery 40.77 per cent (Taiwan: 47.45 per cent). South Vietnam also absorbed more than 85 per cent of Taiwan's cement exports and about 74 per cent of the export value of chemical fertilizers (Naya, 1971, p. 43). The implications of these developments for Japan's own exports to those countries are self evident. More importantly, the industrial spurt engendered by the Vietnam War permitted, for countries like South Korea, the transition towards export-oriented industrialization by providing institutional channels to the American market as well as a secure cushion of dollar earnings. Yet, the South Korean experience differs substantially from that of Japan. The latter could shelter itself for quite a long time from foreign competition by focusing on domestic full range industrialization, whereas the former was literally thrust onto foreign (US) markets.

The defeat of the United States in Vietnam led, well before 1975, to a decline in aid and transfer payments to the region, thereby reducing the level of effective demand generated within the area by Washington's public expenditure. The South Korean strategy of embarking on an accelerated process of heavy and chemical industrialization was, to a significant extent, a response to the loss of the safety net represented by American public expenditure. From the 1970s onward, Seoul's export strategy can be defined as chasing the composition of per capita demand of the United States, by moving from, say, textiles, to goods for which per capita demand is more dynamic. A similar strategy characterized Tokyo's external policies, except the range of commodities belonged to a higher category. At this point it is important to stress the hierarchical order defining South Korea's heavy industrialization path. The Japanese participated in the drafting of the third and fourth five-year plan, stretching from 1972 to 1982, by targeting the sectors towards which Japanese industries could be transferred (Landsberg, 1993, p. 153). Yet Tokyo did not provide an expanding area of demand for South Korean products. The share of South Korean exports going to Japan tended to decline. More specifically, the possibility of sustaining a growing deficit with Japan came to depend on a large export surplus with the United States. This situation has not changed since then.

The history of the links between South Korea and Japan raises two issues. The first is financial, its relevance being the determinant role played by political considerations prior to the economic ones. The second is structural and has a more long-term character. In the situation prevailing during the 1970s the heavy industry pattern of growth gave rise, in South Korea, to two deficit crises, the most important of which was that occurring in the triennium 1979–81 (Lim, 1985). The solution of the Korean crisis of 1979–81 stemmed from the strong linkage between foreign policy and finance. South Korea became an important terrain for undoing Carter's foreign policy based on triliteralism and arms control.[1] The new line 'sought to counter the Soviets in the Far East through tight US economic *and* security ties with Japan, Korea and the People's Republic of China and – what is much more problematical – among these nations themselves' (Woo, 1991, p. 183). With the ascendance of Reagan to the presidency, Washington took the political lead in securing Seoul's financial position. In this context the Japanese followed suit by providing South Korea with a $4 billion loan making sure that a significant part of it would be turned into purchases from Japanese industry. The dynamic export markets came from the United States, thanks to Reagan's policies based on the revaluation of the dollar and on military driven budget deficits. Seoul's trade with Washington, while mildly in deficit throughout the 1970s, swung to a surplus in 1982 which continued to rise, in tandem with a rise in the deficit with Japan, till 1987. Thereafter, the surplus with Washington declined to end up in a deficit in the early 1990s but the deficit with Japan kept growing.

The structural aspect of the links between South Korea and Japan lies in the different role played by domestic growth in the economic history of the two counties. In an excellent study of South Korea's industrialization Mario Lanzarotti (1993) has quantified the contribution to overall growth stemming from expansion towards the domestic and the foreign markets. It seems that the latter had a greater impact than in the other industrialized countries. Therefore, it stands to reason that productivity in the exporting industries in South Korea has grown more than in the developed countries, Japan included. Although such a conclusion must be corroborated by deeper studies, its tentative acceptance would bring us directly to Pasinetti's principle of comparative productivity change advantage (Pasinetti, 1981). In a nutshell, Pasinetti's principle shows that if the ratio between the rate of productivity growth of the exporting to the domestic industries is higher, as in say, South Korea, than the equivalent ratio in the rest of the industrialized world, the real terms of trade of South Korean exports will worsen. The ensuing fall of export prices implies that part of productivity gains are leaked abroad to the benefit of foreign consumers.

For more than two decades following the end of the Second World War, Japan obtained from the United States a political and economic umbrella enabling it to pursue a determined strategy of full range industrialization. High productivity growth and a small ratio of exports to GDP meant unambiguously that productivity gains were retained domestically. Such a route was not open to either South Korea or to most of the rest of East and Southeast Asia, not because Washington did not 'help' but because of the ties established with Japan. What matters is the structural aspect of the surpluses that Japan obtains with countries like South Korea, requiring maximization of exports rather than concentration on product development. The dependency, which *mutatis mutandis* operates even more strongly in the rest of East Asia, of South Korea *vis-à-vis* Japan, revolves around issues determined by its high external exposure: heavy subordination to Japan in relation to machines and parts, discretionary transfer of technology by Japanese firms, relocation of Japanese firms operating in South Korea. In the first case, the large share occupied by Japan in supplying machines and parts to Seoul creates structural, non-substitutable links between the South Korean and the Japanese industries. When South Korean products end up competing against the Japanese ones, especially during the phases of the appreciation of the yen, Japanese firms were able to select and reorient the transfer of technology precisely because such a large part of South Korea's stock of capital remained tied to Japan's (Landsberg, 1993).

The South Korean case is the most significant in the capitalist development of Asia outside Japan because it was based on a deliberate linkage between the objective of creating a national capital in the country and the role of both Japan and the United States which accepted and sustained the above objective. In many other East Asian countries such as Thailand, Malaysia and, eventually, Indonesia, industrial accumulation takes place via multinational investment of which Japan's corporation is the strongest component. The local ruling classes retain strong comprador elements giving high speculative features to their financial markets and institutions.

5. CONCLUSIONS

The observations made above have both a developmental and an effective demand implication. From the point of view of development paths, it is likely that East Asia is, for the time being, locked in a situation in which it keeps surrendering an important part of productivity gains abroad, with specific industries displacing the corresponding ones in the more advanced countries. The competitive international position of specific industries will improve insofar as their own rate of productivity growth relatively to the country's overall productivity growth, is greater than the corresponding ratio in the advanced countries (Pasinetti's industry specific principle of comparative productivity change advantage). The persistence of this trend may well generate further protectionist reactions from the advanced countries. However, Japan is in a different position from the rest of the industrialized world, and it is unlikely to be crucially affected by displacement effects. As aptly described by a former Japanese Ambassador to Thailand:

> Japan is creating an exclusive Japanese market in which the Asia–Pacific nations are incorporated into the so-called 'keiretsu' system. The essential relationship between Japan and Southeast Asia is [one of] trading captive imports, such as products from plants in which Japanese companies have invested, for captive exports, such as necessary equipment and materials. (Tabb, 1994, p. 32)

This brings us to the second implication concerning the problem of effective demand. The surplus with Asia has become for Japan the main source of profitable external demand. Although trade between East and Southeast Asia is growing, the clearance of the deficit with Japan requires a third external market, as suggested by Kalecki. Such a market is provided mostly by the United States, rather than by Japan. Unless the United States is willing to fund this deficit indefinitely, through imports, thereby accepting the necessity of sustaining the industry-specific displacements, an immanent problem of effective demand emerges. The rest of Asia must keep exporting but Japan is not taking the onus of getting rid of their surplus. Indeed, the whole post-war history of Japanese growth can be read as building an institutional oligopolistic position in its area of dominance. In other words, the problem facing the rest of Asia is significantly different from that which Japan faced at the end of the war. For the political reasons outlined earlier, Japan was guaranteed markets by US actions. As a result, current account problems did not constitute any fetter to economic growth. This is in marked contrast to the rest of Asia, which is characterized by deficits with Japan. In order for the current account no longer to fetter growth, the USA has absorbed much of their output, enabling some balance. This has alleviated potential demand problems enabling these countries to concentrate on the supply factors which most commentators have focused on. However, this is only because the question of markets has been relieved by US actions, as discussed earlier. There is a further important link between the two sides of the discussion, often called the 'Verdoon Law' (Kaldor, 1966) whereby rises in the gross level of output allowed by the extension of demand and markets itself induces increased productivity, leading to a virtuous circle of development. This, however, is a matter beyond the scope of the current chapter.

As a concluding remark, it is important to observe that due to the strict interconnection between Japan's economic expansion and the role of the United States in the area, the formation of an East Asian zone of capitalist accumulation has altogether different characteristics from the European one. The role of Germany – both positive and negative (Halevi, 1995) – in the dynamics of Europe's effective demand has been such that the Continent's monetary system gravitated towards that of the Federal Republic, especially from the end of the 1970s onward. In fact, Germany is both the largest exporter to and the biggest importer from the rest of Europe. If Germany reflates, the rest of Europe will follow suit. At the same time if, say, Italy reflates, Germany is likely to benefit more than the other European countries given the dominant role of the FRG in providing capital goods to each country of Europe.

In East Asia by contrast, from the Plaza Accords in 1985 until Thailand's financial crisis of spring–summer 1997, currencies other than Japan's were pegged to the US dollar. Under conditions of a prolonged revaluation of the yen *vis-à-vis* the American currency (1985–95), the *de facto* existence of a *dollar standard* in East Asia helped those countries expand exports by passively relying on Japanese technology and direct investment. At the same time it was also a cause of systemic imbalances in the current account position of those countries leading to endemic financial instability. The specific oligopolistic nature of Japan coupled with the reliance on the *dollar standard* has put the burden of adjustment on the United States and has actually prevented Japan from acting as a reflationary factor.

NOTES

1. Carter's foreign policy was consistent with the attempt to stem the decline in the international position of US manufacturing by allowing the dollar to float downward. The best account of the changed power relations within the monetary system, as well as the best argument on the nature of the monetary conflicts and the international level is still that of Parboni (1981).

REFERENCES

Amsden, A. (1989), *Asia's Next Giant*, New York: Oxford University Press.

Blum, R. (1982), *Drawing the Line: The Origin of the American Containment in Asia*, New York: Norton.

Calder, K. (1988), *Crisis and Compensation: Public Policy and Political Stability in Japan, 1949–1986*, Princeton, N.J.: Princeton University Press.

Halevi, J. (1995), 'The EMS and the Bundesbank in Europe', in P. Arestis and V. Chick (eds), *Finance, Development and Structural Change: Post-Keynesian Perspecitives*, Aldershot, UK: Edward Elgar, 263–92.

Hughes, H. (ed.) (1988), *Achieving Industrialization in East Asia*, Cambridge: Cambridge University Press.

Itoh, M. (1990), *The World Economic Crisis and Japanese Capitalism*, London: Macmillan.

Johnson, C. (1982), *MITI and the Japanese Miracle*, Stanford, CA: Stanford University Press.

Johnson, C. (1995), *Japan: Who Governs?* New York: W.W. Norton.

Kaldor, N. (1966), 'Causes of the slow rate of economic growth in the United Kingdom', reprinted in N. Kaldor (1978), *Further Essays on Economic Theory*, London, Duckworth Press.

Kojima, K. (1979), 'Newly industrializing countries', *Monthly Report*, Institute of Overseas Investment [*Kaigai-toshi Kenkyu-jo*], November.

Kosai, Y. (1986), *The Era of High Speed Growth*, Tokyo: University of Tokyo Press.

Landsberg, M. (1993), *The Rush to Development: Economic Change and Political Struggle in South Korea*, New York: Monthly Review Press.

Lanzarotti, M. (1993), *La Corée du sud: une sortie du sous-développement*, Paris: Presses Unversitaires de France.

Lim, H. (1985), *Dependent Development in Korea*, Seoul: Seoul National University Press.

Nakamura, T. (1981), *Postwar Japanese Economy*, Tokyo: University of Tokyo Press.

Nakamura, T. (1983), *Economic Growth in Prewar Japan*, New Haven, CT: Yale University Press.

Naya, S. (1971), 'The Vietnam War and some aspects of its economic impact on Asian countries', *Developing Economies*, **9** (1), 38–57.

Nester, W. (1990), *Japan's Growing Power Over East Asia and the World Economy*, London: Macmillan.

Nester, W. (1991), *Japanese Industrial Targeting: The Neomercantilist Path to Economic Superpower*, London: Macmillan.

Parboni, R. (1981), *The Dollar and its Rivals*, London: Verso.

Pasinetti, L. (1973), 'The notion of vertical integration in economic analysis', *Metroeconomica*, 25, 1–29.

Pasinetti, L. (1981), *Structural Change and Economic Growth*, Cambridge: Cambridge University Press.

Pasinetti, L. (1993), *Structural Economic Dynamics*, Cambridge: Cambridge University Press.

Rotter, A. (1987), *The Path to Vietnam*, Ithaca, NY: Cornell University Press.

Schaller, M. (1985), *The American Occupation of Japan: The Origin of the Cold War in Asia*, New York: Oxford University Press.

Tabb, W. (1994), 'Japanese capitalism and the Asian geese', *Monthly Review*, **45** (March), 29–40.

Woo, J. (1991), *Race to the Swift: State and Finance in Korean Industrialization*, New York: Columbia University Press.

Yamamura, K. (1967), *Economic Policy in Postwar Japan*, Berkeley, CA: University of California Press.

PART III

Finance and Investment in the Context
of Underdevelopment

7. Finance and investment in the context of development: a post Keynesian perspective

Victoria Chick

1. INTRODUCTION

While neoclassical economics aspires to find laws which transcend institutions, it is an article of faith in both post Keynesian economics and development economics that institutions matter. Indeed, the justification for development economics as a separate subject is that the institutions of developing economies differ significantly from those of developed economies. Failure to understand institutional structure and the appropriateness of a theory to it leads at best to misunderstanding and at worst to thoroughly bad advice. The dominant concern of mainstream development economics has been the adequacy (or otherwise) of saving, whether this takes the form of two-gap analysis or the current prescription of financial liberalization: both find the fault in inadequate saving. This concern ignores Keynes's demonstration that investment, the engine of growth and industrialization, preceded intentional (*ex ante*) saving.

The 'Washington Consensus' of the World Bank and the IMF is that slow growth of developing countries is the result of inadequate domestic saving, which in turn is a result of excessive regulation of financial markets and interest rates. These features have 'repressed' domestic saving, and this repression has inhibited investment. Their policy prescription is to deregulate financial markets and free interest rates to rise above current levels; these actions are supposed to encourage domestic saving and hence investment.

Similarly, to Keynesians, the belief that higher saving rates should mean higher growth, and the (unsuccessful) search of the data for this correlation (for example, Sen, 1983), is misguided, on two counts: first, investment leads intentional saving (which cannot be measured), and second, *ex post* saving and investment are equal, so the data purporting to measure saving independently of investment are a mystery. If what is being said is that economies with higher investment grow faster, that is not surprising – but the theory with which these economists are working leads them to look at saving.

It is remarkable how enduring is the idea that saving is required in order to foster investment. The theory that saving is the precondition for investment and growth comes from Ricardo, and was developed for an agricultural, pre-industrial economy. The Washington prescription is based on the financial pattern experienced in Britain in the early stages of industrialization – a pattern which ended somewhere in the latter half of the nineteenth century. The countries developing now are going through a similar process of industrialization, but they have access to a sophisticated global banking system. What they lack is not access to finance but mechanisms for the funding and eventual retirement of debt.

The reversal of causality between saving and investment, one of Keynes's theoretical breakthroughs in *The General Theory* (1936), was similarly dependent on institutions. Two new factors entered the financial picture somewhere in the latter half of the nineteenth century: bank deposits became widely held and the form of business ownership altered. Those institutional changes remain in place, indeed they have intensified, since Keynes wrote. Today they pertain as much to most developing economies as they do to the developed world. Thus those of us who take our inspiration from Keynes are in a position to offer a strong counterweight to the Washington Consensus, on sound theoretical grounds.

In particular our framework suggests that financial liberalization will not do the job which is intended and diverts attention from what needs to be done, namely to provide a means of funding expansion after it is underway in a manner which is no more inflationary than expansion needs to be. As things stand in many countries, the absence of adequate funding mechanisms means that the government or its agencies are often made responsible for funding. Typically, this will add to deficit finance accentuating the financial imbalance. By contrast, advanced countries have solved this problem either by equity shares traded in capital markets or by universal banks, strongly capitalized, who hold equity on a long-term basis. Both are dependent on private capital, which almost by definition will not be adequate for rapid development. Nevertheless, arrangements could be better than they are at present. The attention of policy-makers should shift from the abstract and ill-defined aggregate, 'saving', to the concrete institutional structure of a country's financial system to try to deal with this problem.

The two institutional changes which transform the place of saving in the growth of an economy are the stage of development of the banking system and the form of ownership of the means of production. As an economy develops today, the ownership of its production gradually tends to conformity with this modern Western norm, out of the need to acquire sufficient capital. This is true of agribusiness as well as of industry. And while banking in developing countries may not have become as widespread as in most Western countries, it has penetrated at least to the extent which characterized nineteenth century Britain. These differences affect the appropriate theory and policy advice. Let us begin at the beginning, with the onset of the Industrial Revolution.

2. ONCE UPON A TIME SAVING PRECEDED INVESTMENT

Today development is a conscious aim. At the time of the first industrialization, the vast changes which were taking place were happening piecemeal, without plan or direction, in an extremely decentralized world where communication was poor and regional economies strong. Now, communication is global and rapid; the demonstration effect which economists began talking about in the 1960s now operates with a vengeance. Competition is also global, rapidly shifting and harsh. First-world techniques are not just available; they must be implemented if developing countries are to compete.

Financial institutions, both banks and the stock and money markets, developed along with the changes in the economy and in economic organization. At the beginning of industrialization, sole proprietorships and partnerships were the rule, for banks as well as enterprises. Finance of business could seldom be separated from family finances. Savings derived from profit and were reinvested. The banks saw themselves chiefly as suppliers of finance for trade and for working capital, though they did supply renewable loans; larger sums of money, needed for major investment projects, were typically sought from relatives and acquaintances with money to invest for long-term income or a share of profit. The stock market developed quickly after the establishment of the Bank of England (1694) as a market for gilts, but a market in business debt, and of course equity, had to await the joint-stock form of organization. In the circumstances described, and even much later, it was entirely correct to say that saving was necessary to, and preceded, investment. Self-financing and intermediation – in the strict sense of passing on prior savings, making a profit by providing wholesaling and information services – were the order of the day. Even the banks played this role. They were, at the beginning of industrialization, limited geographically and in the range of their customers. They were also limited in the extent to which their liabilities were acceptable as means of payment; their note issues had a limited range of acceptability and deposits were mainly held as a form of saving.

This form of organization permitted only moderate, incremental growth. Most historians for this reason do not favour the term 'Industrial Revolution' for what was surely an evolutionary process. The modest changes, year on year, were possible to finance in the way described, even though for some, unlimited liability led to grief. Extolling the moral virtue of saving further contributed by shifting the saving function. But investment on the scale required for modern industry would have been impossible, because of its large capital requirements, without development of financial and industrial institutions beyond this point.

Even before the coming of the railways, capital demands were increasing beyond the capacity of individuals' networks, supplemented by working capital and some rollover credit from the banks, to meet them. The risks being borne by entrepreneurs, their backers and their bankers, were becoming unacceptably large. The joint stock method of organization began to come back, after the setback following the burst of the South Sea Bubble. As the demands for capital grew, so did the capacity of banks to meet those demands. The permissible number of banking partners was expanded in the 1830s, so that joint stock banking became a reality, but unlimited liability was retained in England until 1858. Meanwhile the Scottish banking system was developing into a national system of branches, a pattern to which the English banks would also later conform.

With the joint stock form of organization comes another novelty: the balance sheet, and the separation of the need to finance investment from the need to fund it. Finance is what you need to spend beyond your income; funding is what you need to balance assets with long-term liabilities: debt or equity. This distinction can remain unclear in a sole proprietorship or partnership, for whereas the household may estimate its net worth, it need not persuade anyone to 'hold' it. If a family chooses to work for a low rate of immediate return in order, say, to build up a business, that is their affair, as long as they meet their commitments. The joint stock company, not being a natural person, is owned by its shareholders. The rate of return on shares, allowing for the prospect of growth, provides limits on the firm's activities which do not constrain the household. Capital must be 'willingly held' by long-term creditors or shareholders, and the expected rate of return must be competitive. An activity can be financed by short-term lending and later funded; the funding pays back the short-term loan.

The trouble with the Washington consensus is that it follows a theory which has not kept up with developments. Saving and finance are quite separate activities; saving plays a role in funding, not finance. There is little difficulty getting adequate finance; if the domestic banking system is not up to it, countries have access to international banks. The difficulty is developing institutions which provide funding. Once that is done, it may be appropriate to worry about increasing the rate of saving.

3. THE DEVELOPMENT OF BANKS AND THE REVERSAL OF CAUSALITY

Gradually, the use of bank notes and then deposits, gained wider and wider currency. Even so, Keynes, as late as 1930 (in *A Treatise on Money*), distinguished between 'money proper' and bank liabilities. Yet the widespread, though far from universal, acceptance of bank liabilities as means of payment had been a fact for about 60 years, and for even longer they had been accepting and clearing each others' cheques, thus acting as a system rather than the individual, geographically separated banks of early industrialization. These facts had fundamentally altered the role of banks in the finance of investment and the growth of the economy, and Keynes was soon to incorporate this change in *The General Theory*, though without explicitly making the connection.

In *The General Theory*, as is well known, saving responds to changes in income arising from investment: investment precedes and causes changes in saving. Investment is able to initiate the change in income because a crucial part of it is financed independently of saving. This is possible in an advanced banking system because the results of bank lending, new deposits, are generally acceptable and represent not only saving; rather, all money-flows which use transfer by cheque, whether they support consumption or represent saving, flow through the advanced banking system. Deposits held for transaction purposes are just as useful in funding the banks' balance sheets as are deposits which represent saving. These deposits may change hands but they are unlikely to leave the banking system. This state of affairs is elsewhere (Chick, 1986) called Stage 2 banking, in contrast to the stage of simple intermediation (Stage 1) described above. It is not until after *The General Theory*, in the later articles which have now become so familiar to those studying the finance motive and allied problems (Keynes, 1937a, 1937b, 1939) that Keynes fully exploits his new theory and develops its implications. In these articles he makes the distinction between finance and funding, hinted at above, and assigns to 'the credit system (which is solely concerned with finance and never with saving)' (Keynes 1939, p. 284) the role of providing the purchasing power to initiate investment. On the role of the banks he is unequivocal: 'banks hold the key position in the transition from a

lower to a higher scale of activity' (1937b, p. 222). In saying this he agrees
with Robertson, that saving cannot possibly finance investment, for
finance must be had at the beginning and saving is only available at an
increased rate in response to the rise in income which investment pro-
vokes: 'Credit, in the sense of "finance", looks after a flow of investment.
It is a revolving fund which can be used over and over again. It does not
absorb or exhaust any resources. The same finance can tackle one investment after another' (Keynes, 1937a, p. 209).

To assert the importance of bank credit in the finance of investment
does not preclude other means – indeed, it is well known that self-
financing accounts for the bulk of investment finance in the UK and
economies with a similar financing structure. The point is that bank
finance is needed at the margin to raise the level of activity independently
of saving, while the old level of activity may be financed by a variety of
other means (Chick, 1988).

The deposits resulting from the increased lending do not, typically,
leave the banking system, but return to it. As deposits become more and
more central to the payments mechanism, the cash drain arising from
expansion has systematically reduced. To this extent bank credit is self-
funding for the system as a whole: a rise in advances is more or less
equally matched by a rise in deposits. However, an expansion of the
banks' collective balance sheet leaves the banks less liquid in the important sense that they have a lower reserve to deposit ratio than before.
Indeed if the ratio is binding, new bank credit will not be forthcoming.
This is the sense in which I argued (Chick, 1986) that Stage 2 banks are
reserve-constrained but not deposit-constrained.

If bank credit is to play the crucial role just assigned to it, where does
that leave the role of saving? First we must distinguish, for the record,
that Keynes included not only intentional holdings of money (deposits)
in saving but also the unintentional acquisition of deposits as a result of
income payments made from overdrafts, as a result of the extension of
bank lending. By contrast, Robertson and all loanable funds and classical theorists before him identified saving with lending – in the present
context with the purchase of securities. If we take Robertson's definition
for a moment, the role his sort of saving may play in this system is to
fund the investment: '[T]he increment of current investment over prior
investment can only be cared for permanently out of the increment of
current saving' (Keynes 1937a, p. 284; Keynes's italics removed).

In the nature of a banking system such as the British, which has
responsibility for the payments mechanism, long-term lending is quite
risky, as it increases the mismatch between the asset and liability sides of
banks' balance sheets. Firms could count on rolling over their bank credit

but this would increase their uncertainty. Thus firms might wish to issue long-term debt at an opportune time and repay their bank loans. If this were done systematically, the reduction in liquidity which banks experience, *ceteris paribus*, when they increase their lending would be constantly reversed and their liquidity restored as the investment is funded. From a macroeconomic point of view, this happens as the rate of saving increases in the multiplier process.

The development of the stock market in Britain allowed just such action to be taken, at least by firms large enough to have access. Stock markets however, as Keynes stressed, are double-edged: they provide liquidity to individual investors while simultaneously offering the opportunity for speculation. The Victorian investor, inhibited by less well-developed stock markets than in Keynes's time, was often locked in to his portfolio, but by the same token he was forced to take the long view.

The development of a capitalist economy and its financial support was not without its upheavals, to put it mildly: there were many financial and commercial crises throughout the process. Nevertheless, it is worth paying attention to the possibility of smooth development arising from the articulation of the finance and funding mechanisms outlined above combined with a fairly slow rate of growth. The slow rate of growth forestalls both sharp declines in bank liquidity – or even banks hitting the reserve constraint very often – and sharp rises in the rate of increase in the money supply consequent on new bank credit. If the funding mechanism is working well, monetary increases are kept within the range which can be absorbed by increases in productive activity and not spill over into any more rises in prices than are dictated by the redirection of activity which is implied in the new investment. Rapid rates of growth and high investment/income ratios pose much more difficult problems of illiquidity in the banks and too much liquidity outside them.

4. TAKING STOCK OF THE KEYNES STORY

It can be seen by contrast to the pre-Keynesian story that the story told by Keynes reflects and pertains to a particular set of institutional structures. The economy which conforms to that story is one dominated by joint-stock enterprises and banks, which have an arm's-length relationship, where there exists not only a banking system whose liabilities are widely accepted as means of payment but where broad, active markets in long-term securities and equities also exist. Much investment may be self-financed, but the growth potential (sadly, not always the performance) of the economy is greater than in the 19th century because of the freedom from the need to generate saving to finance investment. The potential for instability will also have increased, and in particular, little is left of the pre-Keynesian story of the equivalence of the rate of interest and the rate of profit.

The story one would tell for Germany would have to be different, for finance and funding are both provided by the banking system, which is not at arm's length from firms. The different development of Germany has been attributed (Gershenkron, 1962) to the larger capital requirements associated with later development. The story one would tell for Britain today would also be different. One would have to emphasize the role of the pension funds and other institutional investors, and – most important for the ultimate focus of this paper – until recently one would have to bring in the state-owned or state-subsidized firm and the connection with the government budget. This we shall now do in the context of newly-industrialized or semi-industrialized developing countries. The one thing we shall not have to do in that context is to consider the argument that saving is a precondition for investment, except to consider another facet of that argument and lay it to rest. It is a principle of loanable funds theory that investment which is not financed by (prior, intentional) savings but by the creation or activation of money is *ipso facto* inflationary. It is partly this prospect which lies behind Washington Consensus policy. The proposition derives from the quantity theory, where the inflationary potential can be judged from increases in the money stock or velocity alone. Again, Keynes in *The General Theory* takes pains to contradict this proposition, with the whole apparatus of Chapter 21. The crucial elements of inflation in that chapter are (a) increases in the quantity of money (yes!); (b) the extent to which new money flowed into idle balances or into holdings of securities, where it may affect interest rates but not prices; (c) the degree of excess capacity; and (d) the volume of unemployment. From the institutional perspective of this chapter the most obvious difference between developed and developing countries is the availability of financial assets to absorb monetary shocks; thus the presumption must be for a greater potential for inflation in developing countries from the same monetary increase on that account. This is likely to be offset by a larger volume of slack labour.

Even the sophisticated treatment of Chapter 21 does not include a dynamic factor which in the present context I believe to be of great importance: the speed of monetary increase(s). If all monetary increases are the result of output-supporting credit, the first round is no problem (though prices may increase if there are diminishing returns or inadequate capacity). But the money remains in the system to support induced expenditure. The faster the money supply increases, the less able is the economic system to anticipate and produce to meet the increased expenditure with increased output; thus the more likely is inflation (see Chick, 1984). The sheer pace of modern development gives some cause for concern about inflation, if not on quantity-theoretic grounds. This concern must be balanced against the aspirations which give rise to the problem; the political dimension of the problem deserves recognition.

5. FINANCE IN TODAY'S DEVELOPING COUNTRIES

We have, I hope, demonstrated the applicability of, first, the prior saving theory and second, the Keynes story of bank finance followed by saving/funding to particular institutional frameworks existing at different historical times. We have also hinted that the organization of production has changed yet further in developed economies. It is now necessary to examine that organization in at least the more advanced developing countries, to ask whether Keynes's framework is applicable to them. As for the Washington Consensus, it is far too late for loanable funds and the quantity theory in most LDCs: most have Stage 2 banking of their own and many have access to the international banking system. The World Bank and the IMF are guilty of anachronism.

The organization of production in the developed countries has been marked, since the end of the Second World War, by the rise of multinational companies. These are typically based in the first world but have affiliates in many developing countries. There they often stand alongside the state-owned enterprises as the largest capital-users and the leaders in development. Then there are nationally-based private firms, of varying size and importance, and family-based enterprises which are often quite small. Both the capital requirements and access to capital vary enormously across these types of firms.

Most developing countries by now have banks which, even though their depositors do not include more than the upper reaches of economic society, still find their deposits sufficiently widely used as means of payment to count as Stage 2 banks. Taking the domestic, private firms and the banks together we approximate the institutional arrangement for financing existing in early twentieth century Britain. In both we also observe small, family-based enterprises which are largely self-financing, though in the developing world, kerb markets also serve these enterprises, at high interest rates. To this we must add two new features: the state banks, including institutions dedicated to the financial support of development, and the international banks/money markets. In some countries, in addition the government takes upon itself the mediation of foreign currency loans to domestic clients.

The state-owned or state-run corporations are normally independent of the central government budget but general budgetary policy does play the key role in their credit availability. This may be mediated through a 'development bank' which may not be a deposit-taking institution at all but rather is funded through taxation. State corporations may also benefit from the government's decision to borrow on international money markets in its own name. In the case of Brazil, the government transformed its foreign-currency borrowing into domestic-currency loans to parastatal and other firms, thus generalizing the foreign earnings and exchange risks to the country as a whole.

Affiliates of multinational corporations also have access to the international money markets, though not on sovereign-lending terms. They also have some access to the internal funds of the parent company, the extent depending on local tax laws and exchange control regulations as well as the policies of the parent company. These and the larger private firms can expect preferential treatment from domestic banks, though they nevertheless tend to exhibit a fairly high percentage of self-financing. The preference for self-financing can be attributed to the market power usually exercised by these firms, which allows them to control both their prices and their retention ratios, along the lines suggested by Eichner (1976) and FitzGerald (1995), or to inadequate provision for funding (Studart, 1995). Both these factors may be operating. There is surely little doubt that in most developing countries the stock market is thin and particularly vulnerable to speculation (Studart, 1995; Singh, 1994).

From this brief examination of the institutional structure of the 'representative' semi-industrialized country we may conclude that under-investment is surely not due to a lack of saving to provide direct finance, since even if domestic banks are insufficiently developed (which is itself unlikely), there is substantial access to the most sophisticated banking and money markets. If saving is a problem in developing countries it is not its inadequate volume but a lack of well-developed institutions which channel it into funding for investment. This lack often leaves the problem of funding up to the government, one way or another. It is often undertaken by development banks. Although their brief may extend beyond the support of parastatal companies, development banks usually reach further than these, at least to the support of large private firms. In any case their role is usually substantial, both in financing and funding investment. In some countries there may be an implicit understanding that repayment is not expected.

Even where repayment is expected, the connection thus forged between government finance and the pursuit of development can have perverse effects in the long run, even when it solves some short-run problems. If the rapid pace of development and the inadequate funding arrangements give rise to a fiscal deficit which itself cannot be financed by borrowing, inflation can confidently be expected.

6. CONCLUSION

The progress of development never did run smooth. The nineteenth and early-twentieth century British (and American) experience was marred by bankruptcies and financial manias, panics and crashes. The panics and crashes consolidated the role of the lender of last resort, so that similar episodes today are worked out by inflationary means, which spreads the risk over the economy as a whole. A similar phenomenon is observed in the rapidly-industrializing countries; indeed it is exacerbated by the absence of adequate funding mechanisms, a much accelerated pace of change and a significantly higher ratio of investment to income than that characterizing the so-called Industrial Revolution. Despite these heavy requirements, we argue that finance is not the problem. Finance is available from a banking system which has progressed, in all but the least developed countries, to the point where their lending is not dependent on saving, and there is the further possibility of access to a global banking system.

The problem is funding, and here saving does play a role. However, while the World Bank/IMF is concerned to increase the level of saving, the real problem is that there is nowhere for it to go which will be effective. Thus financial liberalization is a misguided recommendation: it is poorly aimed, since finance is not the problem, and while it may succeed in inducing saving – itself a problematic statement – this will not provide much in the way of funding. The central problem of most developing countries is to develop the institutions which would make saving do its job of providing funding.

'[T]he characteristics of the special case assumed by the classical theory happen not to be those of the economic society in which we actually live, with the result that its teaching is misleading and disastrous if we attempt to apply it to the facts of experience' (Keynes, 1936, p. 3).

ACKNOWLEDGMENTS

I owe a great debt to Rogerio Studart, who developed my ideas on finance and funding (adding many which were strictly his own) in the course of writing his PhD thesis under my supervision. I am now borrowing many of them back in their new, improved form. I thank all my

Brazilian postgraduates for teaching me what little I know about the Brazilian economy and for provoking in me an interest in development economics. Another paper which greatly influenced this one is FitzGerald (1995). I have also had most helpful comments from David Coady, Gary Dymski, Peter Kriesler and Jean-Marc Fontaine. None of those thanked is responsible for any shortcomings of this paper.

REFERENCES

Chick, V. (1988), 'Sources of finance, recent changes in bank behaviour, and the theory of investment and interest', in P. Arestis (ed.), *Contemporary Issues in Money and Banking*, London: Macmillan; revised version in P. Arestis (ed.) (1993), *Money and Banking: Issues for the Twenty-first Century*, London: Macmillan

Chick, V. (1984), *Monetary Increases and their Consequences: Streams, Backwaters and Floods*, reprinted in Chick (1992), *On Money, Method and Keynes: Selected Essays*, Aldershot, UK: Edward Elgar.

Chick, V. (1986), *The Evolution of the Banking System and the Theory of Saving, Investment and Interest*, reprinted in Chick (1992), *On Money, Method and Keynes: Selected Essays*, Aldershot, UK: Edward Elgar.

Eichner, A.S. (1976), *The Megacorp and Oligopoly: Microfoundations of Macrodynamics*, Cambridge: Cambridge University Press.

FitzGerald, E.V.K. (1995), 'Hamlet without the prince: structural adjustment, firm behaviour and private investment in semi-industrialised economies', in P. Arestis and V. Chick (eds), *Finance, Development and Structural Change: Post Keynesian Perspectives*, Aldershot, UK: Edward Elgar

Gershenkron, A. (1962), 'Economic backwardness in historical perspective', in *Economic Backwardness in Historical Perspective*, Cambridge, MA: Harvard University Press.

Keynes, J.M. *The Collected Writings of J.M. Keynes* ed. D.E. Moggridge, 30 vol (abbreviated to *JMK* below). Original dates given and used in references where appropriate, though page references are to JMK.
Vols V, VI: *A Treatise on Money* (1930).
Vol. VII: *The General Theory* (1936).
Vol. XIV: *The General Theory: Defence and Development.*

Keynes, J.M. (1937a), 'Alternative theories of the rate of interest', reprinted in *JMK* XIV, pp. 201–15.

Keynes, J.M. (1937b), 'The "ex ante" theory of the rate of interest', reprinted in *JMK* XIV, pp. 215–23.

Keynes, J.M. (1939), 'The process of capital formation', reprinted in *JMK* XIV, pp. 278–85.

Sen, A.K. (1983), 'Poor, relatively speaking', *Oxford Economic Papers*, **35** (1), 153–69.

Singh, A. (1994), 'The stock market and economic development: should developing countries encourage stock markets?', UNCTAD Review, **4**, 91–106.

Studart, R. (1995), *Investment Finance in Economic Development*, London: Routledge.

8. Capital mobility and the problem of effective demand in underdeveloped economies

Prabhat Patnaik

1. INTRODUCTION

The optimism of the Keynesians regarding the efficacy of demand management for achieving near-full employment under capitalism derived from underplaying two basic features of the capitalist system: first, that it is characterized by antagonism between classes, including antagonistic claims upon the social product, which in normal circumstances is contained because of the discipline imposed upon the workers by unemployment. In a situation of near-full employment workers would 'get out of hand', one consequence of which would be inflation. Second, capitalism exists, and has always existed, as an international system. The picture of a capitalist state bringing about full employment through demand management within particular national boundaries is flawed because it ignores the ramifications of this essential fact.

While much has been written about the first of these constraints, though not necessarily from the perspective mentioned above, the discussion of the second constraint remains, to my mind, inadequate. For a long time, it was believed, invoking Tinbergen's proposition about the number of instruments and the number of objectives, that through a mix of appropriate exchange rate and fiscal policies the twin objectives of full employment and balance of payments equilibrium can always be achieved; this is assuming of course that the first constraint does not intervene, that is, the relative stability of the wage-unit is not seriously disrupted by full employment *per se*. In other words the possible subversion of Keynesian demand-management by the fact of the economy's being inserted into an international context could be prevented, it was assumed, through the pursuit of an appropriate exchange rate policy.

Kaldor's was an early dissenting voice. He argued that the use of the exchange rate instrument, precisely where this use is essential, would seriously disrupt the stability of the wage-unit. Accelerating inflation in other words would arise even if we ignore the fact of spontaneously intensified class conflict in the neighbourhood of full employment (or the usual reasons mentioned by the Monetarists which represent a refracted perception of this very fact). It would arise because in the event of a balance of payments deficit accompanying full employment, the use of the exchange rate instrument, since it would involve a terms of trade loss, would necessarily entail a squeeze on the wage-share (assuming 'mark-up' pricing). Since this is untenable, the government may not really have the required freedom in using the exchange rate instrument.

Kaldor's argument took it for granted that a country should more or less balance the current account of its balance of payments. It generally ignored the whole question of capital flows. As a matter of fact once we take capital flows into account, it follows that a country's income does not have to remain limited to a sum which equals exports times the foreign trade multiplier. What then is the constraint upon demand stimulation in an economy which is inserted into a world of free capital flows?

This chapter is devoted to a discussion of this question, though from the perspective primarily of an underdeveloped economy.

2. A SIMPLE OPEN-ECONOMY FRAMEWORK

To facilitate discussion I use the framework of a simple open-economy macro model, adding to it and subtracting from it as I go along. It may be useful therefore to establish its point of departure from standard textbook open-economy macroeconomics by developing first a brief critique of the latter, especially of the Mundell–Fleming approach which played such a leading role. The original Mundell–Fleming model did amount to saying that in a regime of fixed exchange rates and free capital flows there were no palpable constraints upon demand stimulation by the government. But in a regime of flexible exchange rates the scope for using the fiscal instrument did not exist, the level of activity being determined essentially by the magnitude of money supply. Because of this strikingly non-Keynesian result which emerged in the flexible exchange rate case, let us concentrate upon this latter case.

This model involved a logical structure which relied on a system of recursive, rather than strictly simultaneous, determination of variables. Since, at some internationally prevailing interest rate the supply curve of foreign exchange on the capital account was infinitely elastic for the country in question, its own domestic interest rate was thereby determined. With a given money supply, this meant that the money income in terms of the wage unit was determined unambiguously from the LM curve. Finally, with the interest rate and the level of income so determined, the exchange rate had to be such as to make the IS curve cut the LM curve precisely at this predetermined point. It followed from this analysis that with given money supply, fiscal policy was incapable of having any impact upon income, employment or output.

There are two obvious problems with models of this genre. First, they assume that there is zero substitutability on the demand side between foreign exchange and domestic currency. If foreign exchange could be substituted for domestic currency, then, given the infinitely elastic supply of foreign exchange at the prevailing interest rate, it would be impossible to maintain that money income is determined by something called a given money supply. Or putting the matter differently, in a world where foreign exchange can substitute for domestic currency and where the supply of foreign exchange is infinitely elastic at the prevailing interest rate, it would be impossible for the Central Bank to *sterilize* foreign exchange inflows and hold money *supply* constant in any relevant sense.

More generally, these models visualize the demand for foreign exchange inflows entirely in flow terms, that is, as a means of settling the current balance. The fact that there may be a stock demand for foreign exchange is completely ignored by them.

The second problem consists in the assumption that there is an infinitely elastic supply of foreign exchange at the prevailing interest rates, from which follows the conclusion that a country can never be foreign exchange constrained as long as it maintains this interest rate. Now, this assumption, no matter what its relevance to the context of the US, is certainly of questionable validity in the case of most other countries, especially third world countries. In the case of the latter, while it is reasonable to presume that an interest rate lower than that which prevails internationally would result in zero or negative capital inflows, an interest rate equal to that prevailing abroad is unlikely to bring in anything more than a finite amount of capital inflows; and an interest rate which is higher would no doubt bring in a larger amount, but even this would necessarily be finite. It follows then that a basic assumption of the Mundell–Fleming-type models makes them inapplicable in the context of third world economies.

3. AN ALTERNATIVE APPROACH

In this section I shall develop the alternative single period macroeconomic framework for an open economy which does not suffer from the two limitations mentioned above and which would be used for developing in stages, the basic argument of this paper. The point of departure of this model, to recapitulate, is the recognition, first, of the fact that the inflow of foreign exchange can relieve monetary stringency in an economy, and, second, of the fact that the supply curve of foreign exchange on the capital account is not infinitely elastic at the internationally-prevailing interest rate.

Let us assume that there are two income-earning financial assets, one international and one domestic. Let the international asset give a rate of return i^* which is certain. Which of the two assets wealth-holders would wish to hold would depend upon a comparison of their respective rates of return. However, they would in fact hold a mix of the two on account of the principle of increasing risk operating with respect to the domestic asset for which there is a probability distribution of the expected returns. For any given magnitude of wealth in terms of foreign exchange of the wealth-holders, the value of the domestic asset in terms of foreign exchange which they would wish to hold therefore is determined, *inter alia*, by a comparison of the best guess return from this asset (henceforth denoted by r) with i^*.

The additional value (in terms of foreign exchange) of the domestic asset sought to be held is the difference between the desired absolute magnitude and what is already held. This additional value however is nothing else but the net capital inflow into the economy (assuming that desired stocks are actually held at the end of the period). The net capital inflow into any particular economy, however, cannot be determined solely by a comparison of rates of return. Two economies offering the same rates on their domestic assets would not obviously experience the same absolute magnitudes of net capital inflow; the sizes of the economies must also matter. I shall, however, ignore this factor here both because it would keep the total number of variables in the model limited, and also because it does not in any essential way affect the argument presented below.

Denoting the value of the domestic asset that is already held by these agents in terms of the domestic currency, by D, the total wealth of the *rentiers* by W, the price of the foreign currency in terms of the home currency by e, and the net capital inflow by F, we can say that

$$D/e + F = W. f(r - i^*) \tag{8.1}$$

where $f' > 0$.

This total inflow F should equal the sum of the flow demand for foreign exchange for meeting the current account deficit and the accretion to the stock-demand for foreign exchange which arises for the following reason. There is in any given period a transaction demand for money. If the money supply happens to be less than this, the domestic interest rate would increase inducing a larger net capital inflow. Normally the banking system would give domestic currency in exchange for this, at a fixed exchange rate in a fixed-rate regime and at the going rate in a flexible exchange rate regime such as we are considering. If perchance the banking system did not do so and suspended foreign exchange transactions, then economic agents logically should directly use foreign exchange in lieu of the domestic currency. In other words the scope for a stock demand for foreign exchange arises in a flexible exchange rate regime to the extent that the money supply created against internal debt falls short of the demand for money (which following our assumptions is nothing else but the transaction demand for money). In what follows I shall assume that all foreign exchange stocks are held by the Central Bank. If the money supply created against internal debt is denoted by M^o the demand for money (which because of our assumptions will necessarily only be transactions demand) by M_d, the ratio of total money-supply to reserve money by q, and the stock of foreign exchange already held in the economy by H, then the accretion to the stock demand for foreign exchange is given by $\{[(M_d - M^o)/eq] + H\}$. The assumption of exogenous money therefore amounts simply to saying that M^o is given.

Equilibrium in the foreign exchange market is given by:

$$F - [(M_d - M^o)/\ eq] + H + N = 0 \qquad (8.2)$$

where N denotes the net current balance.

The best-guess rate of return on holding the domestic asset must be the sum of the yield on the asset, its expected appreciation in terms of the domestic currency and the expected appreciation of the domestic currency itself in terms of the foreign currency; that is:

$$r = i - (\ \delta i / i) - (\delta e / e) \qquad (8.3)$$

where i denotes the yield on the asset, and the second and the third terms on the right-hand side denote respectively the expected rates of appreciation of the asset price and of the domestic currency.

For notational convenience I shall introduce a term n:

$$n = i - (\delta i / i) \qquad (8.4)$$

The transactions demand for money is a function of money income y, but the income velocity of circulation is dependent upon the return on the financial asset (inclusive of capital gains). We therefore have:

$$M_d = M\,(n,\,Y) \tag{8.5}$$

where Y is:

$$Y = C + I + G + Ne \tag{8.6}$$

Exports are unlikely to be much affected by the exchange rate in the short run, no matter how significant the latter's effect may be after a time lag. As for imports let us for simplicity assume that all imports are of final goods. We can think of two constituent components of imports, one which is physically invariant in the short run (a part of capitalists consumption for instance), and the other which is also invariant but only in terms of the domestic currency, and hence is fully responsive to changes in the exchange rate for any given level of money income. Both constituents are symptomatic of the fact that only limited adjustments to exchange rate movements are possible in the short run. Altogether therefore we can give a stylized expression to the current balance as follows:

$$N = R - vY/e \tag{8.7}$$

where R is a constant expressed in terms of the foreign currency.

It is customary to make investment a function of the domestic interest rate, but it seems to me more appropriate to assume that it depends upon the rate of return on the financial asset inclusive of the rate of capital appreciation; that is:

$$I = I\,(n) \tag{8.8}$$

Finally, to keep things simple, I ignore taxation and assume that all government expenditure is deficit-financed. If capitalists' consumption is assumed to be composed of two autonomous physically-given components one of which is imported (this is precisely what was assured in equation 8.6) and the other domestically-produced, if all wages are consumed, and if prices are a markup over unit wage cost which is constant up to full capacity, then consumption will become simply a linear function of total incomes so that:

$$C = a + bY \tag{8.9}$$

This completes the description of the model. We have nine equations for determining ten variables, that is, C, I, Y, e, n, r, i, N, F, and M_d, which makes the system underdetermined. This however is not some logical fault of the present model, but arises because of a deeper reason, namely that since both the interest rate as well as the exchange rate play the role of equilibrating the foreign exchange market there is simply no way of assigning a separate equilibrium value to either. True, we have rolled the money and the foreign exchange markets into one and that, some may feel, is the reason for the indeterminacy; but to the extent that our assumptions underlying this are not unrealistic, it points to the fact that in a situation characterized by capital flows with exchange rate and interest rate flexibility, we have no way of arriving separately at an equilibrium value for each of these rates.

It is not surprising that other open-economy macroeconomic models have invariably closed their systems by assigning in effect a value to one of these rates by postulating either rigidities, infinite elasticities, or corner solutions and so on. Thus, Mundell and Fleming take the interest rate as given, while Kaldor takes the exchange rate as given. An indirect way of coming to the Kaldor specification is to take the real wage rate as given (with imported inputs and markup pricing this reduces to the Kaldor proposition). Or alternatively one can assume identical prices for foreign and home commodities in which case the money wages and markup margins at home and abroad implicitly give us an exchange rate. Finally one can also bring in NAIRU-type considerations to get a closure of the system.

None of these considerations however is very persuasive, at any rate in the context of an underdeveloped economy. It is highly unrealistic to think that underdeveloped economies face an infinitely elastic supply curve of foreign exchange on the capital account at the ruling international interest rates. Likewise, to say that real wages cannot, or do not, fall below a certain level, or that workers, in their totality, are organized enough to prevent such a fall does not carry conviction. The same holds for the NAIRU argument. One can of course bring in the government and its political apprehensions about letting wages fall below a certain level as justification for postulating a floor to wages and thus closing the system. But that immediately takes us away from the regime of flexible interest and exchange rates which we have been talking about and brings us to a regime where one or both the rates are administered.

To conclude, if we take the stylized context of an underdeveloped economy and assume that it is demand-constrained with wages given in the short run, then it turns out that a flexible-rates regime cannot give a unique equilibrium but is compatible with an infinity of equilibria, which is but another way of saying that such an economy would necessarily have to have one or both the rates being administered bv the government. A completely flexible-rates regime in other words is inconceivable in such an economy.

4. SOME IMPLICATIONS

To see the implications of administered rate(s), I assume to start with that it is the exchange rate which the government stabilizes, leaving the interest rate to be determined by the market. And let us suppose that the level at which it is stabilized is such as to ensure an acceptable level of wages to the workers (to avoid cluttering up the argument with NAIRU-type considerations I assume that this level is independent of the level of activity). I also assume, to simplify the argument and not unrealistically in my view, that the elasticity of price expectation in the market for the domestic financial asset is equal to unity, which means that the expected rate of appreciation in its price is a constant (whether positive or negative). So the regime I visualize is one in which there are static expectations in the foreign exchange market, because the government instructs the Central Bank to buy and sell foreign exchange at a pre-determined price, and where there are unit-elastic expectations in the financial asset market.

However, if this is all that the government does then it is by no means certain that an equilibrium will exist in the system at all. An essential condition for an equilibrium to exist is that the best guess rate of return which the domestic financial asset offers must be higher than the international rate of return. And for this the level of domestic activity must be high enough to ensure a high interest rate (i) and with it a high best guess rate of return (n). If the government simply stabilized the exchange rate and fixed its expenditure at some arbitrary level of G then there is nothing to ensure that the level of the domestic rate of return would at all exceed the international rate of interest; and if it does not, then there is no equilibrium. It follows then that while stabilizing the exchange rate, the government must simultaneously manipulate its deficit in such a manner that the level of activity is high enough to ensure a meaningful equilibrium.

Now, this requires freedom on the part of the government to fix its own fiscal deficit. In most of the third world, however, this freedom does not exist. A combination of tax cuts to induce direct foreign investment and sound finance (that is, keeping budget deficits within limited bounds) to placate the IMF has meant that, no matter how large the net foreign capital inflow, the government's hands are tied in the matter of boosting public expenditure.

The question, however, is not merely one of boosting public expenditure. In underdeveloped economies where the prime need is for boosting investment, the government's capacity to do so even when there are immense foreign exchange inflows on the capital account of the balance of payments, gets severely constricted. It cannot increase public investment, because in addition to the overall constraints on public expenditure referred to above, there is enormous pressure on the state to wind up its role as an investor, to privatize public sector units and to refrain in particular from undertaking investment. On the other hand it cannot coerce the private sector to undertake any investment. That sector has its own logic, and interference with it, which is difficult in the best of circumstances, becomes impossible particularly in conditions where the entire effort of the state is directed towards appeasing it in a bid to revive its so-called Schumpeterian characteristics.

It is fashionable these days to decry state ownership. Even those sceptical about the virtues of the free market who recognize the need for state intervention in the development process, fall short of endorsing state ownership, and often fall back on the proposition that the question of ownership is secondary. But one fundamental argument for state ownership, and I mean ownership as practised under old *dirigisme*, not just nominal ownership of autonomous market-driven enterprises, is that it permits the state to influence the investment ratio. State ownership in other words is a necessary means for the socialization of investment. What is essential of course is that the state should be made more accountable. But the retreat of the state and the privatization of its domain serves the purpose neither of greater accountability nor of achieving the desired levels of investment.

To come back to the original argument, where the fiscal freedom of the state is restricted, an equilibrium may not exist even in a fixed-exchange rate regime. Typically therefore governments intervene not only in stabilizing the exchange rate, but also in stabilizing the interest rate. This is a matter not of volition but of practical necessity owing to the pitfalls inherent in the functioning of the market.

If both the exchange rate as well as the interest rate are given, and the government's fiscal freedom is restricted, then of course the foreign exchange reserves become free of all feedback effects; they can be extraordinarily high or low (though of course there are limits to how low they can get), depending upon parameter values, and no mechanism exists to bring them to the right magnitude. But the level of money supply gets detached from the level of reserves and becomes endogenously determined: to equal the demand for it at the prevailing interest rate. In terms of our model, as n gets fixed q becomes a variable.

But the *modus operandi* of such an economic regime is not as simple as it sounds. To say that the government fixes something does not, contrary to my assumption so far, mean that the market necessarily always has static expectations about the future value of that variable. Not only is it the case that the government would not always succeed in maintaining a particular value of the variable in question, but, what is more, the market would begin to build up expectations about whether the government would be able to maintain a particular value or not. In other words it would still have price expectations, but based on data other than the actual price movements which may not have occurred at all. Once we recognize this, it follows that even in a regime of fixed exchange rate and fixed interest rates there would be problems about the equilibrium, not about its existence but about its stability.

In establishing this proposition I shall assume that the fixed interest rate, whatever its level, is expected to remain unchanged, but the exchange rate, even though it has a fixed current value, is expected to take on a value in the future which depends on the change in foreign exchange reserves. Since expectations about the future exchange rate enter the argument through their effect on the magnitude of net capital inflows, what I assume in effect is that equation (8.1) above becomes:

$$D/e + F = W(H_1 - H)F \; ; \; F'(.) > 0 \qquad (8.1')$$

where H denotes the reserves at the end of the current period.

Now, with interest and exchange rates fixed, the level of money income gets determined, and together with it the level of the current balance N, which is thus independent of F. Since by definition:

$$F + N = H_1 - H$$

we have two separate equations linking F with H_1 whose intersection would give us the equilibrium levels of F and *n*. That such an equilibrium would exist is not open to doubt, especially when we keep in nind the fact that the position of F(.) depends on the interest rate fixed by the government. But this equilibrium would be unstable in two cases: the first, which is obvious is when $W.F' > 1$; the second, which is less obvious and requires our going beyond single-period analysis, is when $W.F' < 1$ but the intersection of the two curves occurs at the wrong point.

To see this second case let us assume that the economy is stationary, that is its income remains the same period after period. Now, if equilibrium H_1 is higher than H then this would mean that the economy would be building up more and more reserves despite its lack of growth. And if there is some ceiling to the process, for example if there is a maximum level of the external debt–income ratio, at which, when it is reached, net capital imports become zero, then the economy would move in a downward spiral with dangerous consequences. In short, stability requires that at the equilibrium point not only should the relative slopes of the two curves be right but also that the level of reserves should also be right (though the scope for this second condition does not exist in our single-period model), which is an extremely stringent condition.

When the economy does move in a downward spiral the government has to make frantic efforts to halt the slide. These efforts can take many forms, more or less centring around the offer of more lucrative rates of return for any inflowing capital. In addition to jacking up interest rates, domestic assets and domestic natural resources are sold cheaply to whoever is willing to pay for them in terms of foreign exchange. Now, even if such offers do not continue *ad infinitum*, there is an irreversibility about what has already happened during the crisis: that bit of property (especially government property) which has already changed hands, that bit of natural resource which has already passed into the ownership of some international *rentier*, continue to remain with their new owners. And since the crisis is not just a one-shot affair but is likely to repeat itself, a denouement where the country remains stagnant but becomes progressively owned by international *rentiers* is by no means difficult to visualize. In this scenario, when capital flows in, it is not really put to any productive use because there is no agency for doing so: the government has no fiscal freedom while private investment is determined by considerations to which the inflow of capital *per se* contributes nothing positive (if anything, the maintenance of high administered interest rates to attract this inflow has a detrimental effect on private investment). On the other hand when capital tends to flow out, bits of the country's assets or natural resources are 'denationalized' to prevent this outflow.

Needless to say, the kind of denouement we have visualized above is of great advantage to the financial interests in the advanced capitalist countries. To obtain control over the third world assets and resources against debt which the latter might have incurred for productive purposes is one thing; but to do so against debt which was not even put to any productive use is quite another. The latter requires that growth rates in the third world are kept low. In this way these countries cannot become growing users of scarce natural resources, which would make them suppliers of primary commodities at enhanced supply prices. In other words, it is required that third world countries do not embark upon a growth trajectory that would cause inflation in the advanced capitalist economies, which finance capital abhors above everything else. But at the same time control is obtained over third world resources and assets at throwaway prices.

Even this is not all. I have argued so far that capital inflows are not put to any productive use and simply build up reserves. As a matter of fact, when these reserves are built up, there is pressure from the international financial agencies like the IMF and the World Bank to reduce the level of reserves through increasing the import propensity of the economy. The argument put forward in support of this is the following: with higher reserves there is higher money supply (the latter in their view is not demand-determined) and hence higher inflation. If reserves are brought down through raising the import-propensity of the economy, then the inflationary pressures would abate. *This* argument would have some validity if the economy were supply-constrained; as a matter of fact however this demand is made in the context of economies (such as India today) which are saddled with enormous unemployment and unutilized capacities.

The real purport of the argument, however, is different. If the accumulating reserves on account of capital inflows are liquidated through larger imports, then this would expand the markets for the producers in the advanced economies and would spell deindustrialization in the third world economy. In other words the latter would not only have stagnated but would have even retrogressed, in the process both creating markets for metropolitan producers, and preventing inflationary pressures in the metropolitan economies. At the same time, however, the possibilities open to metropolitan financial interests to capture third world resources and assets would have not only remained open, but would have even been strengthened since the more the reserves are frittered away the sooner is the crisis point likely to arrive when third world assets begin to be sold very cheaply. In other words, by enforcing further import liberalization and by using up burgeoning reserves in that way, the metropolitan financial interests make doubly sure of their own potential gain, and at the same time a bloc is formed with metropolitan industrial interests who also gain markets in the bargain. The imposition of this consensus upon the third world works to the great advantage of metropolitan capital, especially metropolitan finance capitals and has in my view precisely the consequences for the third world economies that are described above.

Putting it differently, the restrictions on the fiscal freedom of third world states, the insistence on supply-side measures as if full employment prevails everywhere, the prevention of demand stimulation by third world states even in situations of burgeoning reserves, especially demand stimulation that would have led to crucially significant capital formation, are all measures which are in the interests particularly of metropolitan finance capital.

Authors such as Kaldor saw the constraints upon demand management by capitalist states in open economies as arising from the downward inflexibility of real wages. In other words it was the workers' stubbornness which in their view thwarted the efforts of the capitalist state to achieve full employment, a position shared by a large number of otherwise radical scholars. Now in the context of the third world one can scarcely argue that the workers in their totality are so well organized as to prevent downward movements in their real wages. What the case of the third world economies throws up therefore is something quite different from what all these scholars have argued, namely that the barrier to demand stimulation is put up, not by workers but by metropolitan financial interests.

Certainly, demand stimulation through larger public investment in a situation of burgeoning reserves is not without dangers of its own. It amounts in effect to a state of affairs where the country is borrowing short to invest long. But the dangers involved in this kind of financing can be reduced insofar as the direction of public investment is towards quick-yielding sectors with an export potential: investment in agricultural infrastructure which increases output is a case in point. And in any case expanding public investment in this manner is much less dangerous than stimulating luxury consumption through larger import of final goods catering to such consumption, as the Bank and the Fund have been advocating. But the whole question of how, in what direction, and in what manner public investment can be expanded becomes irrelevant since the international financial agencies simply do not allow any fiscal freedom to the government of the third world economy. No doubt they have powerful domestic support, so that the contradiction is not between them and the third world society as a whole, but they are the chief actors.

5. CONCLUSIONS

The argument usually advanced in favour of *free market* policies is that capital has become much more mobile in the present world than ever before in the history of capitalism; no matter what the nineteenth century experience might have been, today we live in a world where if the underdeveloped countries open their doors to foreign capital, they can experience large capital inflows and high rates of growth. This argument fails to distinguish between *capital-in production* and *capital-as-finance*. The argument would have some validity if capital-in-production had indeed become more mobile internationally. But as a rule this is not the case. What has become genuinely more mobile across countries is capital-as-finance, and in the case of such capital, simply having more of it is not synonymous with having a higher rate of growth. It is true that such capital does represent command over resources which is put at the disposal of the country in question, and hence is potentially investible. But to convert it into actual investment requires an agency, and it is only the state which can act as that agency. But paradoxically at first sight, the very ambience which brings about the far greater fluidity of finance capital is one which insists upon a retreat of the state from the arena of production. The very condition under which capital-as-finance could have been useful to the country is denied as a part of the bargain for its entry.

Demand stimulation in today's world has to be done in third world countries only in the face of opposition from finance capital. If a country is to take advantage of financial inflows while stimulating demand, it must first be willing to fight the dictates of finance capital. This is by no means impossible; large underdeveloped countries like India are certainly potentially capable of putting up this kind of a fight. But any such fight also presupposes an internal fight against the neo-comprador elements who have come to occupy important positions in civil society as well as in the state.

9. Technical change and the dynamics of comparative advantages: implications for the LDCs

El Mouhoub Mouhoud

1. INTRODUCTION

The purpose of this chapter is to analyse the role played by technical change in the evolution of the international specialization of specific sectors and in the patterns of industrial location of multinational firms. The stylized fact on which this study is based is that the industrialized countries of the North has witnessed during the 1980s a movement of industrial locations at the expense of the underdeveloped countries of the South, and even an influx from the south of units belonging to firms which had previously moved there. The fragmentation of the productive process at the international level – usually discussed in the literature dealing with trade in intermediate goods (Sanyal and Jones, 1982) – had favoured during the 1970s the relocation of industrial units to countries with an abundant and cheap supply of labour. International specialization followed, therefore, a pattern based on segments and components of a productive process reflecting the hierarchies of comparative advantages at the world level. Thus, the movement towards developing countries constituted a form of *de-specialization* of the industrialized world because of the loss of the comparative advantage hitherto held in the affected sectors. Conversely, the tendency for industry to migrate back to the North may be seen as a regain of comparative advantages by the industrialized countries. Often this process is accompanied by significant restructuring within the industrialized regions of the world.

The appearance of the phenomena of reverse industrial migration and of internal restructuring has coincided with the diffusion within the advanced countries of innovations based on electronics and information technologies. Their expansion across different branches is engendering sizeable structural changes within the economy and, in particular, inside

121

the industrial sectors. Some authors have come to liken the impact of information technologies to the rise of a new techno-economic paradigm but I prefer to speak in terms of a new technological system (Dosi *et al.*, 1988). The new information technologies have determined a change in the supply conditions and in the nature of industrial organization, whereas demand has been shaped by its own greater flexibility and by the versatility induced by the uncertain character of the economic environment. In a somewhat schematic but didactically useful manner, we can say that, as a result of the above mentioned processes, product differentiation has become the dominant form of competition, thereby compelling firms to be located near and amidst their markets.

However, the unevenness in the diffusion of technological change allows for the simultaneous existence of altogether different techniques of production and of unequal capital–labour ratios even within the same sector. Thus, the non-uniformity of production techniques inside each sector means that the coexistence of outward and reverse migrations may be found even for firms belonging to the same industry. This consideration is strengthened by the systemic nature of product innovations, especially those occurring in outputs which are substitutes to raw materials, as they enable the innovating country to conquer a comparative advantage in natural resources.

The issue of the reversibility in comparative advantages has not been adequately addressed in the literature. The latter has mostly attempted to integrate monopolistic competition with the approach based on comparative advantages by taking into account imperfections which are specific to the firm, as well as traditional elements such as productivity differentials and relative factors' proportions (Dunning, 1988; Mucchielli, 1985). In this chapter I will try to build upon the contributions made by the economic theory of industrial innovations, in order to explain the novel phenomenon of reversibility in comparative advantages. Thus, the second section will analyse the impact of technical change on the factors determining, at the international level, the segmentation of productive processes by referring to the role played by economies of scope and by the versatility of demand. Section 3 will discuss the conditions in which it is possible to obtain a partial reversibility in the dynamics of a country's comparative advantages and the coexistence, within the same sectors, of conflicting movements of industrial redeployment. The fourth section will provide a measurement of the size of the phenomenon, along with specific examples of relocation occurring both inside traditional sectors such as textiles and apparel, as well as in the knowledge intensive sectors such as electronics. Finally, the conclusion will deal with the implications that the changes might have for the position of the countries of the South in the international division of labour.

2. PRODUCTION FLEXIBILITIES, ECONOMIES OF SCOPE AND RESTRUCTURING

In the post-war period the restructuring and the relocation of production took place under conditions of increasing product standardization which was conducive to greater economies of scale. Expectations related to trends in the composition of demand were more or less stable denoting an environment characterized by a low level of uncertainty. This conjuncture made it possible to deal with unforeseen quantitative fluctuations in the level of demand by means of inventory management or by subcontracting parts of productive capacity. By contrast, in an increasingly uncertain environment firms must confront a dynamic form of flexibility determined by the versatility of demand. Uncertainty requires that information be made constantly available to firms which, in turn, carries a substantial management cost. These factors are therefore diametrically opposed to those favouring the relocation processes of the post-war years, thereby pointing to a new set of modalities in the international restructuring of productive processes.

Technical change can, under these circumstances, influence the dynamic tendencies of comparative advantages in two ways: through a classical mechanism of technical progress involving substitution of capital for labour, as well as through the specific effect engendered by the new information technologies. In the former case traditional substitution would simply lower the degree of labour intensity in production and, with it, also the relative weight of wage costs in the value of manufacturing output. The latter case would, in its turn, open up the possibility of producing both a wide variety of the same product and a series of joint outputs, without however giving rise to unsustainable capital costs. It follows that economies of scope are most likely to ensue from the spreading of the new information technologies.

The notion of economies of scope has been extended to the case of flexibilities arising from programmed automation in multiproduct firms. A scope effect is obtained whenever the average cost of the multiproduct firm is less than the average cost of each of the joint products if they were to be produced separately (Baumol *et al*, 1982; Bailey and Friedlaender, 1982). Unlike traditional scale economies, whose advantage lies in maximizing the utilization of a given productive capacity, economies of scope presuppose the existence of a flexible set of machines and equipment. Their benefits stem from the possibility of reutilizing and shifting machinery for the production of a variety of outputs. The flexibility brought about by the new technologies allows the minimization of the adjustment lag to become an objective in firms' behaviour alongside the traditional cost minimization procedures. Just the same, in the case of flexible equipment economies of scope are conditioned by the degree of product differentiation permitted by that very equipment. For this reason I prefer to distinguish between economies of scope proper, economies due to product range and economies of scale in the dynamic sense (Cohendet and Lléréna, 1990). The first type of economy can be ascribed to firms producing more highly differentiated goods while using the same inputs. A classical example is that of a railway company providing both passenger and freight services, two altogether different outputs. In the second instance the firm produces goods which differ in terms of quality and content. Flexible technologies thereby allow changes in the composition of the firm's output without significant delays and adjustment costs (Chamberlin, 1927; Lancaster, 1966). The third case, pertaining to dynamic scale economies, typifies situations in which equipment is elastic enough to respond to changes in the volume of demand while capable, in the longer run, of generating new products. Traditionally, with inflexible equipment, changes in the mode and volume of demand were met by adding new machines in new production lines to the old ones, often leading to overinvestment. In principle this phenomenon is eliminated with the introduction of flexible and mobile automation.

New technologies have a significant impact on the industrial competitiveness of the countries from which they originate. Indeed, according to the theories of the product cycle the advanced countries should have permanently lost their ability to gain comparative advantages in sectors characterized by labour intensive techniques of production. Yet, the relative fall in labour costs and the greater adaptability to demand conditions stemming from the flexibility of production technologies may, in fact, compensate for the benefits arising from locating the labour-intensive segments of production in labour abundant areas. Relocation back to the North may, therefore, constitute a regain of specialization in hitherto discarded sectors.

A number of studies have shown that the transformation of the process of production affects directly the firm's division of labour. The firm's logic is deemed to be shifting from one based on the link between techniques and returns to scale to one centred on knowledge and learning. The new principles guiding the division of labour are thought to derive from the growing economic importance of knowledge and information. This factor leads to the grouping of similar and mutually compatible knowledge-intensive activities. Yet a significant degree of heterogeneity may exist between each of the clusters of knowledge-intensive activities. As a consequence, the need arises for new methods of coordination aimed at connecting and transmitting the different forms of knowledge. The ensuing selection process between firms is bound to occur mostly in the developed world, where clustering of knowledge-intensive activities is more widespread. The cognitive division of labour thus requires a cultural and geographical proximity of production activities.

The diffusion of new technologies does not necessarily translate itself in the elimination of specialization. Firms tend to give priority to accessing a specific set of factors embodying a specific set of skills (Moati and Mouhoud, 1994, 1995). Hence, countries whose sole advantage resides in the low cost of labour or in the abundance of raw materials, are not the main target in the multinationals' decisions about plant relocation. Furthermore, product innovations in intermediary goods favour, in principle, trade between the developed countries while strengthening intra-industry trade in intermediate products. Given the system of intersectoral relations, the diffusion of new technologies in manufacturing engenders an equal transformation in the nature of industrial and raw material inputs, thereby affecting the import flow from the developing countries. In this context, an interesting example is provided by UK exports of date palms to the Middle East. Britain could engage in this sort of export, for which she is not naturally endowed, thanks to the application of new biotechnologies.

The spread of the new technologies turns out to be uneven for two fundamental reasons. First, national systems have different ways of fostering R&D and in coordinating the application of its results. Second, the tempo of the introduction of the new methods may differ between final demand products and input products. Thus we obtain overlapping layers of technological systems at the international level as well as within the sectors themselves (Moati and Mouhoud, 1994). The outcome is by no means unidirectional since relocation tendencies may prevail in some sectors, while in others the introduction of new technologies may lead to a new form of sectoral clustering. In the latter case the fragmentation of the industrial processes will entail an expulsion of segments of industry from the developed areas. The foregoing analysis of technical change leads to the formulation of three hypotheses concerning both the reversibility of comparative advantages and the contradictory tendencies operating within the international division of labour. These hypotheses pertain to the coexistence of different technological systems at the international level with the developed countries displaying a monopolistic position over innovations; the existence of economies of scope with flexible technologies; the prevalence of product differentiation in all the branches where competition is linked to the versatility of demand.

3. CHANGE OF TECHNIQUES AND THE REVERSAL OF COMPARATIVE ADVANTAGES

In order to explain the phenomenon of reversibility back to the North of comparative advantages I will start from a discussion of some theoretical approaches to international trade specialization. In the traditional Heckscher–Ohlin type of analyses based on relative factors' proportions, the phenomenon can be explained on the basis of three conditions (Mouhoud, 1993). The first requires that the technologies for the production of the same good differ between the two areas. The second condition demands that the North – where the new technologies are both created and applied – produce differentiated goods in a variety of range, while the South keeps producing a homogeneous commodity. It is then shown that North–South trade becomes more oriented towards intra-industry exchanges but with lower overall intensity. The third condition implies a hierarchical structure in comparative advantages so that the South can compensate the disequilibrium with the North by expanding trade within itself and with intermediate countries.

Also the models based on technological gaps between countries and on horizontal and vertical product differentiation, fail to account for the case of reversible comparative advantages (Krugman, 1979; Flam and Helpman, 1987). These models, in which the dynamics of international trade is ascribed to technical progress and population growth, assume that the North initiates the new productive cycle by generating new goods while discarding old ones. It follows that the flows of industrial relocation are only directed towards the South and that the latter is inherently capable of catching up with the more advanced area. In their turn, endogenous growth theories explain the reversal of comparative advantages in terms of the innovator–imitator dichotomy. The asymmetry between the two areas lies in that the South is only an imitator and devotes to that effect its own R&D expenditure. The North, by contrast, is in a position both to invent new products and to innovate the existing ones thanks to public subsides of R&D. The imitating activity of the South is thereby disadvantaged (Grossman and Helpman, 1991).

The major difficulty with the explanations outlined above resides in their inability to account for the simultaneous existence of processes aimed at relocating in the South with tendencies in the opposite direction. In other words, the interesting phenomenon is represented by the concomitant loss and reacquisition of sectoral comparative advantages. For this reason preference will be given to an analysis based on the spectrum of available techniques for the production of a given good. The relative position of a country within the range of the spectrum will determine whether or not the country will obtain a comparative advantage.

According to this interpretation, the countries situated at the polar extremes of the technological range would obtain a comparative advantage for the same differentiated product. At the developed end of the spectrum countries can cumulate both cost advantages and those accruing to the economies of scope. This set of countries is therefore able to maintain its comparative advantage over the whole range of produced commodities. At the opposite end of the spectrum traditional factor intensity advantages will prevail but without the benefits arising from the scope effects. Lastly, countries belonging to the intermediate group would mostly benefit by specializing in certain types of models. They will tend therefore to relocate elsewhere the production of goods belonging to inferior ranges. In this context, the firms which have progressed most in the adoption of flexible technologies will prefer to install their facilities in countries where technological innovation and its diffusion are systemic. The tendency to relocate back to the North arises from this set of units. The intermediate countries will be subject to contradictory processes. On one hand, firms might be capable of gaining full advantage from flexible technologies for some of their models, giving rise to a flow towards the developed pole of the spectrum. On the other hand, however, for a different set of products, they may also benefit from pure cost advantages thereby generating a movement toward the less developed pole. It follows that this kind of firm is the source of movement in either direction.

The analysis in terms of a spectrum of techniques permits the identification of the nature of the recouped advantages. In the long run, the reacquisition of sectoral comparative advantages can accrue only to the countries which create new technological systems. In the short and the medium term what matters is the capacity by firms to reclaim their own specific advantages. The next sections will present some concrete cases showing the coexistence of contradictory movements in the mechanisms of industrial relocation.

4. SOME RECENT TENDENCIES IN INTERNATIONAL INDUSTRIAL LOCATION

The relative marginalization of developing countries possessing in the main labour and natural resources, appears from the study of the factors affecting the flows of foreign direct investment (FDI) as well as from the analysis of the concentration of the ensuing stock of capital. Since the second half of the 1980s the world economy has witnessed the phenomenon of the relocation back to the industrialized North of production activities previously subcontracted to low wage countries. Such tendencies seem to reverse the logic of segmenting and relocating industrial processes in order to exploit the natural comparative advantages of the developing economies. During that period the aggregate value of FDI operations increased very rapidly, displaying new geographical and sectoral characteristics. Moreover, also the nature, the form and the determinants of FDI changed significantly during the last decade.

From the mid-1980s onward, developed countries have been generating 95 per cent of total FDI while receiving 80 per cent of it. As a consequence the share going to the LDCs has shrunk substantially (Hummels and Stern, 1994).The overall shift in foreign direct investment has been compounded by an increased concentration of the flows staying within the group formed by the United States, Japan, Germany, France and the United Kingdom (Julius, 1990). By contrast, the share of FDI going to the developing countries, including the newly industrializing ones of East and Southeast Asia (NICs), declined from an average of 30 per cent in the 1970s to 15 per cent by the end of the 1980s. Two thirds of the last meagre figure are absorbed by only ten countries formed by the East and Southeast Asian NICs and by some Latin American countries. The latter have also experienced during the 1980s a remarkable divestment in industrial activities by multinational companies. For example at the beginning of the 1980s, 70 per cent of the FDI stock of German automotive corporations was in Latin America only to be reduced to 30 per cent by the middle of the decade following a shift back to the industrial countries (Mouhoud, 1993). By 1993 the share of FDI flows to developing countries was 40 per cent of the total. Yet the reversal of the decade-long negative trend occurred mostly in relation to foreign investments in China and in East and Southeast Asia. (This happened not just because of lower labour costs but also for reasons linked to market expansion.)

At the sectoral level FDI has declined in the primary industries in favour of the industrial sectors and, especially, in favour of services, notably financial services, whose share of total FDI grew from about 25 per cent in the 1970s to 40 per cent in the 1980s (Chesnais, 1994). Within the industrial sectors FDI flows have tended to focus on technology-intensive branches and on those having a high level of marketing expenses. In this context, the oligopolistic nature of many of the sectors absorbing FDI flows implies that the two characteristics just outlined are coterminous. Finally, a number of studies have shown that the firms operating in these sectors are also characterized by specific knowledge-intensive endowments (Markusen, 1995). Until the end of the 1970s foreign direct investment followed, by and large, the logic of vertical production. Today FDI seems to have taken a horizontal connotation. Against the 30 per cent share of intra-firm exchanges relative to world trade, the bulk of the output of multinational companies' foreign affiliates is sold in the market of the host countries. Thus American multinationals export back to the United States only 13 per cent of their output, while the foreign multinationals operating in the USA export to their home countries no more than 2 per cent of their production (Brainard, 1993; UNCTAD, 1993).

Alongside the changes in the nature, size and direction of FDI flows, the factors determining the flows have themselves undergone substantial change. Rather than relative factors' endowments, the forces shaping foreign direct investment tend to reside more in the possible technological gains, in the existence of a given set of skills (Dunning, 1988). The role of demand has emerged particularly in a study conducted by the European Commission. It has been found that labour costs do not play a critical role even in traditional sectors. In fact, the weight of labour costs has given way to the greater importance attached to being close to a market with a high level of per capita and aggregate demand such as that of the European Community. The direction of investment by multinational corporation (MNCs) towards areas of high aggregate income levels and in product lines corresponding to a high level of per capita demand, implies that they tend to concentrate in branches with a high share of R&D and with a high percentage of technicians and engineers over their total employment. These are also the sectors most oriented towards product differentiation and product complexity. Lastly, the forms taken by the FDI flows have changed as a result of the financial orientation of contemporary advanced economies. Investments aimed at acquisitions, mergers, and joint ventures have taken priority over the building of branches and fully controlled affiliates.

Globally, FDI has increased among countries having similar levels of per capita income and with weak trade barriers. Markusen and Venables have developed a convergence hypothesis in order to explain the evolution of FDI patterns and international trade (Markusen, 1995; Markusen and Venables, 1995). They maintain that the greater the similarities between different economies, the more international economic activities will be dominated by multinational companies. The key elements which have to be roughly similar belong to the realm of size, technical efficiency and relative endowments. The leading role acquired by transnational companies in the globalization process seems also to explain the tendency to the polarization of trade within the so called *triad*, that is, between the United States, Western Europe and Japan. This is also the consequence of the fact that the dynamic of per capita demand tends to guide the process of investment at the international level. Yet the exploitation of cost-based comparative advantages by means of relocation of industrial activities outside the three developed areas of North America, Japan and Western

Europe, has not ceased altogether. It actually continues to occur in the form of subcontracting.

5. INTERNATIONAL SUBCONTRACTING AND INDUSTRIAL RELOCATIONS

During the 1960s and the 1970s the splitting of production by relocating some of its segments in the developing countries followed a logic of vertical separation. The firms' objective was then to import back into the developed world a part of the final product. Nowadays the search for industrial locations has become far more selective. Market demand acts as an important factor in these decisions for traditional industries as well, with the consequence of penalizing the countries with an abundant and low-cost labour supply. At any rate, movements back to the United States and Europe of outputs previously subcontracted to low-wage countries have been taking place since the last decade. Hence, the developed countries' competitiveness is re-emerging in products which only ten years earlier were considered as a dead economic weight.

Industrial relocation is in general the outcome of two key factors. The first of these is the process of increased automation which tends to reverse in favour of the developed economies the real cost of production per unit of output. In these cases the migration of industries back to the North involves a mutation in the previous methods of production. Instances to that effect can be found in the electronic, automobile and toy industries. The second factor pertains to the versatility of demand. These forms of relocation are governed by the conditions of production flexibilities dictated by the need to improve, at the microeconomic level, the adjustment of supply in response to shifts in demand. The requirements of flexible production flows tend to privilege the restructuring of the technical methods of production into skill- and learning-intensive ones. The frequency with which goods have to go back to the drawing board, as it were, increases in relation to both technological content and duration. Indeed the competitiveness of products with a high technological content and a relatively short lifespan depends very much on the speed with which firms can react to market demand. Therefore, their assembling facilities tend to be located near the areas of final demand and near to the design and engineering centres.

6. THE CASE OF TWO INDUSTRIES: TEXTILES AND ELECTRONICS

As mentioned above, traditional sectors are not immune to the process of relocation back to the North. German textile firms, for instance, are no longer showing a strong tendency to migrate outside the developed areas. If anything, any migration that might still take place is determined by the objective of expanding market shares in countries where the automation of production is now feasible. During the late 1950s Germany witnessed a movement in textile industries towards Eastern Europe because of domestic difficulties in finding an adequate supply of labour. Benefiting from traditional ties with Eastern European countries enabling them to combine productivity gains with low wage rates, German firms could accommodate outward relocation with exports back to the mother country. This interaction between relocation, productivity gains and exports to Germany, has come about thanks to a tight cooperation with the subcontractors by dispatching to Eastern Europe German technical and managerial personnel. Yet since the 1980s movements from Eastern Europe have taken place in the opposite direction mostly towards Germany itself as well as towards Portugal, Spain and Ireland.

A different picture emerges, by contrast, as far as the behaviour of France's textile companies is concerned. It appears that automation processes and just-in-time methods are slow in coming. Moreover their introduction has led only to an acceleration in the flows between the different manufacturing stages. The market power of distributors, who impose their conditions as to purchase prices, product variety and delivery schedules, translates itself into further industrial migration away from France as well as into increased automation. Firms which split up part of their production by locating it in low-wage countries, managed to maintain their responsiveness to changing market demand through the use of telecommunication technologies and also by adopting labels which actually conceal the country of origin. In a standard oligopolistic fashion, retail prices are set at the French or European levels, the difference being shared between the distributor and the manufacturer. A few of the large companies have undertaken a restructuring process in order to bypass the power of the distributors. The strategies most followed involve the introduction of more flexible technologies and coordination of activities with firms specializing in logistics. These textile companies, although few in number, relocated back to France with interesting results. Their production has acquired greater variety and flexibility in relation to shifts in demand, while the companies concerned have succeeded in establishing a much broader degree of control over the conditions determining their competitiveness.

On the whole outward industrial migration has become more costly even in this kind of industry because of the risks involved in being removed from the areas where demand mostly originates. In the final analysis, in traditional sectors location decisions are also taken on the basis of criteria pertaining to (a) the size of the market resulting from the composition of per capita demand, and (b) the structural interconnectedness of the productive system. In general these two factors go hand in hand.

In the electronics industries relocation back to the developed areas seems to be determined by the discontinuity in the learning process whenever the assembling facilities of the final product are in a low-wage–low-skills country. A further factor militating in favour of industrial relocation to the developed world is the difficulty of coordinating the many skills which contribute to the creation of the final product. Lack of appropriate skill coordination may indeed lead to inefficient behaviour on the part of subcontractors. In knowledge intensive sectors, such as the electronics and computer industries, locating plants in low-cost countries may cause, at a later stage, the uncoupling of final production from the whole web of skills which precede the actual assembly phase. Given that in these kinds of sector the rate of technological innovation and the ensuing product rotations is very high, subcontracting final production to a low-cost area carries the risk of freezing the characteristics of the product for a period longer than that required by the technological race. In the electronics industry competition requires rapid product innovation and differentiation, creating the necessity to bring together the many skills which contribute to the final product.

7. CONCLUSIONS

The analysis developed in this chapter has been conducted in terms of sector-specific technological transformations. I have argued that, once East and Southeast Asia are excluded from the picture, the rest of the developing world is subjected to a form of marginalization due to industries relocating back to the North. For this group of countries, the possibilities of embarking on a process of growth and technological transformation via foreign direct investment is indeed becoming increasingly remote. Hence a process of globalization based on learning and skills is not consistent with the economic exploitation of generic factors of production.

Yet globalization is not the only tendency in the world economy. There are alongside it processes of regional integration which are backed by nation states and other institutions which also include some of the developing countries. The movements towards regional integration may well constitute the form of active integration of the countries of the South in the world economy. For if the process of specialization is left to the action of multinational firms only, the countries possessing only natural endowments will be marginalized. Hence, institutionally supported agreements of regional integration may operate as a counterweight to marginalization. Given the coexistence of many different technological systems and configurations, the exploitation of the comparative advantages of the Southern countries lies in the ability to develop, by means of public investment activity, advanced transportation and telecommunication networks. As shown by the experience of some French and European companies in the textile sector, firms tend to combine the segmentation of the production process with the imperatives of international competition requiring rapid responses to shifts in demand. The capacity of the less developed countries to attract segments of the production processes depends on the ability to combine comparative cost advantages with the creation of an efficient public infrastructure.

REFERENCES

Bailey E. and A.F. Friedlaender (1982), 'Market structure and multiproduct industries', *Journal of Economic Literature*, **41** (3), 1024–48.

Baumol, W.J., J.C. Panzar and R.D. Willig (1982), *Contestable Markets and the Theory of Market Structure*, New York: Harcourt Brace Janovich.

Brainard, S.L. (1993), 'A simple theory of multinational corporations and trade with a trade off between proximity and concentration', NBER working paper, no. 4269, Washington, DC: National Bureau of Economic Research.

Chamberlin, E.H. (1927), *The Theory of Monopolistic Competition*, Cambridge: MA: Harvard University Press.

Chesnais, F. (1994), *La Mondialisation du capital*, Paris: Syros.

Cohendet, P and P. Lléréna (1990), 'Nature de l'information, évaluation et organisation de l'entreprise', *Revue d'Economie Industrielle*, **51**.

Dosi, G., C. Freeman, R. Nelson, G. Silverberg and L. Soete (eds) (1988), *Technical Change and Economic Theory*, London: Pinter.

Dunning, J.H. (1988), *Explaining International Production*, London: Unwin Hyman.

Flam, H. and E. Helpman (1987), 'Vertical product differentiation and North–South trade', *American Economic Review*, **77** (5), 810–22.

Grossman, G. and E. Helpman (1991), 'Quality ladders and product cycles', *Quarterly Journal of Economics*, **106** (2), 557–86.

Hummels, D.L. and R.M. Stern (1994), 'Evolving patterns of North American merchandise trade and foreign direct investment 1960–1990', *World Economy*, **17** (1), 5–29.

Julius, D. (1990), *Global Companies and Public Policy: The Growing Challenge of Foreign Direct Investment*, New York: Chatham House Papers, Council on Foreign Relations Press, for the Royal Institute of International Affairs.

Kim, W.S. and E.O. Lyn (1987), 'Foreign direct investment theories, entry barriers, and reverse investments in US manufacturing industries', *Journal of International Business Studies*, **19**, 53–66.
Krugman, P. (1979), 'A model of innovation technology transfer, and the world distribution of income', *Journal of Political Economy*, **87** (2), 253–66.
Krugman, P. (1991), *Geography and Trade*, Cambridge, MA: MIT Press.
Lancaster, K. (1966), 'A new approach to consumer theory', in K. Lancaster (1991), *Modern Consumer Theory*, Aldershot UK: Edward Elgar.
Markusen, J.R. (1995), 'The boundaries of multinational enterprises and the theory of international trade', *Journal of Economic Perspectives*, **9** (2), 169–89.
Markusen, J.R. and A.J. Venables (1995), 'The increased importance of multinationals in North American economic relationships: a convergence hypothesis', in M.W. Canzoneri, W.J. Ethier and V. Grilli (eds), *The New Transatlantic Economy*, Cambridge: Cambridge University Press.
Moati, Ph. and E.M. Mouhoud (1994), 'Information et organisation de la production: vers une division cognitive du travail', *Economie appliquée*, **47** (1), 47–73.
Moati, Ph. and E.M. Mouhoud (1995), 'Division cognitive du travail et localisation des activités industrielles dans l'espace mondial', paper presented at the conference *La Connaissance dans la dynamique des organisations productives*, Aix-en-Provence, 14–15 September.
Mouhoud, E.M. (1989), 'Les stratégies de relocalisation des firmes multinationales', *Revue d'economie politique*, **99** (1), 96–122.
Mouhoud, E.M. (1992), *Changement technique et division internationale du travail*, Paris: Economica.
Mouhoud, E.M. (1993), 'Changement technique, avantages comparatifs et délocalisation–relocalisation des activités industrielles', *Revue d'economie politique*, **103** (5), 735–61.
Mucchielli, J.L. (1985), *Les Firmes multinationales: mutations et nouvelles perspectives*, Paris: Economica.
OECD (1989), *Technologies de l'information et nouveaux domaines de croissance*, Paris: OECD.
OECD (1992), *La technologie et l'économie: les relations déterminantes*, Paris: OECD-TEP.
Rauch, J.E. (1986), 'Production transfer from rich to poor countries', *Journal of Development Economics*, **23** (1), 41–53.
Sanyal, K.K. and R.W. Jones (1982), 'The theory of trade in middle products', *American Economic Review*, **72** (1), 16–31.
Teece, D. (1986), *The Multinational Corporations and the Resource Cost of International Technology Transfer*, Cambridge, MA: Ballinger.
UNCTAD (1993), *Annual Report*, Geneva: UNCTAD.
United Nations (1991), *World Investment Report: The Triad in Foreign Direct Investment*, ST/CTC/118, New York: UN.
Vernon R. (1966), 'International investment and international trade in product cycles', *Quarterly Journal of Economics*, **80** (1), 190–207.
Vernon, R. (1979), 'The product cycle hypothesis in a new international environment', *Oxford Bulletin of Economics and Statistics*, **41** (4), 255–67.

PART IV

Effective Demand in Eastern and Western Europe

10. The importance of effective demand in the transition from a supply- to a demand-constrained economic system

Louis Haddad

1. INTRODUCTION

The transition from a centrally planned economy (CPE) to a market economy implies a drop in demand below potential supply. However, the process of transition in Eastern Europe and the former Soviet Union has resulted not only in such a drop but also in a contraction of both actual and potential supply. We have now the worst of both systems: output is severely curtailed by both supply and demand. The dramatic falls in output, which have exceeded expectations, are worse than those experienced during the Great Depression of 1929–33.

The focus of this chapter is on effective demand, which has been deliberately discarded by the standard transition strategy. The chapter argues that in the initial stages of transition effective demand should be allocated a role equal to that of supply. This may seem at first sight paradoxical, given the objective of transition is to create a demand-constrained economic system and given also that the former CPEs suffered from chronic shortages. However, it has to be remembered that the root cause of these shortages is 'systemic', the product of central planning and administrative controls. Arguably, if central planning were to be discarded much of the excessive demand and shortages would evaporate, and hence there would be no need for contractionary policy.

2. SYSTEMIC FEATURES OF CENTRALLY PLANNED ECONOMIES

For the purpose of this chapter it is necessary to focus on certain systemic features of the former CPEs that have been either ignored or imperfectly understood by newcomers to Eastern Europe and the former

Soviet Union. Once these features are properly understood it will become apparent that conventional macrostabilization policies are at odds with the environment of economies in transition that have abandoned central planning and administrative control and have not yet established functioning markets.

First and foremost, the former CPEs were 'inherently' inflationary, although this fact was not reflected in rising prices but in long queues and shortages. However, since planning was conducted primarily in physical terms the suppressed inflation had no major adverse effects on the rate of investment, the employment level, the balance of payments, or the distribution of income and wealth (Haddad, 1977). Of course, shortages of consumer goods reduced work incentives and consequently labour productivity. Such shortages were the result of a deliberate policy to keep the level of consumption as low as possible in order to maximize the rate of investment. In particular, the emphasis on capital goods and defence (non-marketable products) created disposable income without a corresponding increase of consumer goods. This resulted in chronic shortages of consumer goods and accumulation of a large volume of savings (the monetary overhang).

Shortages of producer goods and labour were the result of 'systemic' factors, of 'taut planning' and 'planning from the achieved level'. The former kept annual demand ahead of supply, while the latter compelled enterprises to increase their output from year to year. Both planning practices encouraged enterprises to hoard labour and inventories and to conceal their productive capacities, thereby aggravating existing shortages. Additionally, inefficiencies of state-owned enterprises (SOEs), caused by absence of competition and threat of bankruptcy contributed to chronic shortages.

Second, and related to the first feature, the former CPEs were geared for production and investment, not consumption. Until the late 1970s their growth rates were very high by international standards (Summers and Heston, 1988) but in the 1980s they recorded very low growth rates and were indeed stagnating. The causes of the decline and stagnation were many and varied. Some were policy failures and others systemic. In particular, the adherence for too long to a policy of high investment, especially in capital goods ('the law of the preferential growth of heavy industry'), and low consumption destroyed incentives and reduced labour productivity. More importantly, the decline in economic growth is due to an apparent inability of the planning system to generate the required rate of innovation to offset the law of diminishing returns. Despite the low consumption level, policy-makers continued to accumulate large volumes of savings and invest them in traditional priority sectors yielding smaller and smaller output.

Thus output was already falling in much of the region before the collapse of the system and before the transformation process had started. But the fall in output was due to the inefficiency, not the lack, of investment.

A third feature of the former CPEs is the general inefficiency of SOEs and the relative absence of small and medium-size firms. Many SOEs failed to cover their costs from the sales of their products and accordingly received subsidies, mainly in the form of bank credits which were never paid back. This is the familiar 'soft budget constraint' so thoroughly analysed by Kornai (1980). It is the result of the fundamental principle that money in a CPE is 'passive', that real output should not be constrained by financial consideration. Thus the existence of the soft budget constraint in a climate of chronic shortages meant that SOEs were free from financial and marketing problems, but were still very much constrained by the availability of inputs allocated to them by the supply bureaucracy. However, despite their inefficiency, SOEs were 'highly productive'; they fulfilled and over-fulfilled their production plans and provided welfare services (health, housing, vacations) for their employees.

A fourth feature of the former CPEs is 'over-full employment' and the hoarding of labour by SOEs to fulfil and overfulfil their production plans. Contrary to a common fallacy among newcomers, a genuine labour market did exist, though it was far from perfect. The great bulk of the labour force was allocated indirectly through a differential wages structure. Workers were free to move from one occupation to another and labour turnover was quite high. However, because of housing shortages, the movement of labour from rural to urban areas was normally restricted by an internal passport system. The hoarding of labour, absenteeism and inadequate consumer goods reduced labour productivity.

A final feature of the former CPEs that has been much criticized is their foreign trade conduct, particularly within the Council for Mutual Economic Assistance (CMEA). The extent of this trade varied from one country to another (from about 25 per cent in the case of Hungary to over 80 per cent in the case of Bulgaria). Trade within CMEA was conducted mainly on a bilateral basis using adjusted world prices. It was a seller's market. Members did not face the rigours of international competition and thus were not compelled to innovate or improve the quality of their products. However, there was a tendency to sell their better quality products outside CMEA for hard currencies which they then used to finance essential imports, particularly machinery and equipment embodying advanced technology. Indeed imports from and exports to the West were strictly controlled and treated as a single activity. Thus it paid to dump or sell below marginal cost to finance essential imports and bottlenecks whose value in terms of contribution to GNP exceeded the marginal costs of exports.

Arguably, conventional macroeconomic stabilization policies are ill-suited or, at best, inadequate to deal with the peculiar properties of economies in transition. In particular, they did not take into account the depressing effects on aggregate demand and output of the collapse of both central planning and CMEA trade. Accordingly, instead of maintaining an adequate level of effective demand which is warranted by the new environment of the former CPEs, standard macrostabilization policies sought to restrict further the level of demand. Such policies have led to a downward vicious circle in which falling demand generated less supply and in turn falling supply created less demand. Thus the aggregate supply and demand curves pushed and pulled each other inwardly.

3. THE DECLINE OF OUTPUT

This section discusses the dramatic output decline which has occurred in the former centrally planned economies. Although there is general agreement that the decline is caused by several factors, there is much debate on the relative importance of the causal factors and on the extent of the actual decline as distinct from the nominal decline recorded in the official figures. In particular, there is a tendency to underplay the extent of the decline by suggesting that some 10–20 per cent is not actual but a mere statistical illusion (Osband, 1992; Borensztein, Demekas and Ostry, 1993; Aslund, 1994; Berg, 1994).

The collapse of CMEA in January 1991 has been frequently cited as the major cause of the output decline. All countries except Poland, which applied its 'big bang' strategy before the collapse of CMEA, experienced the greatest fall in output in 1991. Further, Bulgaria, which depended on CMEA more than any other country, recorded the largest drop over the 1991–93 period. According to Kornai (1994), the breakdown of CMEA, including the former Soviet market, has been the most important cause of the recession. Others suggest the collapse of CMEA is responsible for some 20–30 per cent of the total output decline (Borensztein *et al.*, 1993; Laski and Levcik, 1993). In our view, this figure seems consistent with the importance of CMEA trade for their national economies, except of course in Bulgaria. In other words, falling exports were not the main cause of contracting demand.

Another common explanation suggested for the output decline is in terms of structural and transitional processes. Liberalization of foreign trade and prices, it is often argued, leads to changes in relative prices which cause a shift to a new equilibrium characterized by a decrease in demand for the goods in surplus sector and an increase in demand for those in the previous shortage sector. Kornai insists: 'It is not simply that aggregate demand is insufficient. The demand for some sectors of the economy fell dramatically while the demand for that of other sectors did not fall at all' (Kornai, 1994, p. 47). But the decline in Russia (and elsewhere) occurred in all major industries.

The statistical evidence on the shifting of resources from declining to expanding industries is not very strong. With the opening of their economies to foreign competition one would expect a significant reallocation of resources in line with orthodox comparative costs principles. However, the study by Borensztein *et al.* (1993) indicates no strong tendency for resources to be moving towards those sectors with relatively low domestic resource costs. Further, if structural change is taking place on the scale claimed by Kornai then there should have been a significant increase in investment. But investment has been declining everywhere and net investment in some countries is near zero. In fact, there has been 'quiet disinvestment, depletion of the assets invested earlier' (Kornai, 1994, p. 54).

A further indicator of structural change, or the lack of it, is the changing composition of imports. Given the relatively backward state of industries in the former CPEs, one would expect a significant increase in the imports of machinery and equipment embodying advanced technology needed for restructuring. Instead, these items have declined while imports of consumer goods, especially of the luxury kind, have grown since the liberalization of imports. In Poland the share of machinery and equipment declined from 24.6 per cent in 1991 to 23.9 in 1993. In Russia the import of machinery and equipment in 1993 fell by 48 per cent over the previous year (Gaidar, 1994).

Clearly, the attempt to explain away the depression in the transition economies largely in terms of 'statistical factors', the collapse of CMEA (an 'external factor') and structural change is not very convincing. A more plausible explanation, though by no means the sole one, is to be sought in terms of mismanagement of the transformation process, and, in particular, the application of inappropriate policies. There is little doubt that conventional macrostabilization policies designed to check the high inflation rates resulting from premature liberalization of trade and prices led to a decline in credit, real wages, investment, output and employment. Calvo and Coricelli (1993) found that monetary contraction in Poland, the former Czechoslovakia and Hungary, had a significant effect, ranging from 5.4 per cent to 15 per cent of the output decline. It is interesting that in Hungary, which experienced the smallest credit contraction and the smallest output decline in 1989–90, wages increased by 2 per cent, whereas in Bulgaria, Czechoslovakia, Poland and Romania, they fell below the norms established by governments (Calvo and

Coricelli, 1993, p. 49). Similarly, Borensztein *et al.* (1993) and Kornai (1994) suggest that binding credit ceilings imposed on SOEs had significant effects on the contraction of output from both the supply and demand sides. Firms were unable to finance their inputs causing a contraction of supply and accumulation of inter-enterprise credits. In Hungary, the proportion of firms that considered insufficient financing to be an obstacle to growth rose from 20–30 per cent of the respondents in 1987 to 40–45 per cent in 1993 (Kornai, 1994).

Finally, we come to a more controversial cause of the output decline, the fall in aggregate demand. There are diverse views on the relative importance of this factor: some writers regard it of secondary importance – 5 per cent of the total decline (Berg, 1994, p. 398); others estimate the proportion of decline contributed by insufficient effective demand to be over 66 per cent (Laski and Levcik, 1993); while yet others still take an intermediate position. Ellman (1994) attributes some of the decline in aggregate output to the lack of export markets and the fall in domestic demand resulting from the fall in real incomes. Kornai (1993) states that the situation in Hungary is 'half-Keynesian'. However, later he shifted his emphasis somewhat by stating the decline to be more Schumpeterian than Keynesian (Kornai, 1994). Industry studies and surveys of enterprise managers reveal that the great majority of enterprises are suffering from a lack of effective demand. According to Gaidar (1994), the overwhelming majority of enterprises in Russia are feeling restrictions of 'solvent demand' on the part of both the population and other enterprises. Further most enterprises in Eastern Europe are operating well below capacity (Amsden *et al.*, 1995).

Similarly, surveys of industrial enterprises conducted in Bulgaria, Czechoslovakia and Romania in 1991 revealed the perceived relative importance of demand and supply factors in the output decline. In early 1991 about half of the managers viewed supply factors (import shortages, raw materials) as the most important causes underlying the decline, while only about 10 per cent cited demand factors (for example, lack of orders and loss of markets). However, by mid-year demand factors had become the most important element for about half of the enterprises (Borensztein *et al.*, 1993). In Hungary, 'only half of the firms consider the insufficiency of demand as the main obstacle to production' (Kornai, 1993). However, in the revised version of his 1993 paper Kornai (1994, p. 44) states: 'the recession cannot be explained solely in terms of insufficient demand . . . only two-thirds of firms consider the lack of demand an obstacle to production'. This is clearly inconsistent with his view that the recession is more Schumpeterian than Keynesian.

This is not to deny that supply factors are no longer a constraint. There are still shortages caused largely by the collapse of traditional trade flows, but it is quite clear that supply factors have moved to the background. Enterprise surveys in Russia indicate that only 10–12 per cent of factory managers complained about shortages (Gaidar, 1994, p. 109). According to Kornai (1994, p. 42): 'the shortage economy in Hungary has ceased'.

Another important indicator of the role of effective demand in the output decline is the sharp decline in investment. We have already referred to tight credit policies and high interest rates (the product of macrostabilization policies) but these only explain part of the fall. Uncertainty about the future has discouraged investors even when credit was readily available (Calvo and Coricelli, 1993). It has also caused a massive outflow of capital and 'smuggling of profits' abroad. In Poland, gross capital formation fell by 52.2 per cent during 1989–92. In Hungary, it fell by 27 per cent over the same period (Kornai 1994, p. 53), while in Russia business fixed investment fell 30 per cent during 1991–93 (United Nations and IMF, 1995a).

Finally, the significant and in some cases the dramatic falls in real wages, as shown in Table 10.1, must have been responsible for some of the decrease in effective demand.

Table 10.1 Percentage change in real wages

	1989	1990	1991	1992
Poland	8.3	−24.4	−0.3	−3.6
Hungary	0.7	−3.7	−4.0	−3.9
CSFR	0.1	−5.4	−25.2	−10.1
Bulgaria	3.0	7.3	−43.0	22.5
Romania	2.7	6.0	−16.6	−15.1
Russia	−9.0	−10.5	−46.5	

Source: Amsden *et al.* (1995)

In summary, much of the output decline, possibly as high as 50–60 per cent, can be explained in terms of insufficiency of demand for both consumer and producer goods, as well as for exports. The causes of the decline in aggregate demand are very low wages and investment and the collapse of CMEA. The decline in these components of effective demand were primarily due to the collapse of the planning system, but macroeconomic stabilization policies designed to control inflation caused further deterioration in aggregate demand and subsequently further output decline. In other words, the transformation process itself is contractionary; hence no explicit contractionary policy and wage cuts are needed on top. It is argued in the next section that an alternative strategy that would have anticipated the emergence of the problem of effective demand would have been more successful in preventing an unnecessary fall in output and would have provided a better climate for structural and systemic change.

4. THE IMPORTANCE OF EFFECTIVE DEMAND

There is convincing evidence that conventional macroeconomic stabilization policies which focus on the supply side have undermined stability by causing contraction of both aggregate demand and supply, and in addition have created an unfavourable environment for investment and restructuring (Taylor, 1994; Amsden *et al.*, 1995). It is bad economics, especially at the macro-level, to focus solely on demand or supply. Aggregate demand and supply curves are interdependent. Just as supply can create demand, so too demand can generate supply. It is quite clear from the discussion in the previous section that what is needed now is a reversal of the downward cumulative effect of aggregate supply and demand.

However, it has been argued that 'unemployment may be necessary to reduce wages so that the private sector can expand sufficiently' (Chadha *et al.*, 1993). This is a major fallacy. The abandonment of central planning will result in the shedding of excess labour by enterprises, and consequently there will be a fall in real wages which are already low. Also since wage costs are a small proportion of total costs, the fall in real wages would not give strong incentives to increase production. If wages fall below the subsistence level, as has happened in some of the former CPEs, particularly in Russia and Ukraine, consumer demand for wage goods will fall below potential supply. Moreover, very low wages have adverse effects on productivity and labour supply.

An alternative policy that seeks to maintain real wages at their previous level, or under certain circumstances to increase them, will maintain the demand for wage goods and will prevent the emergence of excess capacity without necessarily endangering price stability. Indeed, the traditional argument of 'the economy of high wages' may well apply in the circumstances of the former CPEs. After decades of low wages and shortages which had damaged productivity and morale, a policy that tries to improve rather than depress workers' living standard is likely to raise productivity, and thus may turn out to be anti-inflationary.

One of the main reasons why macroeconomic stabilization policies seek to restrict domestic demand by keeping real wages low is to promote exports. But the domestic and foreign demands for manufactured goods of economies in transition are not perfect substitutes. Wage cuts and other forms of regressive income distribution will reduce domestic consumption. Moreover, given the extreme uncertainty and unpredictable behaviour of economic agents, in the environment of transition, there is no guarantee that the expected high profits resulting from falling wages will be reinvested. Indeed, there is ample evidence that profits are smuggled abroad and used to import luxury consumer goods from the West (Gaidar, 1994; Yavlinsky and Braguinsky, 1994).

The second major component of aggregate demand that should have been the focus of attention by macrostabilization policies is investment. The sharp fall in investment should have been anticipated by policymakers as the logical consequence of the collapse of the central planning system with its in-built bias towards a high rate of accumulation. However, it is not necessary to maintain the pre-reform rate of accumulation, if the efficiency of investment can be raised. But without a developed capital market and an effective banking system, investment funds are likely to be wasted rather than used for successful restructuring (Rostowski, 1993).

Contrary to conventional opinion, it is necessary to maintain a high rate of investment by the state in the initial stages. State investment if intelligently planned complements private investment, both domestic and foreign. Smooth and swift transition requires the establishment of new infrastructures (financial, industrial, innovational and social), which only the state can perform. The reduced investment activities of the state throughout the former Soviet Union and Eastern Europe have led to the decline in the quality of the physical infrastructure (public utilities) as well as the social infrastructure, health, education. Such a decline undermines long-term growth. Thus Kornai (1994) has urged an increase in the investment proportion of government spending in order to overcome the recession.

We have already noted the need to maintain effective demand by households so that private investment in consumer goods and services can be stimulated. Private investment can also be stimulated by reducing the climate of uncertainty. Policy-makers must provide incentives in the form of low taxes on productive investment and high taxes on speculative and casino-type activities. They must also provide credit facilities and low interest rates to new firms to engage in high value-added industries. Such measures may increase the budget deficit and thus undermine the stability objective. Yet, if they encourage the emergence of genuine entrepreneurs willing to invest in productive activities then the short-term budget deficit will be a small price to pay for creating a dynamic private sector, which is the ultimate objective of the transition.

The rapid decline in the physical and social infrastructure as well as uncertainties relating to privatization and other transition problems have discouraged the inflow of foreign capital and the outflow of domestic capital. Indeed, there is a net outflow of capital from the economies in transition. Foreign direct investment in all transition countries increased from $200 million in 1989 to $6 billion in 1993 and then fell slightly in 1994 (United Nations and IMF, 1995a). By contrast, the estimated outflow of capital from Russia alone was $20 billion annually during 1991–93 (Gaidar, 1994). Russia, it is claimed, could attract $20–30 billion annually but has attracted only $2 billion in five years (ibid.).

The third component of effective demand, that of exports, is the most difficult to stimulate and sustain. The low quality of their manufactured goods and low productivity due to inefficiency and low rate of innovation cannot compete on the world markets. To increase exports there has to be a restructuring of industries and an increase in the rate of innovation. Massive devaluation and wage cuts will do very little to sustain a growth of exports. There has to be also a temporary protection of industries capable of becoming internationally competitive in the near future. Such industries require time and much investment as well as advanced technology from the West. Currently, there is very little prospect of this kind of restructuring occurring across industries. Foreign exchange is being dissipated on imports of luxury goods instead of equipment and machinery embodying new technology.

5. CONCLUSION

It is quite clear from the foregoing analysis that a great deal of the output decline and the accompanying economic and human costs could have been avoided, without jeopardizing the transition process, had the policymakers and their advisers paid attention to effective demand. Further, it is not clear that standard stabilization policies will lead to genuine restructuring and transformation of the former CPEs into well-functioning market economies. The expansion of economic activity particularly in Poland over the last two years, which is now widely seen as a success indicator and vindication of those policies, may not be sustained, if it is largely a recovery from a deep depression. Unless major structural changes occur, for which there is no hard evidence yet, the level of output will not increase beyond the level of the previous peak.

Proponents of conventional stabilization policies admit the fall in output has been too large but assert 'no plausible alternative has been presented to date'. It is further asserted 'a better demand management can be accomplished but this belongs to unrealistic fine tuning' (Aslund, 1994). This point of view appears to preclude the possibility of designing macroeconomic policies that give equal attention to both aggregate supply and demand. Further, it is not obvious why the accepted policies are more realistic than those that are concerned with problems of effective demand. Indeed, we have shown in this chapter that the application of orthodox macroeconomic stabilization policies have overshot their targets and generated a deep depression that has not been witnessed since the Great Depression of the 1930s.

REFERENCES

Amsden, A., J. Kochanowicz and L. Taylor (1995), *The Market Meets its Match: Restructuring and the Economies of Eastern Europe*, Cambridge, MA: Harvard University Press.

Aslund, A. (1994), 'Lessons of the first four years of systemic change in Eastern Europe', *Journal of Comparative Economics*, **19** (1), 22–38.

Berg, A. (1994), 'Does macroeconomic reform cause structural adjustment? Lessons from Poland', *Journal of Comparative Economics*, **18** (3), 376–409.

Borensztein E., D.G. Demekas and J.D. Ostry (1993), 'An empirical analysis of the output declines in three Eastern European countries', *IMF Staff Papers*, **40** (1), 1–31.

Calvo, G.A. and F. Coricelli (1993), 'Output collapse in Eastern Europe', *IMF Staff Papers*, **40** (1), 32–52.

Chadha, B., F. Coricelli and K. Krajnyak (1993), 'Economic restructuring, unemployment and growth in the transition economy', *IMF Staff Papers*, **40** (4), 744–80.

Ellman, M. (1994), 'Transformation, depression, and economics: some lessons', *Journal of Comparative Economics*, **19** (1), 1–21.

Gaidar, E.T. (1994), *Institute for the Economy in Transition. Russian Economy in 1993: Trends and Prospects*, Moscow: Russian Academy of Sciences.

Haddad, L. (1977), 'Inflation under socialism', *Australian Economic Papers*, **16** (28), 44–52.

Kornai, J. (1980), *Economics of Shortage*, Amsterdam: North-Holland.

Kornai, J. (1993), 'Transformational recession: a general phenomenon examined through the example of Hungary's development', *Economie appliquée*, **46** (2), 181–227.

Kornai, J. (1994), 'Transformational recession: the main causes', *Journal of Comparative Economics*, **19** (1), 39–63.

Laski, K. and F. Levcik (1993), 'Alternative strategies for economies in transition', in E. Hochreiter (ed.), *Alternative Strategies for Overcoming the Current Output Decline of Economies in Transition*, Vienna: Oesterreichische National Bank.

Osband, K. (1992), 'Index number biases during price liberalization', *IMF Staff Papers*, **39** (June), 287–309.

Rostowski, J. (1993), 'Problems of creating stable monetary systems in postcommunist economies' *Europe Asia Studies*, **45** (3), 445–61.

Summers, R. and A. Heston (1988), 'A new set of international comparisons of real product and price levels estimates for 130 countries 1950–85', *Review of Income and Wealth*, **34** (1), 1–25.

Taylor, L. (1994), 'The market met its match: lessons for the future from the transition's initial years', *Journal of Comparative Economics*, **19** (1), 64–87.
United Nations and IMF (1995a), *Economic Reviews 16, 1994: Russian Federation*, Washington, DC, March.
United Nations and IMF (1995b), *World Economic Outlook*, Washington DC, May.
Yavlinsky, G. and S. Braguinsky (1994), 'The inefficiency of laissez-faire in Russia: hysteresis effects and the need for policy-led transformation', *Journal of Comparative Economics*, **19** (1), 88–116.

11. Some thoughts on the possible contribution of the economies in transition to the rehabilitation of demand

Wladimir Andreff

1. INTRODUCTION

This chapter deals with the transitional economies (TE) formed by the Central and Eastern European Countries and by the republics of the former Soviet Union, which include the Commonwealth of Independent States (CIS) as well as the Baltic states. At the time of the collapse of the communist regimes and the beginning of the transition process – intended as a reform strategy aimed at transforming the centrally planned economies into market ones – these countries were in a situation of severe economic crisis and external indebtedness (Andreff, 1993b). From the outset of the transitional process TE countries have enforced a set of stabilization policies following the conditionality criteria laid out by the IMF. These policies involved drastic liberalization measures in price fixing and in the determination of internal and external trade. They were also based on strategies of structural adjustment centred on privatization programmes which could not possibly be implemented in the short run (Andreff, 1992a, 1993c). Furthermore, consistently with the objective of building a market economy, measures were devised to create viable labour and capital markets and a system of private property rights.

As argued in the first section of the chapter, those 'orthodox' economic policies – despite some initial successes – have not so far resulted in the stabilization of the TE countries. We may, of course, see in this fact an additional confirmation of the failure or of the inadequacy of IMF–World Bank types of adjustment policies for countries affected by supply inelasticities and just coming out of a regime based on systemic shortages. However, it is more interesting to point out that the non stabilization of the TEs is due to the persistent underestimation of variables having a significant impact on the actual outcomes of the stated policies. Thus, the impact of the changes in the distribution of income on the rate of inflation will be discussed in the second section of the chapter, while the third section will analyse the neglected implications of a sudden opening of the external sector towards the developed market economies. The discussion of the underestimated factors will allow us to ask in the fourth section whether a change in economic policies may stimulate domestic demand thereby halting the recession gripping the transitional economies. It is in this sense that the hypotheses about the rehabilitation of demand formulated in the industrialized economies acquire a specific research interest for solution of the present difficulties of the non-stabilized TE countries. The rehabilitation of demand as well as the reintroduction of the very concept of effective demand as a key policy variable in the transition process, appears as an indispensable step. Nevertheless, given the present systemic transformation of Eastern Europe, it would be a mistake, as argued in the conclusions, to neglect altogether the structural aspects of supply conditions inherited from the previous economy of shortages (Kornai, 1980).

2. THE EASTERN EUROPEAN ECONOMIES IN TRANSITION: NOT YET STABILIZED

Five years from the inception of transition, the policies of stabilization and of structural adjustment have yet to succeed in stabilizing the TE countries of Eastern Europe and of the CIS. This observation seems to hold whether we take just one indicator, for example the rate of inflation, or whether we look both at the rate of inflation and the current account balance. Finally, the lack of success appears *a fortiori* evident if the budget deficit, the growth rate, the unemployment rate and the stability of the exchange rate are all taken as indicators of the policies' achievements. In this context, the attainment of macroeconomic stabilization, in the wider sense, may be defined by the following six characteristics: the way out of recession, an unemployment rate as low as possible, a rate of inflation which no longer causes socially unacceptable changes in the distribution of income and wealth, a stable budget, a current account balance capable at least to service, if not to reduce, the external debt, and a stable exchange rate. In a narrower sense, stabilization is associated with the capacity to attain and control a low rate of inflation, which in the TEs is usually calculated at a rate of less than 1 per cent a month. According to the stricter definition the control of inflation – which in Eastern Europe is the first policy objective – is far from being attained, regardless of whether these countries followed a shock therapy or a more gradual approach .

An overall examination of the macroeconomic situation in the TEs in 1993 reveals that in the majority of cases the six stabilization criteria have been satisfied neither as a whole nor even separately. The policies of stabilization and of structural adjustment were believed to yield trade surpluses in terms of hard currencies at least during the first two years of transition. The reduction of the external debt burden was indeed the second most important objective in the rank of priorities. By contrast, during the years following the implementation of the policies most of the countries concerned displayed a deficit in hard currency trade balances, thereby obtaining no relief on their level of external indebtedness which, as of 1993, has again reached dangerous levels. Thus, setting aside measures of external aid, postponement of repayments (Poland) or a certain attractiveness to foreign investors (Hungary), stabilization policies have failed to achieve their second objective. In 1990 and 1991 all the TEs have repeatedly devalued their currencies with many of them enforcing also a sliding exchange rate policy which brought about a continuous devaluation of the national currencies. Exchange rate stability is presently beyond reach while inflation remains high and the external accounts show no significant improvement.

As to the attainment of budgetary stability, it must be observed that deficits generally stayed at a higher level than the targets fixed by the IMF. The increase in fiscal revenues has been much smaller than expected, partly because of the recession and partly because of the low revenue raised by the new taxes. The latter phenomenon ought to be ascribed to the inefficiency of taxation authorities as well as to the high rate of tax evasion practised by both the private sector and state-owned firms. TEs' budget deficits are also generated by a lesser amount of expenditure cuts than envisaged by the IMF, because the need to cover part of the social costs of transition has exceeded the reduction in the subsidies to state enterprises. As a consequence part of the budget deficit can be interpreted as a political concession to the higher than expected costs of transition, but it can also be read as a latent support of aggregate domestic demand relative to the harsher austerity implied by a more faithful enforcement of IMF conditionality. Domestic demand has been broken by wage austerity and the vanishing of investment opportunities, but less than would have been otherwise the case.

The expansion of production and of employment – although viewed as the ultimate objectives of austerity policies – are not at the centre of the short-term priorities of the stabilization and structural adjustment programmes. The size of the recession in the TEs has surpassed even the most pessimistic forecasts. By 1993 only four countries showed a positive growth rate in their national income data; there were ten in 1994. It is worth noting in this context, that Poland's growth rate of 3.8 per cent in 1993, has been heralded as a success of the stabilization programme. Yet after 1992, for reasons of political instability, the Polish authorities no longer followed the programme very strictly, opting instead for a slight stimulus of the economy. The ensuing recovery is without doubt due to the stimuli as much as to the depth of the preceding austerity. Apart from a specific group of countries, the decline in supply (output) has led, with a two year lag, to a strong rise in unemployment whose rate hovered in 1993 and 1994 around 15 per cent.

Hence, in 1993 none of the TEs has been effectively stabilized in the wider sense of the term. The overall growth performance improved in 1994 and 1995, but the policies of stabilization devised by Washington's international organizations have not attained most of their objectives over a five-year period despite the urgency with which measures dictated by conditionality principles were ushered in. There are three consequences to such a destabilizing situation. Real wages have fallen significantly in all the TEs, although some of the ensuing impoverishment has been offset by new forms of social spending which explain the lesser decline in consumption expenditure. In fact, given the growing dissatisfaction of the population with every fall in household consumption, most of the TEs are now adopting measures aimed at cushioning consumption demand. By contrast, gross fixed capital formation has literally collapsed. This phenomenon is quickly accompanied by a deterioration of the technical state of productive capacities, thereby jeopardizing the instruments which could serve for the rehabilitation of demand. In those countries suffering the least decline in gross capital formation – Slovenia, Poland, Slovakia, Romania – investment subsidies were maintained contrary to the IMF recommendations. For the economies in transition, the rehabilitation of demand must first and foremost involve strong stimuli to investment demand.

3. THE NEGLECTED VARIABLES OF STABILIZATION PROGRAMMES: INCOME DISTRIBUTION AND INERTIAL INFLATION

The failure of stabilization and structural adjustment programmes is usually ascribed to the fall in demand induced by those very policies. Their effect is negative as far as output growth is concerned, while inflation is reduced by a statistically non-significant amount. The policies have a positive – but not very significant – impact on the balance of payments, but the effect on the current account position is noticeably positive (Edwards, 1989). In addition to being subject to frequent implementation errors (speed, sequencing, incompleteness), the above mentioned programmes were unsuitable to the specificity of the destabilization process occurring in the TEs (Kolodko, 1993). In recalling the experiences of the Latin American countries Dornbusch (1991) argued for instance that it is impossible to move quickly from a situation of hyperinflation to low inflation because of the high social costs involved in the transitional phases. This point is of crucial importance for the TEs in the light of the fact that inflation stems from structural problems following the disintegration of the Soviet regime (Dembinski and Morisset, 1990). Inflation has also originated from the shock caused by the reforms themselves and from structural transformations affecting the distribution of income which ignited a preexisting inertial inflationary pressure (Andreff, 1994a).

It is claimed that international conditions prevented the success of structural adjustment and stabilization programmes. Phenomena such as the disintegration of the Council for Mutual Economic Assistance (CMEA), the reduction in Soviet oil shipments, the sudden and massive opening of trade towards the West, the decline of exports to the USSR (Berg and Sachs, 1992) and, finally, the overestimation of the speed of international integration and of the amount of foreign aid (Andreff, 1994b, d; Andreff and Andreff, 1995b) have certainly contributed to unsettle the policies of transition. Yet it is hard to avoid the impression that these arguments aim at convincing public opinion that the suggested policies were the appropriate ones although their results turned out to be well below expectations. Instead we believe it necessary to envisage new routes and new types of adjustment policies for the economies in transition by taking into account variables neglected by the proponents of both shock and gradualist therapies.

Three basic variables appear to have been neglected by the supporters of economic liberalism. These are:

1. The persistence of a distributional conflict creating an inertial inflationary pressure strengthened by the redistribution of income and wealth caused by structural reforms like privatization.
2. The impossibility of adjusting an inelastic supply without first waiting for the outcome of restructuring policies.
3. The disruptive effects on trade flows of the disintegration of CMEA and of the USSR and the sudden reorientation of these flows towards the West compounded by the need to find a new specialization and by the reemergence in 1992 of hard currency trade deficits (Russia excluded).

The distribution of national income and its effects on inflation before and during the transition has hardly been mentioned at the time of the promotion of stabilization policies. The introduction of market mechanisms, price liberalization, privatization and economic restructuring have a direct effect on distribution thereby inducing agents to devise strategies aimed at maintaining their share of national income. Income's indexation, whether explicitly or implicitly, was a well entrenched strategy by both firms and households of the previous socialist regimes with the consequence that this form of behaviour continued when transition began. It follows that as long as the distribution of income is strongly influenced by the system's transformations, agents' attempt to index their incomes will propagate inflation, compelling the authorities to lengthen the time horizon of stabilization policies.

The theory of inertial inflation was conceived for developing countries having a high level of external debt and a high rate of inflation. In the case of TEs it is increasingly admitted – even in publications of the World Bank – that inflation is not just the expression of excess demand, but that it is linked to inertia and to distributional conflicts. Coricelli and Revenga (1992) for instance, have maintained that inflation depends on the ability of the different actors to bargain for a greater share of the national economy by claiming higher monetary revenues.

The mechanism of inertial inflation in the TEs can be explained in the following historical terms. In the centrally planned economies (CPEs) of the past, whenever wages rose without a corresponding increase in productivity, planners increased prices after a certain lag. At the beginning of every annual plan the Unions negotiated some kind of wage increase giving rise to an inertial inflationary process. In turn, firms tended to fix prices on the basis of a markup on costs higher than the level allowed by price control authorities (Layard, 1991). In this way firms, having to operate in a shortage economy but with a greater degree of freedom introduced by various reforms, financed the stock of inputs as well as the amount of autonomous investment. Such procedures resulted in an implicit form of indexation concerning investment expenditure relative to price increases. Institutionally, indexation took place yearly, during the negotiations between firms and the authorities over the annual distribution of investment funds, usually won by the former. Being in a shortage economy firms also competed for labour by bidding up wages which increased the cost basis of the markup (Bauer, 1991). In this context, the reforms introduced in the socialist economies before transition, including the austerity policies enforced in Hungary and Poland towards the end of the 1970s, were already stimulating an indexation oriented behaviour by modifying each group's share of national income.

In the CPEs centrally determined wages were indexed to average productivity growth at a higher index than the rate anticipated by the plan. Yet, to determine *ex ante* wage rises does not take into account the nature of the ensuing adjustments. Incomes and distributed revenues faced a limited supply of goods caused by the limited growth of productivity. Wage earners' liquidity, a sign of their momentary victory during negotiations, was dissipated in upward price revisions in the subsequent annual plan, as well as in more severe shortages. A similar tendency occurred in the case of implicit price indexation by firms of their investment expenditures. In fact, in the CPEs inflation was the *de facto* instrument preventing a continuous rise of these expenses in the composition of national income. This sort of behaviour has a sufficiently strong inertia to continue also in the TEs. It must be pointed out that when price rises occur in an inertial manner, the real supply of money falls and the growth of the money stock must follow prices in order to avoid a general crisis of liquidity. The supply of money becomes, therefore, an endogenous variable.[1]

Given the inertial character of inflation, successful deindexation must be applied not only to wages, but also to firms, both private and state-owned, which are today in a stronger position to influence prices. Firms use this power in order to save their expenditure and to limit their own collapse. According to the conventional view, incomes policies and wage deindexation are necessary elements of any stabilization policy. However, these kinds of suggestions are not sufficient to combat inertial inflation. Such measures affect only wage earners and for the short and medium term only. As long as the transformations induced by transition will impact significantly on the distribution of national income among social groups, the stabilization policies and Transition itself will not shed their inflationary aspects. Yet, demand has turned out to be less suppressed than in the case of a strict application of IMF conditionality.

4. THE ECONOMIES IN TRANSITION AND THE RESTORATION OF WORLD DEMAND

The recession in the TEs contributes to the international economic situation in a depressionary direction. In this context let us begin by analysing the opening of Western markets to the TEs. The shift towards the West in these countries' external trade at the expense of their mutual trade relations, is both an important element for a successful implementation of the stabilization and structural adjustment programmes and an inevitable consequence of the disintegration of the Soviet Union and the CMEA. The liberalization of external trade and its redirection towards hard currency areas is seen as an initiation to international competition and it is, therefore, part and parcel of the stabilization programmes. At the same time the flow towards the West, stimulated by a severe initial devaluation, is also intended to re-equilibrate the balance of trade thereby contributing to the stabilization of the nominal exchange rate.[2] For this purpose it is deemed necessary that trade with the West rise more than the fall in trade among Eastern European countries and between these and the former USSR. It is also required that commerce with the West lead to the accumulation of hard currency reserves, something that has yet to happen. Paradoxically the failure of stabilization policies to obtain a hard currency trade surplus stimulates, albeit marginally, the level of demand for the products of the developed market economies.

As of 1992 the external deficits of the TEs in hard currency trade confirm the fact that the TEs have created more market outlets for the developed capitalist economies than the other way around. Eastern and Central Europe, but not Russia, have been generating net additional demand for the Western economies. Furthermore by being recipients of net investment flows – which translate themselves into a demand of imported capital goods and technology – the TEs are supporting the fledgling level of investment demand in the West. Hence the paradox whereby the collapse of domestic demand becomes a cushion for the level of Western demand. For such a situation to continue the TEs would have to keep accumulating hard currency deficits without any interruption in the flow of funds from the West. From this perspective the TEs share similar problems with the developing countries.

On the whole the TEs' contribution to the rehabilitation of external demand depends essentially on factors outside those countries' control. By the same token, the possibilities open to the rehabilitation of internal demand must be examined by bearing in mind that the TEs, in addition to having external debts and trade deficits, are following a voluntaristic approach to international integration without any strategy of real investment. These economies appear to be subjected to an exhilarationist regime (Taylor, 1988; Bhaduri and Marglin, 1990; Marglin and Bhaduri, 1990; Fontaine, 1993).

5. IS IT POSSIBLE TO RESTORE DOMESTIC DEMAND IN THE TRANSITIONAL ECONOMIES?

The persistent state of instability has increased the costs of transition while the state of recession has created an unfavourable investment environment. The recent election results (Andreff, 1994c) have signalled that it is time for a new economic policy which, while retaining its reforming character, could become more oriented towards sustaining domestic demand. In the end this policy is the logical continuation of the quasi-recovery observed in 1992, particularly in Poland, based on the support of the lowest income groups, on deepening the budget deficit, and on keeping the level of subsidies to firms in order to limit the decline in investment.

After four years of systemic decline in the level of output, priority should be given to the growth rate of production rather than to the rate of inflation. The growth rate would, in this instance, depend on multiple sources of demand: expenditures originating from the need to absorb the social costs of transition (retirement of personnel, severance payments, unemployment benefits) and investment demand from the newly created private sector. A greater efficiency in the management of the state-owned firms and in the collection of new taxes could make the demand-based expansionary policy compatible with a moderate budget deficit. The cases of China and of Vietnam show that, contrary to the TEs experience, transition may well take place in the context of a dynamic developmental policy sustained by the expansion of demand with a major role of the state-owned firms, obtaining on balance stable results as confirmed by the steady influx of foreign direct investment (Andreff, 1993a).

The response of the TE countries to such a process of demand rehabilitation is not self-evident. It is necessary to know whether these economies operate under a stagnationist or exhilarationist regime. The answer to this question depends on the analysis of the nature of the systems which are now being transformed into market economies. We may therefore relate briefly to whether the old Centrally Planned Economies could be described *à la* Kornai or in terms of non-Walrasian rationing equilibria (Davis and Charemza, 1989). For the latter group of theories, repressed inflation expresses a situation of excess demand which could be eliminated by a corresponding stabilization policy during the transition from a regime of fixed prices to a regime of flexible prices. In the case of the economics of shortage approach (Kornai, 1980), shortage is due to a structural, chronic and institutionally determined insufficiency of supply stemming from the very mechanism of planning (Soos, 1984). It follows that despite their formal similarities (Andreff, 1993b), the difference between a regime of excess demand and a regime of shortage lies in that in the latter the problem cannot be cured by either restricting demand or by enforcing standard adjustment and stabilization policies. By contrast, and considering that in the old CPEs demand was always neglected, a transition facilitating policy would require measures favouring the expansion of supply (economic and technical restructuring, modification – within the respect of property rights – of the powers to determine supply, dismantling of state monopolies and stimulating competition) and measures expanding supply by taking into account the exigencies of demand. In other words, transition reflects a situation in which the economy moves from a state – the old CPE regime – where everything is for production, thereby creating overall shortages, to a state where everything is geared to transactions at the expenses of production. In this case agents abandon productive activities and rush towards transaction and speculative activities.[3] Recession becomes, at this point, an inevitable feature of the economies in transition. The role of demand, in a system where the amount of goods to be distributed among the population displays no significant growth, confirms the exhilarationist character of demand in the Eastern and Central European economies.

As a matter of fact, the transition from a CPE status to that of TE, involves a redistribution of income leading to the impoverishment of a large section of the population and to a minority of winners whose enrichment can be associated with primitive accumulation. Had the TEs been fully fledged market economies their state would be defined in terms of the exhilarationist model in which the economy reacts positively to such a shift in income distribution, thereby favouring the recovery in the level of investment. The fact that this phenomenon has not occurred is due to the behaviour of the *nouveaux riches*. These people belong, by and large, to the old *nomenklatura*, as well as being formed by the former functionaries, and mafia figures whose normal behaviour is rooted in the shortage economy of the past. Today such an inherited behaviour consists in the capitalization of their wealth without investing in real terms (speculation, acquisition of hard currencies, conspicuous consumption and illegal activities), which represents an economic as well as a social obstacle to investment recovery. As pointed out by Kornai (1990) the behaviour described hitherto denotes the absence of an entrepreneurial class and of an upper middle class aspiring to attain the entrepreneurial status. Thus, classes and social groups willing to take investment risks are found to be wanting. In some of the TEs political restrictions prevent the transformation of the old *apparatchiks* into reborn capitalists. In these circumstances profits, although high, are uncertain in nature whereas speculative gains are almost guaranteed, contributing, along with the lack of political and economic stabilization, to the low level of confidence in long-run investment projects. The anti-investment bias of the stabilization policies is therefore multiplied manyfold blocking the exhilaration in investment which would have otherwise occurred.

In the above context, it is understandable that, as soon as the TEs opened themselves to the West the desire to export towards the more certain Western markets has prevailed over the more uncertain investment environment (Fontaine, 1993). This is perhaps the most visible economic revolution differentiating the present TE countries from the old CPEs. In the latter the thirst for investment by firms was coupled by their propensity to import and by their aversion to export.

Evidently the CPEs were based on a fixed price regime. Price liberalization converted these countries into flexible price economies, transforming them from a stagnationist to an exhilarationist regime. Yet supply rigidities have not been overcome in the TEs where in most sectors production is dominated by state-owned firms or by private ones sheltered from all forms of competition. The new political forces which emerged from the last round of elections are tempted to set in motion expansionary policies based on the redistribution of income towards the new poor. The risk of such policies is that the recovery hitting against relatively inelastic supply and upwardly flexible prices is going to be swallowed by inflation.[4] We arrive, therefore, at the frustrating conclusion according to which an actual exhilarationist situation does not become an exhilarationist recovery because of macroeconomic blockages.

6. CONCLUSIONS

A moment of reflection will show that, on the basis of what has been argued so far, an alternative policy to the stabilization programmes should aim at preventing firms from increasing their share of national income via a rise in prices. It is difficult to see which institution other than the state could accomplish the task of blocking the monopolistic formation of prices, collusion practices and the like, which must be accompanied by anti-trust and industrial restructuring policies (Andreff, 1995a). The same consideration applies to a second alternative consisting in the formation of a sufficiently strong consensus among social groups in favour of the transformation of the economic system. This implies a transition process carried out at a pace accepted by the majority of the population, probably slower than the programmes announced in the last four years. Furthermore, it is unlikely that, under democratic conditions, a restrictive wage policy can be enforced much longer without involving workers' representatives.

The real alternative to the traditional policies of stabilization appears to rest upon the rehabilitation of demand. If the analysis about the inherent exhilarationist character of the present TEs is correct, such a rehabilitation policy, instead of boosting investment, runs the risk of exposing the countries concerned to a new bout of inflation. Thus, any demand-oriented policy requires a supply policy as well. In the present analytical framework, the latter turns out to be essential for the stabilization of the inflation rate. In addition to halting the recession and attenuating somewhat the conflict over the distribution of income, supply policies can eradicate the perverse effects of price liberalization stemming from those very practices, by tackling the monopolistic practices of the state-owned firms. Supply policies have the objective of transforming monopolistic firms into price takers, enabling output to become elastic relative to price. In this way price liberalization will no longer give rise to a massive recessionary tendency, nor to rent-seeking situations.

The principal goal of supply restructuring is to make supply conditions more flexible. Contrary to the explanations given by Western advisers – who thereby justified the fall in output with arguments about the necessity to weed out inefficient industries (Sachs, 1993) – the implosion of production in the TEs is not that much the result of supply restructuring (Blejer and Gelb, 1992). The inability of firms to satisfy on a large scale, by means of appropriate restructuring, the new form of demand expressed by consumers is one of the most important causes of the recession. This phenomenon happened despite the existence of the labour surpluses resulting from the past practices of hoarding workers. Supply rigidities come especially from impediments caused by the physical structure inherited from the economy of shortage, entailing uncertainties as to the source of inputs and sectoral disequilibria in favour of the heavy industry rendered more acute by the monopolistic practices of the state-owned firms. The restructuring of the latter acquires a much higher priority than privatization (Andreff, 1995a). In order to avoid being in a situation of stalled exhilaration the TEs would be interested in orienting their productions towards the most flexible forms of supply both in quantity and in price. Such a strategy will allow the TEs to find a way out from the dilemma between a stagnationist regime and an exhilarationist one. Clearly the key variable of this alternative strategy is given by investment provided, however, that its composition be different from that characterizing the centrally planned economies (Nechaev, 1991).

Have we, then, come full circle back to the myth of the pure market economy? We do not think so if we consider that the state's role in the restructuring of supply cannot be bypassed. It will have to play an equally important function in the case of demand rehabilitation policies.

NOTES

1. When in 1990–91 the Polish authorities decided to regain control over the supply of money within the stabilization programme, they succeeded in stopping the acceleration of inflation but not in breaking the inertial part of it which remained in 1992–93 at 40 per cent annually, This policy has generated a serious liquidity crisis among firms which were compelled to establish inter-firm cedit lines or payment arrears. These forms of credit unveil a kind of collusion between the remaining state-owned firms which reminds us of oligopolistic strategies. The reason for such behaviour is to be seen in the need to counter the restictive credit policies which have replaced the bulk of the old central allocation of funds. The same phenomenon is observed in the rest of the TEs.
2. I will not discuss the hypotheses needed to satisfy the criterion of critical elasticities which is assumed to be satisfied, in the stabilization programmes for the TEs. A

supporter of export led growth (Hrncir, 1994), has argued that devaluation is useful only in the short and medium run. In the longer run export led growth can be attained only by means of industrial microeconomic restructuring aimed at inceasing the value added of tradeables.

3. Kregel (1993) has criticized the transformation of the TEs into stock exchange type systems where wealth is reallocated but not created and where, like an original idea of Walras, exchange takes place on the basis of a given amount of goods.

4. The likelihood of this event is strengthened by the coexistence, especially in Russia, of quantitative shortage and strong inflation (Layard in Blanchard *et al.*, 1993; Sapir, 1993).

REFERENCES

Andreff, W. (1992a), 'French privatization techniques and experience: a model for Central Eastern Europe?', in Targetti (ed.) (1992), *Privatization in Europe: West and East Experiences*, Aldershot: Dartmouth.

Andreff, W. (1993a), 'The double transition from underdevelopment and from socialism in Vietnam', *Journal of Contemporary Asia*, **23** (4), 515–31.

Andreff, W. (1993b), *La Crise des économies socialistes. La rupture d'un système*, Grenoble: Presses Universitaires de Grenoble.

Andreff, W. (1993c), 'Internal and external constraints of privatization in Eastern Europe', *History of European Ideas*, **17** (6), 715–23.

Andreff, W. (1994a), 'Quand la stabilisation dure. L'hypothèse d'une inflation inertielle en Europe centrale et orientale', *Revue Economique*, **45** (3), 819–31.

Andreff, W. (1994b), 'Economic disintegration and privatization in Eastern Europe', in L. Csaba (ed.), *Privatization, Liberalization and Destruction: Recreating the Market in Eastern Europe*, Aldershot: Dartmouth.

Andreff, W. (1994c), 'La transition: désorientée ou réorientée?', *Bulletin du ROSES*, no. 8.

Andreff, W. (1994d), 'De la désintégration à une nouvelle intégration internationale de l'URSS et de l'Europe de l'Est', in M. Lavigne (ed.), *Capitalismes à l'Est: un accouchement difficile*, Paris: Economica.

Andreff, W. (ed.) (1995a), *Le Secteur public à l'Est: restructuration industrielle et financière*, Paris: L'Harmattan.

Andreff, M. and W. Andreff (1995b), 'Economic disintegration in Eastern Europe: Towards a new integration?', in B. Dallago and G. Pegoretti (eds) *Integration and Disintegration in European Economies*, Aldershot: Dartmouth.

Bauer, T. (1991), 'The microeconomics of inflation under economic reforms: enterprises and their environment', in S. Commander (ed.) *Managing Inflation in Socialist Economies in Transition*, Economic Development Institute of the World Bank, EDI Seminar Series, June

Berg, A. and J. Sachs (1992), 'Structural adjustment and international trade in Eastern Europe: the case of Poland', *Economic Policy*, **0** (14), 117–55.

Bhaduri, A. and S. Marglin (1990), 'Unemployment and the real wage: the economic basis for contesting political ideologies', *Cambridge Journal of Economics*, **14** (4), 375–93.

Blanchard, O., M. Boycko, M. Dabrowski, R. Dornbusch, R. Layard and A. Shleifer (1993), *Post-Communist Reform: Pain and Progress*, Cambridge, MA: MIT Press.

Blejer, M.I and A. Gelb (1992), 'Persistent economic decline in Central and Eastern Europe. What are the lessons?', *Transition*, **3** (7), 1–3.

Bresser Pereira, L. and Y. Nakano (1987), *The Theory of Inertial Inflation: The Foundation of Economic Reform in Brazil and Argentina*, Boulder, CO: Lynne Rienner.

Coricelli, F. and A. Revenga (1992), 'Wage policy during the transition to a market economy', *World Bank Discussion Papers*, no. 158, July.

Davis, C. and W. Charemza (eds) (1989), *Models of Disequilibrium and Shortage in Centrally Planned Economies*, New York: Chapman & Hall.

Dembinski, P.H. and J. Morisset (1990), 'Les politiques de stabilisation du FMI: une tentative d'évaluation pour l'Amérique latine et l'Europe de l'Est', *Revue d'études comparatives Est–Ouest*, **21** (4), 75–94.

Dornbusch, R. (1991), 'Experiences with extreme monetary instability', in S. Commander (ed.), *Managing Inflation in Socialist Economies in Transition*, Economic Development Institute of the World Bank, EDI Seminar Series, June.

Edwards, S. (1989), 'The International Monetary Fund and the developing countries: a critical evaluation', *Carnegie-Rochester Conference Series on Public Policy*, 31.

Fontaine, J.M. (1993), 'Demande et investissement dans le processus d'ajustement', *Revue tiers monde*, **34** (135), 491–512.

Hrncir, M. (1994), 'Economic recovery and foreign exchange rate regime: the case of the Czech Republic', in J. Gàcs and G. Winckler (eds), *International Trade and Restructuring in Eastern Europe*, Heidelberg: Physica Verlag.

Kolodko, G. (1993), 'Stabilization, recession and growth in a post-socialist economy', *MOCT-MOST*, **1**, 3–38.

Kornai, J. (1980), *Economics of Shortage*, Amsterdam: North-Holland.

Kornai, J. (1990), *The Road to a Free Economy*, New York: W.W. Norton.

Kregel J.A. (1993), 'Exchange versus production as the basis for the design of monetary, fiscal and exchange rate policies for the transformation process: a post-Keynesian view', University of Bologna, mimeo, first draft, 19 March.

Layard, R. (1991), 'Wage bargaining, incomes policy, and inflation', in S. Commander (ed.), *Managing Inflation in Socialist Economies in Transition*, Economic Development Institute of the World Bank, EDI Seminar Series, June.

Marglin, S. and A. Bhaduri (1990), 'Profit-squeeze and Keynesian theory', in S. Marglin and J. Schor (eds), *The Golden Age of Capitalism*: *Re-interpreting the Post-war Experience*, Oxford: Clarendon Press and WIDER.

Nechaev, A.A. (1991), 'The industrial depression in the USSR: a mechanism of development', *Communist Economies and Economic Transformation*, **3** (4), 455–66.

Sachs, J. (1993), 'Réussir la stabilisation monétaire en 1993', *Economie internationale*, **54**, 2nd quarter, 11–24.

Sapir, J. (1993), 'Formes et nature de l'inflation', *Economie internationale*, **54**, 2nd quarter, 25–65.

Soos, K.A. (1984), 'A propos the explanation of shortage phenomena: volume of demand and structural inelasticity', *Acta Oeconomica*, **33** (3–4), 305–20.

Taylor L. (1988), *Varieties of Stabilization Experience*, Oxford: Clarendon Press.

12. Restoring demand in the process of European construction

Jacques Mazier

Up to the mid-1980s, the European construction proceeded through the adoption of common policies. Since then, the process has reached a standstill and the search for harmonization of national legislations has not led anywhere. The European budget, no matter how modest (less than 1 per cent of GDPs), was subjected to harsh negotiations, especially with the United Kingdom. The European Monetary System (EMS) had succeeded in creating a stable real exchange rate system and was held by many to be an outstanding success which was probably due less to some specific institutional factors than to its utilization as an instrument of restrictive policies. Its basic asymmetry shifted the burden of adjustment on Germany's partners and induced an overvaluation of their currencies with a heavy cost in terms of growth and employment. Finally, the technological policies which brought together European firms, no matter how useful they were, mobilized only very small amounts of resources – less than 1.9 per cent of the community budget.

A new perspective was opened up after the White Paper on the completion of internal market integration was adopted and the 'Single Act' was signed in 1986. Reliance on market forces, perceived as a 'European-style supply side policy', was seen as the magic solution to overcome the stalemate in European construction. However, the full liberalization of capital movements, which was one of its essential components, brought the EMS into question, bringing about a new monetary regime. The 1991 decision for a 'single currency' was fraught with difficulties and based upon an unrealistic scenario, as became clear in the wake of the monetary crises in 1992 and 1993.

One can illustrate the inability of these attempts to bring about a new 'growth regime' by analysing two separate episodes: the single market proper (section 1) and the Maastricht-style monetary union (section 2). An alternative path can be thought of, which relies on the restoration of demand and the adoption of structural policies (section 3).

1. THE FAILED ATTEMPT THROUGH THE SINGLE MARKET

1.1 Expectations: Questionable Estimates

Many estimates of the impact of the 'single market' have been presented, especially in the Cecchini report of the European Commission. According to these views prices and costs should normally fall and competitiveness should increase as non-tariff barriers (NTBs) are dismantled and scale economies materialize on the larger market. Freeing capital movements should improve financial conditions and bring rates of interest down. After an initial short-term contractionary adjustment, an increase in the rates of growth and employment were expected to occur in Europe.

Table 12.1 presents the results of macroeconomic simulations run for the Cecchini report which singled out and quantified four primary effects: the elimination of customs controls, the opening of public markets to foreign bidders, the liberalization of financial services and the general supply-side response of firms to their new competitive environment (removal of technical and regulatory fetters, scale economies, weakening of X-inefficiency and cutback on monopoly rents).

Table 12.1　The macroeconomic effects of the single market (EEC 12)

(in %)	Elimination of border controls		Opening of public sector's markets		Liberalization of financial services		Supply effects		Total	
	1 year	Medium term	1 year	Medium term	1 year	Medium term	1 year	Medium term	1 year	Medium term
GDP	−0.01	0.36	0.20	0.55	0.43	1.46	0.51	2.14	1.13	4.52
Inflation rate	−0.21	−1.02	−0.30	−1.46	−0.47	−1.38	−0.60	−2.29	−1.58	−6.16
Real wage rate	0.06	0.29	0.18	0.26	0.26	0.42	0.26	1.25	0.77	2.22
Productivity per head	0.05	0.20	0.15	0.27	0.63	1.11	0.75	1.47	1.57	3.04
Employment (000)	−67	211	62	356	−245	440	−284	859	−533	1 866
External balance (% GDP)	0.17	0.16	−0.01	0.09	−0.03	0.26	0.18	0.45	0.30	0.95

Source: Cecchini Report (1988)

The compound impact of these effects would spur the GDP growth in the medium run (+4.5 per cent), increase employment by nearly 1.9 million jobs and decrease prices by −6.2 per cent. The per capita purchasing power should also increase albeit more slowly than labour productivity thereby entailing a redistribution from wages to profits.

The impact of the elimination of customs controls and of the opening of public markets to foreign bidders is relatively modest (less than 1 per cent of GDP growth and less than 600 000 jobs) while more than half of the beneficial effects arise from overall supply-side measures (2.1 per cent GDP growth and 800 000 jobs) and, to a lesser extent, from financial liberalization (1.5 per cent GDP growth and 400 000 jobs). However the calculations concerning these last two effects are most problematical.[1]

The report also stresses the potential for other growth enhancing mechanisms. With improved foreign accounts (+1 per cent of GDP) and budget balances (+2.2 per cent of GDP) demand could be boosted respecting either the external or the domestic equilibrium. All in all, as shown in Table 12.2, GDP could increase by approximately 7 per cent and close to 5 millions jobs would be created.

Table 12.2   Estimated impact of coordinated expansionary measures at the EU level

Years 1, 3, 7	GDP			Inflation			Current account			Govt. balance			Employment		
	1	3	7	1	3	7	1	3	7	1	3	7	1	3	7
Reduction in personal income tax up to 1% of GDP	0.7	1.7	2.0	0	0.5	3.0	-0.1	-0.2	-0.4	-0.7	-0.3	-0.1	0.2	0.8	1.2
Reduction in employers' contribution (2% of GDP)	0.4	1.8	1.8	-1.0	-2.2	-1.6	-0.1	-0.2	-0.2	-0.8	-0.4	-0.4	0.2	0.8	1.2
2% reduction in interest rates	0.8	0.8	-	0.4	0.6	-	0	0.2	-	0.5	0.6	-	0.2	0.6	-
10% devaluation	0.4	1.1	-	0.5	1.2	-	-0.2	0.3	-	0.2	0.4	-	0.2	0.5	-
TOTAL	2.3	5.4	-	-0.1	0.1	-	-0.4	0.1	-	-0.8	0.3	-	0.8	2.7	-

Notes: GDP, Inflation and employment are shown in terms of annual percentage variations. Current account and government balances are expressed as percentages of GDP.

Source: CEPII–OFCE (1993)

These are the most often publicized figures. However, as indicated, these estimates rest upon frail bases: out of the 5 million jobs announced, 1.3 million would result from the loosely quantified overall supply effects and the financial liberalization, while 2 million would follow from a hypothetical fiscal expansion which stands at the opposite end of the present 'European supply-side' policy spectrum.

The short-term/long-term articulation can also be criticized. The simulations assume that, except for general supply-side effects, the full impact of various measures makes itself felt during the first year while they typically take time to materialize. Complementary studies undertaken to take into account the degree of implementation of the large single market (*grand marché*) indicate that the supply-side measures have probably made themselves felt before 1992, but that the dismantling of NTBs has been delayed. Simulations based upon these new findings yield an altogether different profile: the initial job losses, arising from productivity gains and from the substitution of capital for labour are smaller than previously calculated, but the medium term increase in growth and in employment is roughly halved.

These factors tend to reinforce the doubts expressed *vis-à-vis* the estimates produced in the Cecchini report: *the positive results of the implementation of the single market have been grossly overestimated*. The 1988–90 European recovery was due more to demand factors (delayed impact of the reversal in oil prices following the earlier shocks, relaxation of monetary policies after the stock market crash of 1987, investment recovery brought about by enhanced expectations and by the improved financial position of firms) than to supply factors arising from the single market.

Beyond this macroeconomic observation one should also note that the Maastricht logic assumes that a number of virtuous circles operate which might in effect prove much less potent than expected.

1.2 The Single Market: a Perverse Byproduct of Increased Competition

Competition and economies of scale positively depend on a number of factors and the removal of NTBs will not in itself create a single market. National markets are characterized by strong specificities.

All the anticipated benefits stem from cost reductions and restructuring operations engendered by market forces. The principle of mutual recognition based upon competition, rather than harmonization, between national regulations does allow some progress but will probably favour the least compulsory regulations. As far as labour flexibility is concerned, one sees regressive developments at work with wages and employment falling following international competition.

Public interventions are looked upon by the Commission as factors distorting competition and only specific forms of support are allowed such as aid to R&D or regional development and more generally policies aiming at improving the environment for firms. This position overlooks the institutional specificities of various countries and the variety of ways in which public interventions are conducted in different European countries. Restrictions imposed upon public interventions have not been compensated for by an increase in interventions undertaken by the European Community itself. Technological programmes have not known any new impulses and remain modest and, although the reform of structural funds in favour of less developed regions has allowed their amount to be doubled between 1987 and 1993, they still represent only 0.3 per cent of GDP.

One of the most worrying features is the lack of a common trade policy. The Community only uses a small number of the instruments at its disposal. Opening up public tenders and liberalization of the service sectors are done on a unilateral basis, with no counterpart asked from our non-European partners. This lack of will is the reflection of the deep divergences between European states and contribute to making the European Union a simple free trade zone.

Finally, freeing the capital movements is a far-reaching decision. Financial markets have become the main, if not the sole, reference in judging economic policies, whereas they have only a partial, flimsy and often erroneous view of economic and social realities. And in the end, the compromise realized by the EMS between the fixity of exchange rates, the mobility of capital and the autonomy of economic policies broke down.

2. PERSPECTIVES AND CONTRADICTIONS OF THE MONETARY UNION

The single currency will deeply change the nature of the monetary constraint and will alter the growth regime more profoundly than the single large market (*grand marché intérieur*) has done. Problems specific to the transition period must be mentioned before examining the advantages and drawbacks of the single currency.

2.1 Problems of the Transition Period

No major innovation is expected to take place during the transition period which will extend up to, and probably beyond, 1 January 1999. The European Monetary Institute which was founded in 1994 is only expected to provide counsel and technical advice regarding the implementation of the future European system of central banks but has no power on monetary matters. Instability is bound to be high in this transition period due to the coexistence of free capital movements under fixed rates of exchange. In order to control this instability, governments will most probably resort to very orthodox policies to avoid raising doubts in the minds of financial operators. This will be a first factor slowing growth.

Furthermore, a quasi-fixed exchange rate system with one dominating country, Germany, will inflict high costs on other countries, especially if economic situations and objectives differ. For reasons pertaining to the domestic situation, the Bundesbank will maintain rates of interest above the level which would correspond to the situation of other EEC countries. Participants to the EMS will therefore find themselves handicapped by high rates of interest which, apart from their depressing effect on demand, will push up the Mark and affiliated currencies and downgrade international competitiveness.

Finally, the Maastricht criteria on the public debt (60 per cent of GDP) and deficit (3 per cent of GDP) are very stringent. These criteria, based on much looser analysis than one might think at first, are not justified in terms of domestic macroeconomics. The rationale for these criteria is hard to understand for countries with low inflation and large foreign trade surpluses such as Belgium, Ireland, Netherlands or France. Even the insolvency risk, sometimes stressed in the case of highly indebted countries such as Belgium or Italy, is largely overdone.

Estimates of the fiscal effort required to meet the Maastricht criteria by 1999 produced by the Centre d'Etudes Prospectives et d'Informations Internationales (CEPII) and the Observatoire Français de Conjonctures Economiques (OFCE) show that they will be particularly important for Italy, the United Kingdom, Spain and Greece. The global *ex ante* annual contractionary effect would amount to 0.65 per cent of GDP between 1994 and 2000. The effort required to meet the public debt criterion is even more stringent and would concern all countries except Portugal and Luxembourg. For the EEC at large, the annual contractionary effect would amount to 1.95 per cent of GDP. Satisfying the Maastricht criteria would have devastating effects especially if one considers the high unemployment rate in EEC countries. Furthermore, there is little reason to expect that the fiscal evolution will allow relaxation of the monetary policy and bring interest rates down, since they are determined by the Bundesbank. One must equally add that, when pursued simultaneously in closely interdependent countries, contractionary policies are quite ineffective. The cutback on public spending in each country lowers the growth rates both at home and in partner countries, thus depressing the fiscal revenue all around. These policies eventually depress the rates of growth and push unemployment up without significantly improving the fiscal balances.

The MIMOSA model carried out a simulation of the impact on the EEC of a once-and-for-all decrease of public spending by 1 per cent. In the medium term, this decrease induces a fall in production of 1.5 per cent, a lower inflation and lower rates of interest. The exchange rate falls in the short run, following the decrease in the rates of interest, but it increases in the medium run, due to disinflation. Competitiveness gains and the impact of the reduction in the rates of interest initially mitigate the contractionary effects of the decrease in the public spending but far from fully offsetting them. The *ex post* fiscal improvement is only 30 per cent to 50 per cent of the initial gain: although the drop in the rates of interest alleviates budgetary expenses, fiscal revenue falls with the overall level of activity.

2.2 The Advantages of the Single Currency

The advantages of the single currency should not be overlooked. With fixed exchange rates between currencies no foreign exchange risk premium will be required, which ought to bring rates of interest down and boost investment, improving medium-term growth prospects. By the same token, transaction costs induced by the use of many currencies will disappear and monetary union will display a greater macroeconomic stability when faced with shocks. More generally, price stability, the prime objective of the monetary union, is unanimously regarded as an asset – but this greater command over the inflationary process is not without costs.

One of the arguments most often presented in favour of the single currency concerns the foreign financing facilities it allows. Within a monetary union, intra-European current account deficits do not act as constraints and can be financed by foreign credits written in the common currency at lower rates of interest. The solvency constraint does not, however, disappear with this greater ease in financing the current account. It still bears on debtors, although in a way which is less demanding in the short term than the submission to a macroeconomic contractionary policy induced by a foreign constraint. This selective adjustment might, however, result in a loss of independence which can prove costly. The painless financing of the balance of payments thus has a counterpart which should not be overlooked.

Finally, building the monetary union will bring about two advantages at the international level. First, with the ECU reaching the status of an international currency, transaction costs of EC countries will fall as will their foreign exchange requirements. Second, the homogeneous monetary block will give the EC a greater weight in the process of international monetary coordination and will contribute towards reconstructing a true international monetary system.

2.3 The costs of Monetary Union

The formation of an independent European central bank with price stability as its major objective will have important implications. The autonomy of the monetary policy will push the economic policies in the direction of greater orthodoxy. The underlying notion behind this idea is that monetary policy is the best instrument for controlling inflation, which has not been convincingly demonstrated. In so far as this approach overstresses the demand component of inflation, it might inflict excessive costs in terms of slowing down demand and increasing unemployment. The efficiency of monetary policy varies from country to country following agents' sensitivity to the cost of credit or the constraints on financing. Furthermore, severing monetary policy from other aspects of economic policy might result in an incoherent overall macroeconomic policy.

A number of unresolved questions remain. The European Central Bank will be responsible for the internal monetary policy while the Council of Finance Ministers will determine the general shape of the exchange rate policy *vis-à-vis* other currencies. This is a complex procedure which might, in practice, end up in conflicts between different European institutions. The Maastricht treaty provides no answer to the crucial issue of the regulation of banking and financial systems.

These steps are problematical also in terms of their implications for a democratic polity. A supranational authority would not have any clearly established legitimacy. Members of the Board of the European Central Bank are appointed by the European Council for eight years, not renewable. They have extended powers at their disposal but there are no precisely defined rules and instruments to check those powers. The members of the Board of the European Central Bank will in effect enjoy even greater autonomy than in the USA or in Germany.

The real adjustments required by the deepening economic integration will be hampered by the fixity of the rates of exchange. In peripheral less-advanced countries, specialized in the export of standardized products, inflationary tensions induced by high rates of investment and large intersectoral productivity differentials will affect the exchange rate, whereas in countries where competition proceeds through product differentiation, the improvement of non-price competitiveness will increase their degree of freedom. The need for real adjustments will also stem from specific shocks arising from the persistence of strong national specificities as well as from the deepening of the intersectoral differentiation process.

The changes in real exchange rates entailed by these adjustments will only result from a flexibility in relative prices, that is, from wage and employment flexibility. Such an evolution would require a modification of the system of industrial relations towards a regressive kind of labour flexibility thus aggravating the tendencies which already operate in the present single market framework. Furthermore, since prices are more rigid downwards than upwards, fluctuations contracting output will be amplified compared to those expanding output. Growth will consequently be further slowed down – a tendency which was already at work within the EMS. The perverse effects of competitive disinflation will also be felt. Disinflation operates very slowly, it is very costly in terms of unemployment and its effects are quickly exhausted once the rate of inflation reaches a certain threshold. The rising importance of non-price competitiveness which operates on the quality and diversity of products will weaken these constraints, but only the core countries and in the medium to long term.

The extent of real adjustment which European countries will have to enforce will be larger than the scope offered by relative price flexibility alone. Institutional changes will take time before they influence the dynamics of wages and employment. The US experience shows that the increase in employment is persistently stronger in some states than in others. The large wage and employment flexibility in the USA – as compared to Europe – prevents competitiveness being restored and employment being maintained in states affected by negative shocks. The reduction in income differentials only happens in the long run, following large structural changes such as those which happened during the 1930s and 1940s which allowed the wages in southern states to catch up with the rest of the USA (laws on minimum wages, the mechanization of agriculture and the increase in demand following the outbreak of war). Geographical mobility of workers, on the other hand, is an important factor explaining the smaller dispersion of regional unemployment rates in the USA.

Strong discrepancies will thus appear between European regions, either in the form of trade deficits which will eventually breed insolvency or dependency, thereby jamming the growth process, or through the worsening of unemployment and income disparities between the various areas. Contrary to the situation prevailing in federal states, interregional labour mobility will only marginally reduce these imbalances, and one cannot expect mobility to increase following the monetary union since linguistic, social and cultural barriers will remain strong.

In principle, budgetary policies offer better possibilities. Under fixed exchange rates and capital mobility, the efficiency of fiscal policies will be enhanced while constraints on these policies will be alleviated thanks in particular to the weakening of the external constraint in intra-community trade following monetary union. On the other hand, fiscal policies will face a number of problems: more open domestic markets will reduce their efficiency, seigniorage will contract in more inflationary countries, and European fiscal systems will be subjected to downward competition, as has been the case throughout the 1980s concerning the taxation of savings and profits. More worryingly, the fear that domestic public finance might get out of control will result in very stringent norms concerning public deficits and debt. All in all, national fiscal policies will not be able to provide answers to regional imbalances in case of shocks or of structural adjustments.

Because of its small size relative to national budgets and GDPs the community budget will equally be of limited use. The Commission's proposals that the budget should reach 1.4 per cent of GDP by 1997, be directed on a priority basis to poorer regions inside the EEC and also be used to improve the competitiveness of firms is a step in the right direction, but it does not reverse the diagnosis. The situation in the Community is completely different from that prevailing in federal systems. In the United States, federal budgetary spending amounted to more than 22 per cent of GNP and was 2.1 times the total of the combined spending by the states. Clearly, from a macroeconomic management point of view, federal states are in a much better position due to the potency of the federal budget as policy instrument. Regional imbalances within the European Union will increase with the achievement of the single market and monetary union. Now, because of the limited size of community budgets, the redistributive impact of the European Community's structural interventions can only be very limited in scope.

The deep mutations which will characterize the movement towards monetary union will not allow a stable growth regime to be established. By privileging monetary union as the main instrument of integration the construction of Europe will proceed upside down with no progress on budgetary matters or on Community-based policies. In this context it is unlikely that an agreement will be made regarding political unification and the degree of interregional labour mobility will remain low. The national regulation mechanisms (wage setting mechanisms, social protection and welfare, forms of interfirm cooperation) will go on exhibiting a strong heterogeneity, heavy constraints will bear upon national economic policies and regional imbalances will worsen. Adjustment will mainly operate through changes in the wage system which will evolve towards regressive flexibility, and the overall context will, in the end, prove inimical to growth.

The perspective of European construction via monetary union now seems outdated. From the very beginning of the transition period, monetary instability as well as losses of credibility have been called it into question. The single currency can now be considered only as a long-term objective which would, as it were, crown a lengthy convergence process with many possible scenarios. These may involve the transition from a simple free trade area to a two tier union around a small core dominated by Germany. In the light of what has been pointed out in this section, it might be interesting to explore a new logic which would imply a U-turn as compared to the approach followed since the mid-1980s.

3. REVERSING THE LOGIC OF EUROPEAN CONSTRUCTION

The logic of European construction has to be reversed at the levels of both monetary–budgetary and structural policies. Only then will demand restoration acquire its full significance.

2.4 A Renewed Monetary Europe

For all the reasons expounded earlier, the idea of a single currency as a medium-term objective must be abandoned. After the EMS imploded in August 1993, one could not see a return to flexible exchange rates, albeit managed, as a solution. The EMS must be extended to become a fixed but adjustable parity system. The present floating of exchange rates should be used to define a new grid of exchange rates which would ratify the revaluation of the Deutschmark. This would allow a significant reduction of the European rates of interest. Later on, one should stick to the principle of periodic and dedramatized modifications of the rates of exchange as long as rates of inflation have not converged, as long as development inequalities between European countries have not been reduced and as long as adequate instruments have not been devised at a federal level which would allow asymmetric shocks affecting only one country to be coped with efficiently. Many proposals have been made to improve the workings of the EMS and to give more weight to monetary authorities in the face of speculative movements.

However, re-regulating capital movements is indispensable if one has to proceed further in that direction. This can be done in several ways: forbidding loans in domestic currency to non-residents, as was the case in many European countries up to the late 1980s; increasing the guarantee deposits on future contracts in foreign currency; installing obligatory reserves for financial institutions with a position in foreign exchange markets, as was done in Italy in 1987–78 and in Spain in 1992. Moreover it would be necessary to introduce a Tobin tax, that is, a tax on dealings in foreign currency taking into account the duration and size of dealings in such a way as to penalize operations aimed at realizing financial profit in foreign exchange transactions. Except for the first, none of these measures is aimed at capital controls. Agents could go on doing all these operations but there would be a cost attached to speculation on foreign currency. Central banks would thus be endowed with more powerful instruments to defend exchange parities.

In order to solve the delicate problem of the anchor currency, and to avoid it being the Deutschmark again, one ought to go one step further.

The ECU should be the sole legal external currency while, within the European Union, it would circulate as a simple common currency. This would imply a ban on non-residents holding intra-European currencies, in other words, a return to foreign exchange controls. This is a difficult but crucial step to reconcile an external monetary policy and the possibility of dedramatized intra-European rates of exchange realignments.

2.5 Restoring Demand

In the face of rising unemployment and the failure of the European style supply-side policies, the idea of coordinated expansionary policies at the European level reappeared strongly at the beginning of the 1990s. Indeed, European economies are suffering not so much from a savings deficiency, but more from a lack of investment due to a lack of profitability arising from too high rates of interest and from a lack of favourable demand expectations. All the simulation models show how effective a coordinated expansion would be. Using the MIMOSA model, the CEPII and OFCE have calculated the impact of a programme based on the following criteria.

A fall in household taxes equal to 1 per cent of GDP corresponding to a coordinated expansionary policy at the EU level. This would have strong multiplier effects enhanced by the limited scope of leakages through foreign trade and, in the medium term, it would also have a limited budgetary cost.

A fall in employers' contributions amounting to 2 per cent of GDP, which has a limited expansionary impact, has a good anti-inflationary potential. Such a measure also allows an improvement in competitiveness and favours less capitalistic methods of production.

A fall in interest rates of 2 per cent in the first year and by a small decline of 0.5 per cent in the last year of the policy. The measure would stimulate internal demand and would lead to a depreciation of European currencies.

A 10 per cent devaluation of all European currencies, which would give a boost to competitiveness and would stimulate activity but at the cost of a slight inflationary slip.

All in all, as shown in Table 12.2, such a programme would stimulate the level of activity by 5.4 per cent after three years with no significant cost in terms of inflation, public or external deficits. Employment would improve by 2.7 per cent.

This coordinated expansion would include Germany if it agreed to lower interest rates and devalue. If it did not, the policy could be pushed forward without Germany with a special status granted to the Deutschmark during a transitional period – either as a temporary leave from EMS, or by granting it a wider range of fluctuation, or by appreciating the Deutschmark against other European currencies. As an illustration Table 12.3, still using the MIMOSA model, traces the impact of a break-up of the EMS accompanied by a 3.5 per cent fall in the rate of interest in the first year in all countries except Germany and Benelux, an additional depreciation of their currency by 10 per cent, and a 2.8 per cent reduction in employers' social security and fringe benefit payments acting as a cushion against inflationary pressures. Far from proving catastrophic, such a strategy would, on the contrary, allow for a lasting expansion in all European countries except Germany, an improvement in the external accounts without damage to the budget, coupled with a limited cost in terms of inflation.

Table 12.3 Estimated impact of the disintegration of the EMS

Over a period of 3 years	GDP		Inflation		Current account		Govt. balance		Employment	
	1st year	3rd	1st year	3rd	1st year	3rd	1st year	3rd	1st year	3rd
EEC	1.0	1.2	0.4	0.9	−0.3	0.4	0.1	0.1	0.4	0.5
Germany	0.2	−0.2	−0.1	−0.3	0.4	0.1	0.1	0	0.1	−0.2

Note: GDP, inflation and employment shown in terms of annual percentage change. Current account and government balances are expressed as percentages of GDP.

Source: CEPII–OFCE (1993)

The difficulties one can expect to run into with Germany in relation to monetary policies, highlight a more general phenomenon. The idea of a joint European expansionary policy is not a new one. It was contemplated in the 1970s, but it always stumbled over a number of obstacles. One could, in principle, coordinate expansionary policies but, practically, this proves very delicate owing to the difference in the fiscal, financial and commercial situations between countries. Some heavily constrained countries cannot reasonably implement an expansionary policy while other countries are reluctant to act as 'locomotives'. Furthermore, differing national preferences regarding matters such as inflation, unemployment, fiscal policies or external balances do not make coordination any easier.

The most efficient way to remove the obstacles which had impeded previous attempts would be an initiative at the European level and the privileging of public investment. Yet, designing programmes at the level of the whole European Community is not an easy task. Such development programmes can concern scientific research or infrastructures, but their implementation is always laborious as has been amply demonstrated by the harshness of negotiations over the last ten years.

The various mishaps of the European Growth Initiative from the Edinburgh Summit in 1992 to the Corfu Summit in June 1994 exemplify this point clearly. In December 1992, two supporting mechanisms were devised: direct loans from the European Investment Bank (EIB) to finance infrastructure; and loan guarantees supplied by a new institution, the European Investment Fund, supplemented by the funds (*fonds de cohésion*) established by the Maastricht treaty to promote the catching up of South European countries. All told, these mechanisms could have increased investment by 7 billion ECUs in 1994 and by approximately 5 billion per annum until the year 2000. One should, however, note that this figure is overestimated because it does not properly take into account substitution effects, such as investment projects which would have been realized anyway. The European Growth Initiative (*initiative européenne de croissance*) is then a misnomer because its macroeconomic impact is very limited: *ex ante*, the shock is at most 0.15 per cent of GDP, in the medium term the expansionary effect would be at most around 0.2 per cent of GDP in the EEC at large – but slightly higher for South Europe, 0.35 per cent of GDP.

The White Book on growth, competitiveness and employment (*Livre blanc sur la croissance*) presented by the Commission in December 1993, one year after the launching of the European Growth Initiative attempts to draw more ambitious perspectives and tackles problems from a wider angle. It particularly stresses the need for Europe to build large trans-European transport and energy networks and to prepare itself for the 'information society'. This would require infrastructures worth ECU 20 billion a year until the year 2000. In the White Book's view, these projects should be financed partly by loans from the EIB (6.7 billion), from community budget resources (5.3 billion), borrowing from the European Union itself through the issue of securities (7 billion) and finally a contribution from the companies engaged in the project, also under the form of obligations (1 billion). This proposal raised little enthusiasm from the European partners, especially from the Germans and the British, who stressed the lack of viable and fully elaborated projects, and were hostile to the idea of Community borrowing. This explains why the Corfu summit agreed only to 11 large transport network and eight energy projects totalling ECU 6 billion a year for the coming five years and an extension up to the year 2010 for a total of ECU 68 billion. Despite some progress, we still are far from a genuine European Growth Initiative and the overprudent European governments confine themselves to accompanying the timid recovery which started at the beginning of 1994.

These preoccupations are in line with the proposals formulated by Drèze and Malinvaud in 1993 (see Drèze and Malinvaud, 1994). They cover a wide range of objectives: the reduction of real short-term rates of interest down to zero; the lowering of the cost of labour of non-qualified workers through a tax on CO_2 emissions and an increase in VAT; support policies for a revival of European investment; the reorganization of social security and welfare and the setting of a tax on capital income. Without getting into the various measures of this programme, we shall focus on the investment programme. The authors' opinion is, as we noted earlier, that the financial package agreed upon in Edinburgh is grossly insufficient and they calculate that ECU 80 billion per annum for three years would be necessary, that is, approximately 1.4 per cent of GDP. The content of the programme is quite different since, besides the trans-European infrastructure networks, it focuses on private dwellings, urban rehabilitation and transports, taking into account urgent needs and delays in public housing and investment which have accumulated since the 1970s. The financing methods are also noteworthy: they rely largely on investment incentives which take the shape of employment subsidies designed to interest private lenders (banks and financial markets). Institutions specialized in financing public investment should be mobilized to finance investments which have only a long-run profitability (EIB, European Investment Fund, national institutions).

These proposals go in the right direction. They imply, however, a strong degree of coordination between various actors: European institutions, national states and financial institutions. This point is mentioned, although not discussed, by the authors. But it is a major difficulty on which all proposals of coordinated expansion based on national programmes have so far stumbled.

A coordinated recovery pleads in favour of a vast expansionary programme in which the European dimension would take over and would overcome the coordination problems.

Financing would be supplied for its most part at the community level either from a specific fiscal basis (tax on capital income, VAT, CO_2 tax), which would dampen the expansionary effects, or from an EU budget deficit, contradicting the rule which up to now requires this budget to be balanced. This deficit would be financed by bonds issued in ECUs and collectively guaranteed by all member-states. Such a financing would not induce any further tension on rates of interest insofar as the prospect of a stronger European growth would attract foreign funds and would prompt Europeans to invest more in Europe and less abroad.[2]

In this framework, three kinds of expenditure would be financed in such proportions as to yield significant macroeconomic results.

Classical community programmes would be applied to sectors such as trans-European networks, anti-pollution action and support for high-technology industries and research.

Member-states would be allowed to withhold part of the contributions to the EU budget in order to finance specific national programmes. It seems preferable to leave the definition of priorities to each state rather than, as proposed by Drèze and Malinvaud, to focus systematically on urban transports and urban rehabilitation. In this framework, redistribution would operate in favour of the less-advanced member-states through an increase in Structural Funds and in the Cohesion Funds established after Maastricht. In conclusion borrowing at the Community level would enable the debt constraint which bears upon a number of European countries to be bypassed. The coordination difficulties would be largely bypassed since greater autonomy would be imparted to the states. One should not, however, rule out the possibility of wastage and adequate control and evaluation procedures should be devised.

Aid programmes in favour of East European, African and Arab countries would be devised through the implementation regional co-development agreements. This would contribute to lowering the mounting tensions in these countries while at the same time indirectly supporting European growth through the exports that the EU would generate towards these areas.

2.6 Restoring Structural Policies

The policy sketched above would induce a significant expansionary upturn. It might, however, not last long unless a number of structural handicaps are removed. Some of these are essentially of a national nature, especially regarding the organization of production, the spreading of new technologies, personnel management, education and training systems, industrial relations and welfare systems. In other words these handicaps refer to anything that may contribute to the shift from a defensive to an offensive labour-flexibility. But the problems regarding the competitiveness of Europe's economies have been increasingly acquiring a European, rather than a national, dimension. This dimension is due to the pervasive globalization of production and to the perverse effects of the logic of competition, logic which spread unchecked throughout the Single Market. In order to counteract these tendencies structural policies should be restored at the European level in at least two domains: industrial and research policy, on one hand, and foreign trade on the other.

Industrial policies ought to be much more explicitly recognized than they are in the Maastricht Treaty and, *a fortiori*, than in the Rome Treaty.

The European Commission's reference is, by contrast, represented by the Bengeman doctrine which limits itself to upgrading the policy environment of firms. A more active industrial policy could be grounded in arguments put forward by the new 'strategic industrial policy' which have been put forward over these last years in a number of sectors where scale economies, barriers to entry and product differentiation are important.

The sectoral interventions would link up with research and foreign-trade policies in ways which would differ from one sector to the other. The Commission could have a strategic planning role by drawing the broad directions and ensuring the overall coherence of the various programmes. Competition policy would lose some of its importance as the priorities would shift in favour of industrial policy.

Finally, a larger autonomy should be granted to national policies to take into account each country's institutional specificities. The role of the state and the ways and means of public intervention vary widely from one European country to another. Fitting them into one single identical framework for all countries would not make more sense than trying to homogenize the relationships between banks and firms or the role of small firms in a multifaceted productive system. This institutional diversity should be fully recognized and accepted in all its dimensions, including the role of the state. The scope for national policies in the realm of research and industry should then be restored. This is particularly important for France whose tradition as a mixed economy was an asset in international competition.

Foreign trade policy is, partly, a component of industrial policy. But, beyond specific measures, it should be designed in a broader context. As things stand now, it is one of the weakest links in the construction of Europe.

Defining a common foreign trade policy is a decisive test for the European construction. One first step would be to work out, or rather to reformulate, a central document, equivalent to the American Trade Act. Such a document should list the usual instruments used for retaliation in the case of unjustifiable or discriminatory practices but should also be based upon the principle of reciprocity in case of, for instance, access to public contracts or in the case of the liberalization of services.

The implementation conditions of such a policy are crucial. The incompleteness of the European construction could deprive the possible retaliatory measures of a lot of their potency and a large degree of cohesion would be necessary among European states. Given the present international trade context, one could not do without bilateral agreements, but one should strive to attain a greater transparency and publicize all international agreements. Similarly, one should rehabilitate the customs tariff which is a controllable and transparent instrument with fewer perverse side-effects than many other instruments (one should, for instance, replace anti-dumping long-term duties or certain bilateral arrangements with customs tariffs).

As regards to the often mentioned social dumping much caution is necessary, resorting perhaps to different answers depending upon the issues arising in different regions. The real extent of the phenomenon must always be kept in mind. For instance France's imports from the NICs and Asia represent no more than 1.4 per cent of total imports, although the impact can be quite significant in some sectors. A social clause could be applied in certain circumstances when working conditions are deemed unacceptable, for instance in the form of import taxes, the proceeds of which would be paid back into a co-development fund. For less developed countries with a grossly undervalued currency, it is possible to contemplate bilateral agreements or tariffs. Finally, geographically close countries (Africa, Mediterranean countries, Eastern Europe) must benefit from regional co-development.

All this makes sense only if the rates of exchange are under control, at least to begin with, in the three main trading zones, USA, Europe, Japan. The experience of these last two decades demonstrates that the amplitude of exchange rate fluctuations can be wide enough to counteract the influence of tariffs or of other protective measures. We eventually fall back again on the need for a financial re-regulation to stabilize exchange rates within acceptable 'target-zones'. The foundation of a world trade organization would then find its full justification.

NOTES

1. The first one because it relies upon the *ex ante* introduction of large supply shocks estimated on a purely fixed, lump-sum basis (a decrease in unit costs and prices), the second one because it depends on heavy assumptions (a cheapening of financial services and a fall of rates of interest with fixed rates of exchange) which very inaptly describe the consequences of a liberalization of capital movements.
2. To give an order of magnitude, an increase of expenditures amounting to 1 per cent of the Community GDP (that is, about ECU 57 billion per annum) could be financed through an increase in debt without an undue debt-servicing burden on the community budget. With a debt ceiling of 10 per cent of GDP, the debt service would, in the long term, reach 0.35 per cent of GDP. This would in turn increase, substantially but bearably, the Community budget which today amounts to only 1.2 per cent of GDP.

REFERENCES

Cecchini, P. (1988), '1992: la nouvelle économie européenne', *Economie européenne*, **35**, March.

Drèze, J. and E. Malinvaud (1994), 'Croissance et emploi: l'ambition d'une initiative Européenne', *Revue de l'OFCE*, **49** (April), 247–88.

Eichengreen, B. (1990), 'One money for Europe? Lessons from US currency union', *Economic Policy: A European Forum*, **0** (10), April, 117–87.

Emerson, M. (1990), 'Marché unique, monnaie unique', *Economie européenne*, **44**, October.

Equipe MIMOSA (1993), 'Lutter contre le chômage de masse en Europe', CEPII-OFCE Working Paper, no. 93–01, October.

Equipe MIMOSA (1993), 'La convergence en Europe: bilan et perspectives', CEPII–OFCE Working Paper, no. 93–02, October.

Mazier, J. (1992), 'Intégration économique et monétaire en Europe et régimes d'accumulation', *Mondes en développement*, **20** (79–80), 191–211.

13. The roots of austerity in France

Alain Parguez[*]

1. INTRODUCTION: THE INTELLECTUAL BACKGROUND

In contemporary France measures favouring austerity are akin to President Reagan's 'policy of social surpluses' which broke with the heritage of the New Deal (Wray, 1991). In France, however, it is part of a tradition that goes back at least to the end of the 1920s with the policy of the Raymond Poincaré government. No New Deal ever broke that policy's hold on French minds, a fact that explains the very particular nature of budget austerity in France, and which embodies a vision of the world that is common among France's leading classes. It symbolizes the state's mission: to impose the discipline of the social order on society.

In this context budgetary policy has been governed by three rules:

1. the State's deficit must tend toward zero;
2. interest on the public debt must be paid out of the primary surplus, the amount by which tax revenue exceeds expenditures other than interest charges;
3. government administrations, including the social security, must produce a positive savings balance, that is, a surplus (Rueff, 1958).

The first rule implies that, in the evaluation of the deficit, no distinction be drawn between operating expenses and capital outlays which, therefore, must be financed out of current receipts. The second rule imposes the stringent condition that the primary surplus should grow just to offset any rise in debt charges caused by higher interest rates. Finally the third rule justifies both the increase in tax collection to cover social security benefits and the reduction of social services. It follows that France's budget austerity is harsh and extreme.

* The author wishes to thank Presses Universitaires de Grenoble for permission to use material from his paper 'L'austérité budgétaire en France', published in *Les Pièges de l'austérité*, ed. Pierre Paquette and Mario Seccareccia, Grenoble: Presses Universitaires de Grenoble, 1993.

1.1 The Rueff Report: Financial Orthodoxy at the Dawn of the Common European Market and of the Fifth Republic

The rules of budget orthodoxy were codified in a manifesto that still continues to inform the government's macroeconomic policies. This was the 1958 *Report on the Financial Situation*, written by Jacques Rueff at the request of Antoine Pinay, finance minister in the government of Charles de Gaulle. Jacques Rueff, author of the book *L'Ordre social* (1945) and Director of the Treasury during the Popular Front government in 1936–38, was France's guardian of the orthodox tradition and a stern opponent of Keynes's ideas. By commissioning Rueff to write the report, the government gave him the authority to devise a Budget Charter which, in the eyes of both the sponsors and the author, had a quasi-constitutional importance since it was supposed to cure the financial disorder caused by the Fourth Republic. Indeed, since 1950 French authorities began to distinguish between operating expenses and essential capital expenditures. The former, they felt, should be paid by taxes, the latter financed through borrowing. Since the capital budget was normally in deficit, from an orthodox perspective, it could not but create a drain on available savings.

Rueff rejected this implicitly Keynesian drain altogether. He argued for a single unified budget so that the single deficit would appear as a measure of the state's poor financial management. As a consequence the state would have to aim at a balanced budget regardless of economic conditions thereby eliminating all forms of automatic stabilizers. Hence, if a recession reduced tax revenue, either spending would have to be cut by the corresponding amount or taxes would have to be increased. On the basis of the principle of a single balanced budget, the report stated the necessity that this policy be pursued by all governmental institutions. Thus the assumption arose in the official French literature that the social security account must always be balanced, raising taxes and/or reducing benefits in the case of a deficit. To ensure compliance with the Charter, Rueff recommended that spending proposals, including those related to social security, be strictly adjusted to tax receipts and contribution estimates. In this way the supply of real resources measuring the savings which the state forced upon society, became the absolute constraint governing actual public spending.

By this last principle, Rueff explicitly meant to integrate public sector activity entirely within capital markets. Like Von Hayek, Rueff believed that there existed at every moment an enormous pool of savings resulting from society's voluntary abstinence and taxes. This pool – determined by the desired rate of abstinence and of taxation – would be used to finance both business investment and total public spending. Businesses could therefore spend on investment projects only that amount by which the capital pool exceeded total public spending. The mechanism of supply and demand dictated that the supply of savings, generated by society's choices, was the only normal source of capital for business. Imagine, Rueff argued, that the public sector spends more than the amount of savings collected as taxes. Then, if the state refrained from creating money the deficit would be paid by absorbing part of the voluntary savings pool. Businesses would be deprived of funds and would have to reduce investment proportionally to the amount absorbed by the state for deficit financing purposes. Alternatively the state could create money but with cumulative inflationary consequences. Jacques Rueff was categorical on this point. The only cause of inflation was the creation of money to pay off the budget deficit. Moreover, while private investment was deemed to be productive in the short run as well as in the long run, public spending was viewed as partly productive and in the long run only. Hence the ensuing reduction in the pool of funds available for business investment would be the cause of economic impoverishment.

Rueff ascribed to the budgetary policies of the Fourth Republic the responsibility for France's economic backwardness. According to him the post-1945 growth rate of the French economy had been slowed by a shortage of real capital, the cause of which lay in the budget deficit. The financing of the deficit by means of money creation generated inflation which, by producing negative real interest rates, discouraged voluntary savings. At the same time, negative real interest rates chased away investment by preventing entrepreneurs from counting on high enough real rates of returns on their investments. Rueff therefore assigned to the new Gaullist regime the mission of rationalizing the economy once and for all, by abolishing monetary inflation through the unconditional compliance with the rules of sound budgetary management. Proscribing any deficit in the public accounts was the necessary and sufficient condition for France's integration in the new European order, the Common Market. Rueff concluded his report by stating that France would have to choose between the impoverishment resulting from non-compliance with budgetary orthodoxy, or free trade within the Common Market which would require zero inflation and, therefore, compliance with sound finance principles.

The major political objective of the Rueff Report was the eradication of all Keynesian tendencies from the future Fifth Republic. The fact that the manifesto was signed by some of the highest civil servants in the land, the embodiment of France's technocracy, proves that it owed its success to the fact that it was a condensation of an economic ideology rooted in that community. That virtually no French economist ever subjected it to any scientific criticism is further proof of the intellectual dictatorship of classical finance in France, of the 'Treasury view' attacked by Keynes.

1.2 Renouncing the Keynesian Heritage in France

One of the main opponents of Rueff's views was Jean de Largentaye who, through his translation of the *General Theory*, introduced Keynesian economics into France. In an article originally published in Algeria in 1944, entitled 'The danger of monetary economics', de Largentaye identified the scourge of French society in its blind faith in the doctrine according to which savings are the road to wealth (de Largentaye, 1988). Commonly held by the ruling classes, the doctrine viewed consumption as a barrier to society's wealth. Social wealth grows through investment, the theory went; investment is always limited by the existing pool of savings which stands in an inverse relationship to consumption. The savings pool included corporate profits, which were viewed as savings accumulated for the public by business. According to France's political economists, profits, therefore, always varied in an inverse proportion to consumption and – given that wages form the bulk of it – to the wage bill.

Thus the French 'Ricardian' tradition viewed profits as a pure drawing on income, a kind of gain which in no way derived from the act of purchasing goods and services. As noted by de Largentaye, this approach ignored the role of credit, of banking institutions and of money. Money could only be seen as a form of false wealth created by the state which printed it in order to pay for its deficits. French political economy developed, therefore, a type of financial orthodoxy which was even harsher than that of the British Treasury. The deficit appeared just as a measurement of the state's poor management and as a waste of productive resources.

Writing shortly before the Liberation, de Largentaye asked whether, in an intellectual environment that deliberately ignored the Keynesian revolution, it would ever be possible to undermine the ideology of savings and its policy corollaries: persistent low wages, lack of understanding of the role of money, fear of public deficits. His pessimism was reinforced by the influence of the Ricardian tradition on the socialist and communist Left. The Marxism of the Marxists was ultra-Ricardian, holding that profits were a gain wrung from the working masses through exploitation and that public deficits created inflation, which impoverished the masses even further. The Marxists' view of economics was the same as that of the official political economists. It helped isolate the French intellectual community from the entire new current started by Kalecki (1935) and by Keynes (1936). It was as though the Austrian had defeated Keynes in France, with Hayek's role being played by Rueff.

Events after the war proved de Largentaye correct. The National Accounts, the reference model for all post-war leaders, particularly for the country's senior civil servants, were used to justify the tenets of French economic orthodoxy. As Wray (1991) has pointed out, the entire national accounting system had to record two mandatory equalities: that between investment I and total savings S (inclusive of profits) and that between financial requirements (deficits) and financial surpluses (financing capacity). The interpretation of those equalities could either be 'Keynesian' or 'Classical':

Keynesian meaning	*Classical meaning*
1. I determines S	S determines I
2. Total $S = I$	The S pool is given, I adjusts to it
3. Financial surpluses are made possible by deficits	Deficits are adjusted to prior financial surpluses

In the Keynesian meaning, the accounts showed that deficits *created* equal financial surpluses. By spending more than its revenue, the public sector enabled the private one (businesses, households, financial institutions) to spend less than its revenue thereby generating net savings. These were the amount by which the financial savings of households and financial institutions exceeded the business deficit, which was the amount by which business investment exceeded profits. The Keynesian reading of the accounts had, in fact, revealed to administrators that the public sector deficit, by creating in a Kaleckian fashion a corresponding amount of savings, could not deprive business of savings. The Keynesian–Kaleckian reading of the accounts showed that the public deficit helped create profits (corporate savings), while household savings – being the outcome of withholding demand – reduced them. The French problem was that, from the outset, the classical reading was imposed without discussion. Public accounts were interpreted and acted upon according to the criteria dictated by French orthodoxy. Government accountants quickly concluded that public accounts had to be balanced. By spending more than its revenue, the public sector could only absorb a share of savings which business lacked. The principle that deficits, at one or more point of the structure, were the condition for the existence of surpluses was absolutely foreign to them. The very notion of structure was alien to them since they did not see that the public deficit was a source of savings (profits) for business.

The view of profits as stemming from sharing a given value-added between business, households, financial institutions and the public sector, still governs today's economic policy and official economic thought. As was the case before the Second World War, it is used to justify low wages and budget austerity. Reducing the real income of the employed and erasing the government deficit can only raise the share of business investment in national income. This ultra-Ricardian view was incorporated in economic planning and became the driving force of the growth policy during the Fourth Republic, the major purpose of which was to wring out enough of a surplus to increase the growth rate. France's economic leaders never managed to break out of the 'accumulation-by-tribute' mode of thought, a fact that explains their obstinate refusal to understand the role of consumption in the dynamics of a capitalist economy. These technocrats, most of whom come from the senior civil service, view the public accounts deficit as a scandal, a 'disorder' under the supreme law of economics. Any deficit expenditure is the result of false resources, false currency, and is pure inflation.

So deeply rooted in the dominant ideology was this abhorrence of deficits that the entire social security system was designed to be always in equilibrium. The social security deficit has always been perceived as a greater threat than the government's budget deficit as it might be the result of unlimited growth in social spending which, in its turn, would threaten the economic order. Whether one looks at 1945, 1958 (the year of the Rueff Report and the end of the Fourth Republic), 1981 (when the Socialists came to power) or 1991, de Largentaye's pessimism has come true. The ideas of Keynes, Kalecki and the Keynesians could never have been accepted by the French ruling classes, for whom budget deficits deny the stability of the social order. The hegemony of such a cosmological vision of the order of things encompasses also the left–right cleavages. During the Fourth and Fifth Republics the *dirigistes* (proponents of a planned economy) were perhaps even more attached to budget austerity than the Liberals. The technocrats of the left-wing parties never stopped calling for a rigorous balancing of the public accounts, and were even inclined to denounce the laxity of the conservatives.

With the presidential regime of the Fifth Republic firmly established, the rule of balanced budgets was strictly imposed, thereby eliminating the distinction between pure operating expenses and capital expenditures. All governments of the Fifth Republic would work to eliminate the social security deficit, and then, in the 1980s, they would force the social security system to generate a surplus, which would be the net positive savings of the public sector. These savings would signal that the state was subject to the law of scarcity, and thus act as a guarantor of the social order. General de Gaulle himself established the link, which he deemed indissoluble, between budgetary austerity (Rueff's rules) social order, and the greatness of the nation governed by the value of the Franc, the virtue of the new institutions.

2. PERMANENT AND INCREASING BUDGET AUSTERITY

The necessity for budget austerity is said to arise from the failure of budgetary Keynesianism during the oil shocks of the 1970s and, in particular, from the fatal error of the Socialists' 'New Deal' which ran from June 1981 until the end of 1982.

2.1 The Myth of Budgetary Keynesianism of the 1970s

To assess the alleged degree of Keynesianism in the 1970s, we must consider changes in the net balance of the public sector accounts, including those of the local authorities and of the social security. On the basis of Rueff's rules, these changes provide a measurement of compliance with the discipline of austerity. The data, relative to GNP, must also be compared with those of Germany, which was presented as a model of virtue. Furthermore, given the marked cyclical features of the period, comparisons will be made between changes in structural and full employment balances, which reveal the discretionary action of public finance. A positive balance proves that the budgetary policy is deliberately deflationary, once the figures have been adjusted for the automatic counter-cyclical stabilizers which could otherwise distort the assessment of the action by public authorities. In Table 13.1 the figures are taken from Eisner (1986). Let D_1 and D_2 be the unadjusted and adjusted balances respectively, where the positive and negative signs stand for surpluses and deficits as a percentage of GNP.

Table 13.1 Unadjusted (D_1) and adjusted (D_2) government balances as percentage of gross domestic product: France and Germany, 1970–79.

	France		Germany	
	D_1	D_2	D_1	D_2
1970	+0.9	+1.7	+0.3	−0.1
1971	+0.7	+1.2	−0.1	−0.1
1972	+0.8	+0.8	−0.5	−0.4
1973	+0.9	+0.7	+1.2	+0.9
1974	+0.6	+1.0	−1.3	−0.8
1975	−2.2	+0.1	−5.7	−2.8
1976	−0.3	+1.9	−3.4	−1.5
1977	−0.8	+2.1	−2.4	−0.6
1978	−1.9	+1.1	−2.5	−0.8
1979	−0.7	+2.4	−2.7	−1.5

Source: Eisner (1986, pp. 118–19)

Thus, except for 1973, the unadjusted balances show that the gross level of austerity was much higher in France than in Germany. For the 1970–74 period France was indeed able to maintain a net level of savings in the public sector, whereas the Federal Republic displayed deficits in 1971, 1972 and 1974. From 1974 to 1979 France did have a public sector deficit but of a much smaller size than those of the FRG. The adjusted balances are even more significant: they are always positive for France and negative for Germany, except in 1973. Over the whole 1970–79 period Germany's structural deficits tended to rise while in France surpluses expanded.

These developments prove that France's public finances were governed by three objectives:

1. to limit as far as possible the action of the automatic stabilizers so as to counteract their perceived perverse effect on public spending;
2. to generate increased net savings in the public sector as growth slowed;
3. to use 1 and 2 in order to prevent any British style stop–go policy.

Hence, each time the cumulative effects of the recession and of discretionary austerity undermined the formation of public savings, the government reacted with greater austerity through spending cuts (including social benefits) and greater revenue collections (including social security contributions). The long-term planning of budgetary austerity was perfected under the government of Raymond Barre (September 1976 to May 1981). The purpose of the Barre Plan was to integrate France within Europe through accelerated economic rationalization, which required unconditional compliance with Rueff's rules. Yet the Barre Plan tightened those rules by setting – as with today's Maastricht criteria – a ceiling on public expenditure as a percentage of GNP. It was this threshold, which, if exceeded, brought about an automatic reduction in investment, given the limits to any further compression of households' consumption.

Under the Barre government, which implemented the most brutal budgetary deflation since the Pierre Laval government of 1935–36 and achieved the greatest depression since those years, a new step was taken in that macroeconomic policies were subjected to two forms of Say's Law. The first was the application of Say's Law to the distribution of income, which ran as follows: public spending must be limited by the amount by which the surplus exceeds investment, at any given level of surplus wrung from households there is an inverse relation between public spending and investment, the households whose share must be reduced are, in fact, those of the wage earners. The second form of Say's Law relates to the distribution of expenditures. It states that public spending is limited by the amount by which the given product exceeds private spending; at any given level of private consumption, there is an inverse relation between public spending (including social benefits) and productive investment. With the Mitterrand regime a third form of Say's Law would be added to France's macroeconomic policy-making.

2.2 The Myth of the Keynesian Recovery in 1981–82

To assess the allegedly expansionary Keynesian budgetary policies of the Mitterrand presidency in its early stages (Pierre Mauroy's government, from May 1981 to the end of 1982), let us consider Table 13.2 where D_1 and D_2 have the same meaning as in Table 13.1.

Table 13.2   Unadjusted and adjusted government balances as percentage of gross domestic product: France and Germany, 1980–82

	France		Germany	
	D_1	D_2	D_1	D_2
1980	+0.3	+4.4	−3.2	−1.4
1981	−1.9	+3.3	−4.0	−1.5
1982	−2.6	+3.5	−3.9	0.0

Source: Eisner (1986, pp. 118–19)

The unadjusted balances show that the deficits were incommensurably greater in the FRG; this difference is even more striking with regard to the structural balances (D_2 columns). The Socialists' largesse simply marked a slight decline relative to 1980, when the Barre government's financial deflation was at its peak and succeeded in generating a public sector surplus in the midst of a worldwide recession. It appears, though, that the Socialists were temporarily forced to suspend the action aimed at neutralizing the automatic stabilizers (the first principle of Rueff's rules). The recession – resulting from the twin effects of the international cyclical downswing and the Barre deflation – was so great that the Socialists understood it was impossible to continue inhibiting the automatic stabilizers. This realization explains the increase in budget expenditures and certain social benefits, including unemployment benefits. The idea was simply to spend part of what should have been spent if the effect of the stabilizers had not been distorted by a policy designed to prevent deficits at any cost.

However, the Socialists' discretionary policy was openly deflationary generating structural surpluses beyond comparison elsewhere. Public finance policies did not, therefore, constitute a conscious attempt to stimulate the economy. Budgetary policy, thus, did more than offset the expansionary effect of increased wages and of a less restrictive monetary policy. All in all, the increased gross deficit (D_1 columns) made it possible to increase total corporate profits which halted the economy's descent into depression (Coulombe and Parguez, 1988). That action alone was, however, too mild to restart the economy by rekindling the animal spirits of business.

2.3 The Race to Austerity since 1983

In 1983 the managers of France's public finances restored the traditional practice of the Fifth Republic by making it even more stringent. The application of Rueff's rules became an end in itself in line with the 1926 aphorism of the symbolic figure of French conservatism, Raymond Poincaré: 'Healthy public finances guarantee a strong franc, and a strong franc is the guarantee of the nation's future prosperity.' Evidence of the Poincaré style of orthodoxy is provided in Table 13.3, which shows changes in the overall actual balances of the public sector and their two main components: the state and the social security balances as percentage of GDP.

Table 13.3 Unadjusted government balances, state balances and social security balances as a percentage of gross domestic product: France, 1983–91.

	D_1	State	Social security
1983	−3.1	−3.3	+ 0.8
1984	−2.9	−3.1	+ 0.6
1985	−2.6	−2.9	+ 0.5
1986	−2.6	−2.2	−0.3
1987	−1.6	−2.0	+ 0.2
1988	−2.1	−2.3	+ 0.2
1989	−1.4	−1.7	+ 0.3
1990	−1.3	−1.4	+ 0.2
1991	−1.2	−1.2	+ 0.2

Source: *National Accounts*, Various years.

Table 13.3 reveals the increasingly stifling austerity policies imposed by the Socialist governments as well by the Chirac Conservative government of 1986–88. The first factor in the trend toward the suppression of the public deficit was the full restoration of the rule aimed at neutralizing the operation of the automatic stabilizers. The core of the Socialists' policies after 1982 can be illustrated by means of the chain shown in Table 13.4.

Table 13.4 Causation of France's socialist austerity policies

PHASE A	PHASE B	PHASE C
The recession worsens	The deficit increases as a result of an automatic reduction in receipts and automatic increase in spending.	Automatic increase in revenue collections and automatic decrease public spending.
	PHASE D	PHASE E
	Recession-induced deficit increases disappear and deficits return to their initial level.	Real purchasing power of wage earner's households declines.

PHASE A*

Following E the recession keeps worsening and a new set of Phases B*, C*, D*, E* starts.

According to the logic of the anti-stabilizer effect, if the depression were amplified by the response in Phase C, the government would have to react, as it did after the recession of the early 1990s, with new spending cuts and new measures of revenue collection. The anti-stabilizer programme – which has been running from 1983 to the present day – was designed to make the public sector's balance independent of both the cyclical downswings and the long-term Steindl stagnation which afflicted the economy (Steindl, 1976). It is in this stage that official economics added a third dimension to Say's Law. The deregulation and privatization policies, which – from the end of the 1980s to the present – accompanied budget austerity, eliminate all barriers to the mechanism of supply and demand in the restructuring process. It is believed that the crisis can replace uncompetitive supply with competitive output which will *create* its own demand. Furthermore the third variant of Say's Law aims at inducing positive expectations as to the international value of the Franc, a sign of successful restructuring.

2.4 Say's Law, Interest Rates and the Franc

The figures shown in Table 13.3 are all the more deflationary since the effective deficits correspond to nothing more than interest payments on the public debt. Throughout the 1980s and the early 1990s France's primary deficits were below 1 per cent of GDP, except for 1982 and 1983. Their sharp decline began in 1984 so that government balances climbed to a surplus from 1988 onward. This evolution represents a strict adherence to Rueff's rules which are worth summarizing anew.

First, the amount of interest paid by the public sector must be equal to the amount of the current deficit and primary surplus. This means that interest is paid partly through current indebtedness and partly through the primary surplus. Second, current indebtedness must tend toward zero and all interest will then be paid out of the primary surplus. Third, in the long term there must be a net primary surplus in excess of the primary surplus over interest payable.

The first criterion explains much of the long-term deflationary impact of the management of public finances. The public sector no longer goes into debt in order to make expenditures that, by their direct or induced effects, are highly creative of real value added for the present and for the future. If it does go into debt it should do so only to pay an income to households (with a high propensity to save) and mainly to financial institutions which hold the greatest share of the net public debt. These institutional beneficiaries recycle their incomes on the financial markets which, in a capitalist economy, does not create any additional wealth. Financial markets merely transform or circulate debt corresponding to expenditures already incurred. The second criterion explains how every increase in tax or social collections is absorbed by interest payments to beneficiaries, thus nullifying the effective deficit. This factor leads to the third criterion where the increase in collected revenues finances the accelerated payment of the public debt. That France has one of the lowest ratios of net public debt to GDP should not, therefore, come as a surprise.

The three criteria were supposed to point the way to true austerity. In particular they were meant to cause a drastic redistribution of income by compelling wage earners to give up a portion of their income to the system's beneficiaries. Such a redistribution was apparently the essential condition for a reduction in interest rates because it would fill the hole made in the surplus of the public finances. Redistribution neutralized the deficit implications of a rise in interest rates thereby strengthening the foreign exchange markets' confidence in the value of the Franc as hypothesized by the third variant of Say's Law. Financial authorities recognized that increased interest rates during the 1980s led to a redistribution of income mostly as a result of an institutionalized chain reaction. A rise in interest rates would expand interest payments, which would be met by measures aimed at increasing the primary surplus. These measures would mostly entail extracting revenue from wage earners and retirees, amplifying the redistribution of income and neutralizing the budgetary impact of the interest rate rise.

The automatic chain reaction was the outcome of a comprehensive austerity policy involving monetary and public finance policies in keeping with all the three variants of Say's Law. The increase in the real interest rate has been planned in order to force a rise in the Franc and to convince the foreign exchange markets that the economy was playing by the rules of the law of supply and demand. The institutionalized chain reaction ensured that the impact on the deficit would be neutralized so as not to jeopardize the objective of net public savings. Deflationary policies, both at the monetary and public finance levels, caused a reduction in payroll costs enshrining disinflation. The redistribution of income away from wage earners helped increase the pool of savings, which, according to France's financial orthodoxy, was a good thing. On this basis the Franc was bound to become such a strong currency that the markets would tolerate lower interest rates in France without forcing a depreciation against the Deutschmark.

2.5 The External Constraint

The above account of austerity policies in France should dispel the view, propagated by government officials and economists, that the Socialists resigned themselves to restoring Rueffian criteria because of the external constraint. According to this view, the government wanted to start the recovery by increasing the public sector's deficit, which, however, was absorbed by the growing business deficit which had to be financed through debt. The Franc collapsed revealing that the country tried to recover against the other economies which, like Germany's, were already committed to austerity. At this point, Mitterrand's supporters argued, France faced the disastrous choice of leaving the European Monetary System, and even returning to protectionism, in order to avoid austerity. Reason eventually triumphed, austerity was fully restored and France's place in Europe was saved.

However the libretto of the external constraint opera was based on a threefold misinterpretation of the events.

To begin with, it was incorrect to say that the Socialists practised an all-out budgetary Keynesianism. Table 13.2 attests to the contrary. Nor is it appropriate to say that their economic management went against the grain of the other economies. France's overall budget deficit (D_1) was in 1981 -1.9 per cent of GDP as opposed to -2.7 per cent of the OECD average. In 1982 it was -2.6 per cent for France compared to the OECD average of -4 per cent. In 1983 France's deficit was -3.1 per cent as against -4.1 per cent of the OECD. In every single year it was smaller than that of Germany and it averaged for the 1980–83 period much below the share of the British deficit. Furthermore, the official assertion that the trade deficit reflected the growth of the public sector deficit betrayed a belief in the crudest form of the twin-deficit theory. It is simply false to say that the entire increase in the public sector deficit was absorbed by the trade deficit as a great part of it was transformed into profits for French business.

The real problem was the over-valuation of the Franc with respect to what the market deemed its long-term exchange rate to be. Everyone anticipated a sharp depreciation, a fact which ushered in imports, while over-valuation blocked exports. For France the choice was not between austerity and Europe but, rather, between austerity – which created an over-valued Franc – and a credible long-term exchange rate. Such a standard exchange rate need not be maintained through permanent austerity. The successive devaluations were not enough to lower the Franc to a credible level, particularly against the Deutschmark. To guarantee France's place in the future European monetary union, French leaders saw no other way than to obey Rueff's rules to the letter. As a result of their efforts, the external constraint has become a real yoke.

3. CONCLUSIONS

In the 1990s the French economy has thoroughly verified the validity of the rules developed by Eisner for measuring the impact of public deficits. Harsher budgetary deflation has gone hand in hand with increased unemployment and has stopped private investment growth. Budget austerity has reduced human capital formation and public investment growth in general, while at the same time making the economy more fragile relative to its competitors such as Germany, Italy and Japan. Contrary to official doctrine regarding the virtues of Germany and Japan, France is the only country to have inflicted permanent budget austerity on itself.

The ultimate reason for France's economic crisis is that the failure of the country's economic programme has encouraged its leaders to forge ahead toward more budget austerity. These leaders and experts forget about the resilience of the market economy which they praise so highly. Every effort has been made to break it, to destroy the economy's dynamic animal spirits. The Keynesian view is now absolutely more foreign than ever to the intellectual universe of the leading classes. And the absence of any debate on austerity guarantees that their view will endure.

Observers have wanted to see the Socialists' shift to Rueffian austerity as a sign that they were drifting to the right or as a proof that they had understood the mysteries of the market. The truth is that they have *never* been Keynesian, and still see the world through the distorted mirror of the primordial French political economy. In 1983 they restored an orthodoxy that had been only partly suspended under the pressure of the circumstances. They have never stopped believing in it. Jean de Largentaye was never more right: the obsession with savings is indeed the scourge of French society, at least among its leading technocracy.

REFERENCES

Coulombe, S. and A. Parguez (1988), 'Le rôle des institutions financières dans le circuit dynamique: l'austerité et le capitalisme public en France', *Economies et sociétés* (Séries Monnaie et Production), **22** (9), 85–119.
de Largentaye, J. (1988), 'L'écueil de l'économie monétaire', *Economies et Sociétés* (Séries Monnaie et Production), **22** (9), 11–19.
Eisner, R. (1986), *How Real is the Budget Deficit?*, New York: Free Press.
Kalecki, M. (1935), 'Essai d'une théorie du mouvement cyclique des affaires', *Revue d'économie politique*, **49** (March–April) 285–305.
Keynes, J.M. (1936), *The General Theory of Employment, Interest and Money*, London: Macmillan.
Rueff, J. (1945), *L'Ordre social*, Paris: Sirey.
Rueff, J. (1958), *Rapport sur la situation financière*, Paris: Imprimerie Nationale.
Steindl. J. (1976), *Maturity and Stagnation in American Capitalism*, New York: Monthly Review Press; originally published Oxford: Basil Blackwell, 1952.
Wray, R. (1991), 'Can the social security trust fund contribute to savings?', *Journal of Post-Keynesian Economics*, **13** (2), 155–70

Index